IRISH ARCHITECTURAL AND DECORATIVE STUDIES
Volume XI, 2008

D1709566

IRISH ARCHITECTURAL AND DECORATIVE STUDIES

THE JOURNAL OF THE IRISH GEORGIAN SOCIETY – VOLUME XI, 2008

IRISH ARCHITECTURAL AND
DECORATIVE STUDIES
The Journal of the Irish Georgian Society
Volume XI, 2008

Published by the Irish Georgian Society
© Irish Georgian Society and the authors, 2008.
All rights reserved.

ISBN 978 0948037 702

This annual journal continues the publishing
tradition of the Irish Georgian Society's *Bulletin*
(38 volumes, 1958-1997).

Edited by William Laffan

Produced for the Irish Georgian Society by Gandon
Editions, which is grant-aided by The Arts Council.
design   John O'Regan (© Gandon, 2008)
production   Nicola Dearey
                                Gunther Berkus
printing   Nicholson & Bass, Belfast
distribution   Gandon and its overseas agents

GANDON EDITIONS
Oysterhaven, Kinsale, Co Cork
tel +353 (0)21-4770830 / *fax* 021-4770755
e gandon@eircom.net / www.gandon-editions.com

The Irish Georgian Society acknowledges with
gratitude the support of an anonymous benefactor,
which has made this volume possible.

cover   Hugh Douglas Hamilton (1740-1808)
              Lady Cockburn and her two children
              oil on canvas, 150 x 150 cm
              (detail, see p126) (private collection)

frontispiece   *The Obelisk near Castletown,*
              140 feet high – an engraving of the
              Conolly Folly (1740) from the Noble
              and Keenan map of Kildare, 1752

THE IRISH GEORGIAN SOCIETY

The Irish Georgian Society aims to encourage an
interest in and the preservation of distinguished
examples of architecture and the allied arts in
Ireland. Further information – and membership
application details – may be obtained from:

THE IRISH GEORGIAN SOCIETY
74 Merrion Square, Dublin 2
tel +353 (0)1-6767053 / *fax* 01-6620290
e-mail info@igs.ie / *web-site* www.igs.ie

IRISH ARCHITECTURAL AND DECORATIVE STUDIES

THE JOURNAL OF THE IRISH GEORGIAN SOCIETY – VOLUME XI, 2008
EDITOR: WILLIAM LAFFAN

———

Preface

THE KNIGHT OF GLIN

As ALWAYS, IT GIVES ME ENORMOUS PLEASURE TO MARK THE PUBLICATION OF *Irish Architectural and Decorative Studies*. This is our eleventh volume, and is replete with valuable scholarship on topics from portrait painting in Belfast to shopping in Dublin; from quarrying to travel, collecting, topography, and, of course, architecture. On behalf of the Irish Georgian Society, I thank all the contributors, and especially our editor, for putting together such a stimulating volume. This year, the Journal will be launched in the former Bishop's Palace in Kilkenny, the new home of the Heritage Council, and several of the articles have a Kilkenny focus.

It has become customary for me in this foreword to review recent and forthcoming events and publications of relevance to the scholarship that this Journal promotes. As not all of the aspirations I express here come to pass, it is pleasing to note that the National Gallery of Ireland agreed with my call four years ago for a bicentennial exhibition to celebrate the art of Hugh Douglas Hamilton. Anne Hodge, the show's curator, and the staff of the National Gallery are to be greatly congratulated for this splendid exhibition. Meanwhile, in Cork, the Crawford Gallery – together with our publishers Gandon Editions – are setting new standards for scholarly catalogues with their publication on Daniel Maclise, which elegantly complements their recent book on James Barry. We are still hoping that a major show of the visual and decorative art of Georgian Ireland will be organised, and it is gratifying to note the interest of three American museums in this venture.

The greatly anticipated volume, *Thomas Roberts: landscape and patronage in eighteenth-century Ireland*, by our editor William Laffan and Brendan Rooney, will be published in March. This coincides with a major retrospective on Roberts' work at the National Gallery, which runs until June. All members of the Society are

Fota House, Fota Island, county Cork (opposite and overleaf)
Originally an eighteenth-century hunting lodge, it was extended in the nineteenth-century by Richard and William Vitruvius Morrison (photographs courtesy Irish Heritage Trust)

urged to hasten to Merrion Square for this once-in-a-lifetime opportunity to view almost the entire body of works – many usually inaccessible – by Ireland's greatest eighteenth-century landscape painter. The remarkable set of paintings of Carton will be on public show for the first time in a generation.

Ronald Lightbown has published what is surely one of the most important books on eighteenth-century Ireland, *The Architect Earl, a life of Lord Aldborough*. This is a joint publication of the Irish Georgian Society and Ossory, Laois & Leinster Group. We heartily congratulate Ronald and John Kirwan, who saw the book through to publication. It is available in the IGS bookshop

In these difficult times it is very pleasing to acknowledge some good news stories and exciting initiatives for Irish art and architecture. Primary among these is the imminent reopening of Fota House, county Cork, which has been immaculately restored by the Irish Heritage Trust and hung with a fabulous collection of eighteenth-century paintings unrivalled outside the National Gallery in Dublin. Members of the Society are entitled to free admission to Fota. It is truly remarkable what the Irish Heritage Trust has achieved in the short years since its inception, Again, I strongly recommend a visit.

On the academic front, Dr Lynda Mulvin is organising an important conference, *The Fusion of Neoclassical Principles: scholars, architects, builders and designers in the neoclassical period*, on 21-22 May at the Irish Architectural Archive. Given the list of distinguished speakers, it will no doubt be a stimulating and rewarding event. The Society is also arranging a conference on the Casino at Marino; more details are available from the IGS office.

We are very grateful to the Irish benefactor who has made the publication of this Journal possible, and, as ever, we appeal for your support in continuing the scholarship that is at the heart of the Society's activities. We are anxiously seeking further sponsorship for this remarkable Journal.

Irish Georgian Society

CONTRIBUTING, PATRON AND BENEFACTOR MEMBERS

PATRON AND BENEFACTOR MEMBERS

RA Bartlett
Manolo Blahnik
Glenn Bradshaw
Andrew Coman
Gabriel De Freitas
Bruce Finch
Camilla McAleese
Patrick Murray
Patrick Powderly
Michael Roden
  (benefactor)
Rolf Schmid
Diarmuid Teevan

CONTRIBUTING MEMBERS

Robert Bartlett
Vivienne Boylan
Phillip Braddock
Anne Brady
Revd Gabriel Burke
David Butler
Shane and Emma Cahill
Revd Peter and Rebecca
  Campion
Valerie Coleman

Rosamund Coyle
Eamon and Vivien De
  Burca
Aidan Doyle
Simon Dunne
Garrett Fennell
HE Thomas C. Foley
Jonathan Ford
Lorraine and Desmond
  Gray
Nicolas Griffin
James Harding
David Herlihy
Norma Judge
David and Jane Keating
Garrett Kelleher
Gary Kraut
Paul Lacey
Róisín Laird
Teresa Le Gear Keane
Robert MacKinstry
Hilary Maume
Andrew Maxwell
Noel Meaney
John and Alexandra
  Morley
Nicholas Murphy
Jim and Pauline
  O'Callaghan

Brian O'Carroll
John G. O'Donnell
Paul O'Donnell
Angela O'Floinn
Vivienne and James
  O'Riordan
Chantal O'Sullivan
Fiona Palmer
Eileen and Philip Perkins
Mary Quinn
Brian Redmond
Patrick and Finula
  Riordan
Gaby Robertshaw
Mikal Sanne
Anthony and Tara
  Shanks
John Sheehan
Michael Swarbrigg
Michael Thompson
Karl and Charisse
  Van Kan
Bernard Walsh

Authors' biographies

EILEEN BLACK is a curator of fine art at the Ulster Museum, Belfast. She is the author of numerous articles and catalogues. Her book *Art in Belfast 1760-1888: Art Lovers or Philistines?* (2006) is a major study of art in that town in the eighteenth and nineteenth centuries.

PATRICK BOWE is a garden historian who has written or co-written nine books and many articles on garden history. His last book, *Gardens of the Roman World: an account of gardens in ancient Rome*, was published by the J. Paul Getty Museum, California.

ANNE CASEMENT gained a doctorate from the Queen's University of Belfast for her study of estate management in Ulster in the mid-nineteenth century. She is currently engaged in a survey of the demesne at Glenarm Castle, county Antrim, and her book on the Irish drawings of Lord Mark Kerr is due for publication in 2009.

JANE FENLON is an art historian and has published extensively on sixteenth and seventeenth-century Irish art and architecture.

RACHEL FINNEGAN is head of the Department of Creative and Performing Arts at Waterford Institute of Technology, and author of several related publications, including a new edition of *A Tour in Ireland in 1775 by Richard Twiss* (University College Dublin Press, 2008).

TONY HAND is employed as a planning engineer for a mining company. He was the recipient of the Desmond Guinness Scholarship in 2006. He is currently engaged in postgraduate research at Trinity College, Dublin, on the subject of William Colles and the Kilkenny Marble Works, 1730-1830.

MICHAEL MCCARTHY is professor emeritus of the history of art at UCD. He is the author of *The Origins of the Gothic Revival* (Yale UP, 1987) and *Classical and Gothic: studies in the history of art* (Four Courts Press, Dublin, 2005). Most recently he edited, with Karina O'Neill, *Studies in the Gothic Revival* (Four Courts Press, Dublin, 2008).

JANE MEREDITH was awarded an M.Litt degree from the Department of the History of Art, Trinity College, Dublin, in 2005 for her thesis entitled 'Andrew Caldwell (1733-1808), A Study of a "Guardian of Taste and Genius"'. She is the author of *Around and About the Custom House* (with an introduction by Maurice Craig) (Four Courts Press, Dublin, 1997).

ANNA MORAN is a lecturer in the history of design and material culture in the Faculty of Visual Culture at the National College of Art & Design, Dublin. She is currently completing a PhD at the University of Warwick on the production and consumption of glass in late eighteenth and early nineteenth-century Ireland.

———

Bishop Pocock's improvements to St Canice's Cathedral, Kilkenny

RACHEL FINNEGAN

IN HIS FASCINATING TWO-PART STUDY OF EIGHTEENTH-CENTURY CATHEDRAL restoration, Michael McCarthy claims that the reputation of Richard Pococke (Bishop of Ossory, 1756-65) as the great saviour of St Canice's Cathedral in Kilkenny was due largely to the eulogistic accounts of the bishop's two personal friends, Edward Ledwich and John O'Phelan, on which all subsequent accounts are based.[1] According to these two original accounts (which the author refers to as 'pious hagiography'), the bishop found the cathedral in ruins and single-handedly restored it to its (then) present glory.[2] McCarthy refutes this, however, and cites descriptions of the cathedral by earlier travel writers (including a brief one from Pococke himself, from a tour of Ireland in 1752), all of which fail to note the allegedly ruinous state of the building. He believes that their concern for the memory of Bishop Pococke was a result of the 'lack of appreciation of the alterations he had effected',[3] as witnessed by various subsequent accounts of a more critical nature. In this study, I will give further consideration to the subject of Bishop Pococke's alterations to the cathedral, and look into the question of why it was that his ambitious and costly alterations to this building were so unpopular that some elements survived only a century before being removed to other locations. In doing so, I shall take into account Pococke the man, and analyse the extent to which his earlier life and experiences – particularly his interest in architecture and his undoubted skills in this discipline – may have shaped his responses to his newly elevated position of power and authority as Bishop of Ossory.

1 – Plate XV from POCOCKE'S TRAVELS (vol. II, pt. 1, bk. II), entitled
'A View of One End and Part of the SIDE of the TEMPLE of BAALBECK',
with the artist-author in the foreground holding a measuring stick
(all photographs by David Kane unless otherwise stated)

POCOCKE THE MAN

BORN IN SOUTHAMPTON IN 1704 INTO A CHURCH FAMILY, RICHARD POCOCKE was educated at his grandfather's school in Highclere rectory, and matriculated at (or entered) Corpus Christi College, Oxford, in 1720, aged only fifteen. He received a BA in 1725, a BCL in 1731, and a DCL (Doctor of Laws) in 1733.[4] While Precentor of Lismore Cathedral in 1725, aged only twenty-one (an appointment made by his somewhat unpopular uncle Thomas Milles, Bishop of Waterford and Lismore),[5] his interests appeared to be concerned less with the church than with travel. It seems that the sinecure to which he was promoted required him to be present very little in Ireland, if at all. Several years later, together with his much younger cousin Jeremiah Milles, Pococke made his first Grand Tour to Italy. This is documented through a series of letters to his mother,[6] outlining his six-month tour of the country from December 1733 to June 1734, and is summarised in *A Dictionary of British and Irish Travellers in Italy, 1701-1800*.[7]

In May 1736, Dr Pococke, now having been promoted to Vicar-General of Waterford and Lismore, set out on a second, more extensive journey, this time alone. Travelling for a year through Germany and eastern Europe, he spent a further year in Italy, where he befriended the Irishman Robert Wood, who was to become famous some years later for his two influential books on Palmyra and Baalbec.[8] His departure from Leghorn in September 1738 took him on an extensive tour of the east, where he visited Alexandria, Cairo and Jerusalem over a period of three years, a voyage inspiring his famous travel book on the Levant, in two volumes (discussed below). His trip was almost contemporaneous with one made by another Irishman, William Ponsonby (Viscount Duncannon and future 2nd Earl of Bessborough), and his travelling companion, Lord Sandwich,[9] and it is possible, though undocumented, that they may have met at some stage along the way. They certainly shared the same passion for knowledge about the East, for antiquities and for Turkish dress, all three commissioning portraits in such costume by the artist Jean-Etienne Liotard, and they were all, on their return, to become founder members of two London dining clubs devoted to promoting an interest in the East.

Pococke returned to England in 1742, and in the February was elected a fellow of the Royal Society on the grounds of being 'a Gentleman of Universal Learning, great Curiosity, every way well quallified and likely to be a very usefull and valuable member of the Same'.[10] He worked on his first volume of *A Description of the East and Some other Countries, Observations on Egypt*, which was published the following year, and he dedicated this volume to Henry Herbert, 9th Earl of Pembroke and Montgomery, commonly known as the 'architect earl'. In his dedication, Pococke immediately declared the objective of his book in his statement: 'My Lord, As the magnificent buildings of Egypt, and antient architecture are the chief subject of this book, it could not be more properly addressed than to Your Lordship.'[11] In the preface to this volume, he draws attention to the illustrations in the book, noting:

> The publisher of these observations [Pococke himself] had it only in his thoughts, to give the world the plans he had taken of the Egyptian buildings, together with some drawings of them, and to add an account, and designs of all the different orders of Egyptian architecture. He imagined even plans alone, with proper descriptions, not so defective as they might be with regard to other buildings...

He continues:

> What he has done will, he hopes, give a sufficient idea of the Egyptian manner of building; and if he had gone no further, it would have been very little more than publishing these plates; and it is but a little more at present, by the persuasion of some friends, to give an account of his travels, and of several accidents, that might give an insight into the customs and manners of people so different from our own, in order to render the work more acceptable to the generality of readers.[12]

Volume II incorporates two parts. The first is entitled *Observations on Palestine or the Holy Land, Syria, Mesopotamia, Cyprus and Candia*, and the second is *Observations on the Islands of the Archipelago, Asia Minor, Thrace, Greece, and some other Parts of Europe*. Published in 1745, this volume and was dedicated to Philip Dormer Stanhope, 4th Earl of Chesterfield, then Lord Lieutenant of Ireland, to whom Pococke was domestic chaplain. The dedication was rewarded by his appointment the same year to the Archdeaconry of Dublin, a position he retained until promoted to the Bishopric of Ossory in 1756. This volume of his travels continues in an architectural vein, and includes 178 magnificent plates, the most impressive of which are possibly the ten plans and elevations of temples and 'apartments' in Baalbeck (Pococke's plates X-XX). As was the custom with contemporary travel writers, Pococke frequently included in his illustrations a picture of himself, usually recognisable among the two or three figures present by being depicted either as taking measurements of the buildings or engaged in drawing them (Plate 1).

The same is true of his later works, such as the journal of his travels in Scotland,[13] where he occasionally represents himself sketching the views of castles and other buildings visited. In his Eastern publication, he is dressed in native costume and is recognisable by his beard and turban, whereas in his Scottish memoirs he always appears with a tricorn hat, a long ponytail and a knee-length frock-coat, and is generally accompanied by a man with a shorter coat who is holding or leaning on a long staff. It is interesting that the editor of his Scottish tours refers to the fact that the drawings are by Pococke's own hand ('pen sketches, shaded by brush with Indian ink'), but are reduced for publication by a Mr George R. Primrose. He even describes the method by which Primrose was enabled to 'take tracings from the original drawings, which having been reduced in size about one-third, and arranged as line drawings on prepared paper with transfer ink', were then transferred by Robert Dawson, 'Zincotyper, Edinburgh, to zinc plates, and mounted to print with the text'.[14]

By contrast, nowhere in the actual text of his Eastern book does Pococke refer to the services of a draughtsman or an architectural artist, which, together with the remarks in his preface (already cited), suggests that the architectural drawings are all his own. Nevertheless, certain plates contain, at the bottom left-hand corner in small print, the name of a designer and/or an engraver. Samuel Wale's name appears several times with the abbreviation 'sculp' or 's', denoting that he only engraved the drawing. Wale (1721-1786) is chiefly known as a book illustrator, and, according to his biographer, 'chose not to engrave his own designs, preferring to pass them on to engravers such as Charles Grignion'.[15] However, since his work for Pococke's book must have been among his earlier commissions (he can only have been in his early twenties), he may not have been able to afford to be so particular. The curious illustrations in volume I entitled 'DRESSES Particular to EGYPT' (LIX, 192) are engraved by Charles Mosley.

The only reference to another artist or designer is in the note 'H. Gravelot inv', appearing in the frontispiece of the various sections of the volumes, with 'Grignion sculp' indicating the engraver, and 'G.D. Ehret delin & sculp.' on the botanical prints. In addition, the major maps (such as the 'Map of the Holy Land and Syria' located at the beginning of volume II) are the work of the famous cartographer Jefferys, and are credited as 'T. Jefferys Geographus, delin, et sculp' (Plate 2).

His pioneering book, in two folio volumes, immediately became a standard work on the Levant, and was translated, at the time, into French, German and Dutch. It gained the attention and admiration of many leading academics, including Classical historians and Oriental scholars, and at once earned him a place among the literati of the day. In addition to the book's intellectual appeal was, of course, its practical value, and it is a good example of a Grand Tourist's views on the benefits of foreign travel – a stock subject with travel writers, particularly as a conclusion to their work. His moralistic sentiments and his style are clearly underpinned by his profession as a member of the clergy.[16]

Like many gentlemen of his times, Dr Pococke was an assiduous club member, and throughout his life belonged to a number of learned societies and dining clubs both in Ireland and England. He was, for example, a founder member of the London-based Egyptian Society, which lasted from December 1741 until April

2 – Plate from Pococke's TOURS IN SCOTLAND depicting Tigh-na-Stalcaire on Island Stalker, with the artist-author seated and sketching the castle (reprinted Heritage Books, 2003, 96)

1743, and the more obscure Divan Club, surviving from January 1744 to May 1746. Membership of the earlier association was open to gentlemen who had either already visited Egypt or who intended to do so, while that of the Divan Club (originally named the Turkish Club) was restricted to those who had already visited 'The Sultan's Dominions'. Since travel to these regions was undertaken only by the most committed of individuals, the membership of such clubs was inevitably quite exclusive, and attracted a number of famous scholars, connoisseurs and collectors of antiquities, including, as noted above, William Ponsonby (Viscount Duncannon, and future Lord Bessborough) and Lord Sandwich. Incidentally, he dedicated a plate to each of these gentleman in volume I of *Pococke's Travels* depicting 'The Statue of Memnon at Thebes' (plate XXXVI) and 'A Statue of Osiris. Brought from Egypt' (plate LXIII) respectively. Many of the other plates are similarly dedicated to leading prelates of Pococke's acquaintance, the dedication to whom can be interpreted either as his bestowing a particular honour on those named, or perhaps (and more likely) as acknowledgment of subscriptions donated towards the cost of the engravings for such a costly publication.

Both Pococke and his cousin, Reverend Jeremiah Milles, acted as secretary to the Egyptian Society, with the former, in particular, playing an active role in presenting scholarly discourses on the subject of eastern antiquities. He attended Divan meetings very assiduously for the first year, acting as Reis Effendi (secretary) for its fourth meeting and attending the next eleven consecutive sessions, during which he stood as Reis Effendi for the second time as well as Vizir (chairman). However, he only attended once more, on 24th May 1745, being absent from the last ten meetings, presumably because he was engaged in his clerical duties in Ireland and working on the second volume of his book on the East.[17]

Pococke also belonged to a number of clubs in Dublin, such as the Physico-Historical Society (1744-55), whose purpose was to promote enquiries into the ancient and present state of the counties in Ireland,[18] and the Dublin Florists' Club (1746-66), established for the promotion of ornamental horticulture in Ireland.[19] Membership of such associations, collecting antiquities, coins and other curiosities,[20] and writing scholarly accounts of his travels seem to have been Pococke's major interests outside his actual clerical work, and though obviously close to his immediate family (particularly his mother, his sister, his uncle Thomas Milles and his cousin Jeremiah Milles), he appears never to have married or formed any romantic attachments.

One possible explanation for his unmarried state may have been a realisation that matrimonial duty was incompatible with foreign travel, particularly to those regions considered dangerous. He was well past the usual marriageable age by the time he went on his first Grand Tour (almost thirty), after which he made two more voyages, this time further afield, returning when he was practically middle-aged. In a letter to the celebrated librarian and antiquary Dr Andrew Coltée Ducarel, dated 27th August 1753, Pococke refers to a recent publication by the Bishop of Clogher, containing a description of 'the North-east parts'. He observes, 'I fear no person will be found fit for the journey to the Wilderness that would undertake it. If Swinton were not married, he would be a very proper man, as his talent lies that way.'[21] Though a somewhat curious remark given the homosexual scandal attaching to Swinton's name twenty years earlier,[22] clearly, in Pococke's eyes, travel was an occupation suitable only for the unattached.

As for other insights into his character, it is the unfortunate remark of the celebrated letter-writer Mrs Delaney, wife of Dean Patrick Delany, that seems to have made the most lasting impression on the world since it is quoted in every account of Pococke's life. After meeting him while staying in Bulstrode with the Duke of Portland, she wrote, in a letter dated 2nd January 1761: 'The Bishop of Ossory has been here ever since Monday ... We lose not much entertainment, for he is the dullest man that ever travelled: but he is a good man.'[23] However, the life-size portrait of him by Liotard (Plate 3) shows him in a rather different light, depicting him in a distinctly bohemian manner, with shaven head, and sporting a towering headdress and beard.[24] The portrait was painted in Constantinople in 1740, and depicts Pococke in the 'blew linen garment ... [and] coarse great coat as the common people here wear', as described in a letter to his mother.[25] The adoption of Oriental dress seems to have been a popular, if not necessary part of the experience of visitors to the Levant, though the custom, at least while abroad, was often practiced for considerations quite unrelated to fashion. One such reason was that of disguise to enable easy access to places of interest.[26] A further reason for adopting such dress was for self-protection by blending in with the locals, since it was considered unwise, and even dangerous, for foreign travellers (who were usually quite wealthy) to draw unnecessary and unwelcome attention upon themselves. Thomas Shaw, who published his travels to the Levant in 1738, advised in his preface:

> However, to prevent as much as possible the falling into their [the Arabs'] Hands, the greatest Safety for a Traveller, at all Times, is to be disguised in the Habit of the Country, or dressed like one of his Spahees, For the Arabs are very jealous and inquisitive; suspecting all Strangers to be Spies, and sent to take a Survey of those Lands, which, at one Time or other, (as they have been taught to fear,) are to be restored to the Christians.[27]

Whether such masquerade was an everyday mode of dress rather than one reserved for special occasions is not so clear and would have varied according to the individual, and both the literary and artistic evidence indicates that this type of costume for visitors was almost the norm. It is also clear from portraits commissioned for members of the Dilettanti Society and the Divan Club that the elaborate costumes obtained abroad were occasionally put to good use at home.[28]

The only other known portrait of Pococke (apart from the many miniature self-portrait sketches or 'cartoons' in his Eastern book and Scottish journal) depicts him not only as much older (it was painted a quarter of a century later), but as more in keeping with Mrs Delany's unsympathetic view (Plate 4). This now hangs in the new Bishop's Palace in Kilkenny.

Pococke was to remain as Bishop of Ossory for a decade, during which time (as noted in the so-called Pococke Monument, depicted in Plate 5) he carried out many improvements on other churches in the diocese, as well as establishing and

4 – Portrait of Richard Pococke by an unknown artist in the new Bishop's Palace, Kilkenny

(*courtesy Episcopal Portrait Collection, RCB; photo David Kane*)

opposite

3 – Portrait of Pococke by Jean-Etiènne Liotard, 1740

(*© Propriété de la Fondation Gottfried Keller, dépot au Musée d'art et d'histoire de la Ville de Genève*)

supporting a linen-weaving school at Lintown, just outside Kilkenny.[29] Clearly, he was already a man of independent means, but his promotion to this bishopric greatly increased his income, and, being of a generous disposition, he invested a great deal of his own money in supporting such charitable works. When, in June 1765, the See of Elphin became vacant, Pococke was translated to bishop of that diocese. However, this appointment lasted only a month, after which he was appointed Bishop of Meath. He died on 15th July, as described in the following account:

> 1765, 15 Sept. — He this day confirmed at Tullamore; returned indisposed, went to his chamber, took a Puke, went to bed about 5 o'clock, seemed to rest quietly, but was found dead about 12. He complained of a pain in his stomach, which he could impute to no other cause than a few mushrooms eaten the day before at Ballyboy.[30]

On his death, he left his house and estate in Newtown, Hampshire, to his 'dearly beloved Sister Elizabeth Pococke Spinster', of the same address. The remainder of his estate was left in trust to the Incorporated Society in Dublin for Promoting English Protestant Schools in Ireland, with the interest being used to support

5 – The Pococke Monument, St Canice's Cathedral, Kilkenny

Elizabeth and other members of his family during their lifetime, after which the fortune was to be used for founding 'a School for papist boys who shall become protestants and to be bred to linnen weaving'.[31] This weaving school, which later became known as the Pococke School, was eventually closed and the endowments were amalgamated with the present Kilkenny College. The building, which is situated within the grounds of St Canice's Cathedral, now incorporates the Cathedral Library and the living quarters of the bishop's curate.

It is believed that during his short stay in Meath he planted some cedars of Lebanon in the grounds of the Bishop's Palace, the earliest reference to this being Samuel Lewis's *A Topographical Dictionary of Ireland* (1837):

> The bishop's palace, one of the most elegant ecclesiastical residences in Ireland, was erected by the late Bishop Maxwell: it is beautifully situated, and the grounds and gardens are tastefully laid out; the demesne is embellished with forest trees of stately growth, among which are some remarkably

fine horse-chestnut trees; and there are also two very beautiful cedars of Lebanon, planted by the late Bishop Pococke.[32]

Later suggestions (proposed, for example, by Richard Mant) are that he planted these from seeds that he actually brought back from Syria. It is possible that this is true, given his general interest in horticulture (his membership of the Florists' Club has already been noted) and, in particular, in eastern plants. Chapter 18 of volume I of *Pococke's Travels* is entitled 'Of Egyptian and Arabian Plants', and contains three of the most beautiful plates delineating various plants that 'have not been engraved before or at least, not in a proper manner'. There is also a catalogue of ninety-five different types of plants that Pococke had collected in Egypt and 'Arabia Petraea', seven of which had already 'come up in Chelsea, from the seeds [he] sent'.[33] Whether or not the cedars were part of this collection (though this species is not mentioned in the catalogue), it is a nice story, and, like his Eastern portrait, further immortalises what were probably the most memorable years of his life.

ST CANICE'S CATHEDRAL

THE SEE OF OSSORY BECAME VACANT IN FEBRUARY 1756 AFTER THE DEATH OF Bishop Edward Maurice, whereupon Richard Pococke, at the time Archdeacon of Dublin, was nominated as his successor. His patron was the Duke of Devonshire, who had succeeded Lord Chesterfield, Pococke's earlier patron, as Lord Lieutenant of Ireland. Two months later, on 24th March, he was enthroned 'by proxy', though the exact date at which he actually took up residence in the Bishop's Palace is not clear. By late June, he described his new circumstances in very glowing terms, claiming that 'every one as well as myself thinks I have got the sweetest situation in Ireland, a most exceeding good house, a pleasant garden, wt. we call a noble cathedral, & good neighbourhood, in a fine country, with a good river running through it'.[34] This 'noble' cathedral was described in equally glowing terms almost fifty years later by Peter Shee:

> The cathedral of Kilkenny is second to none of the kind in this kingdom. It may be exceeded in size by one of two others, but it greatly surpasses them in the lightness, beauty and extent of its Nave; and is superior to all in point of situation. Seated on a gentle eminence, it commands an extensive and variegated prospect of the entire city beneath, of the Nore and its winding banks, and of a charming and fertile country all around.[35]

Within two months of his transfer, the new bishop had already turned his attentions to improving the interior of the cathedral church itself, as is evident from the earliest

Chapter Book of St Canice's Cathedral, which contains minutes of the dean and chapter meetings held during his term of office.[36] Largely relating to the financial accounts of the cathedral, these records, which become noticeably more regular and detailed during Pococke's time, continually reflect his genuine concern for the fabric of the building. On 4th June, at the first recorded meeting held since his translation to this post, the chapter refers to the maintenance of the cathedral when arranging the salary of a slater, Richard Coote, whose job involves 'keeping clean the gutters ledds and battlements belonging to the cathedral'.[37] However, the first reference to the bishop's plans for refurbishment appears a week later, on 11th June, when the following is recorded:

> Whereas the Lord Bishop of Ossary [sic] hath communicated to the Dean and Chapter a design for improving and adorning the inside of the Choir of this cathedral and hath for that purpose recommended a general subscription, he himself having subscribed the sum of fifty guineas.
>
> It is therefore unanimously agreed that the thanks of this body be given to his Lordship for this instance of his laudable zeal and for his generous benefaction and it is also in like manner resolved that this body will annually expend in the said improvements until they shall be fully completed such a sum as can be conveniently spared out of the oeconomy over and above the several contributions of the particular members.[38]

According to a later source, the sum of 1,188 guineas was expended on these and other alterations to the cathedral in 1756, with contributions coming from Pococke himself (a hundred guineas), his mother (ten guineas), sister (five guineas) and antiquarians such as Lord Charlemont (fourteen guineas).[39]

However, a letter from Bishop Pococke to the Dean of Exeter, the Revd Dr Charles Lyttelton, dated two weeks later, 25th June, refers not to his plans for the choir, but the chapter house. He notes that he has already sent the dean 'the plan, and uprights [of the cathedral] & in another packet instructions with a very rough sketch of the Chapter House', and is asking the dean to forward these to the Gothic-style architect Sanderson Miller to execute 'his Designs for drawing'.[40] Pococke does not elaborate on the plans and uprights (elevations) that he had supplied, but it is quite possible, considering his knowledge of architecture and skills in drawing evident from his book on the East, that he had drawn his own. The same is true of the rough sketch for the chapter house, though he could have been referring to drawings executed by or for his predecessor (Bishop Edward Maurice), since a meeting of the chapter, held on 12th June 1755 – a year before Pococke's appointment – had ordered that 'the chapel in the north isle of the cathedral be forthwith fitted up for a chapter house for the use of this body by flooring thereof, making a chimney therein and stopping up the arch over it...'[41] It is likely that the new chapter

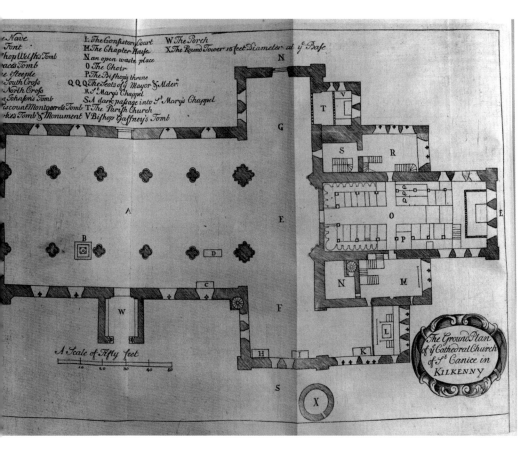

6 – Ground plan of St Canice's Cathedral Church from Sir James Ware's HISTORY OF IRELAND
(courtesy Digital Library @ Villanova University)

house, located in the Lady chapel, was completed in 1763.[42]

To return to the chapter records: what is meant by the reference to the bishop having 'communicated a design' for the choir to the dean and chapter? Had he actually presented rough sketches or designs to this body, or can we interpret the word 'design' as making known his 'intention' to improve and adorn this part of the cathedral? Bearing in mind that he did not actually visit Sanderson Miller at his home in England until September 1756, three months later, and only received the architect's preliminary plans the following October, it is again possible that Pococke had produced his own rough drawings for these alterations. (There is certainly no record of his having consulted or employed an architect locally.) Furthermore, it is likely that these plans were inspired by what he had already enthusiastically admired during his recent visit to the parish church in Hagley Hall, seat of the Lyttelton family, when he stated: 'Sr George Lytelton has adorn'd the church in a most exquisite Gothic taste, Mr Millers design ... all done at ye expence of ye Dean of Exeter.'[43]

In addition to sending the plans, Pococke advised Sanderson Miller to acquire a copy of 'Ware's history of Ireland in wch. is the Cathedral of Kilkenny for a view of the tower'. This revised and improved edition of the book was published in three volumes between 1739 and 1746, and therefore provided a fairly recent, or at least revised representation of the building (Plate 6).[44] This plan appears at the beginning of the section on the See of Ossory, in which biographical details of the various bishops are given up until Pococke's immediate predecessor, Bishop Este. At the end of this account, the author gives a 'Description of the Cathedral in its present Condition':

> It is a large Gothick Pile built in the form of a Cross; the length from East to West takes up 266 Feet in the clear, and the Breadth of the Cross from North to South 123 Feet; being, I believe, the largest Church in the Kingdom, except St. Patrick's and Christ-Church, Dublin; and in the beauty of the Nave it exceeds them both. It is large, spacious and magnificent.[45]

Concerning the principal area to be ornamented by Bishop Pococke, Ware says,

> The Choir hath nothing famous in it with respect to Seats; except a fine old Seat belonging to the Ormond Family. The Compass-Cieling [sic] of the Choir is chiefly remarkable for its fine Fret-work; in which are a great number of curious Modillions; and in the Center a Groupe of Foliage, Festoons and Cherubins, that excells anything of the kind I have seen. A neat set of Organs are a great Ornament to the Choir.[46]

The compass ceiling is still present, of course, but there is no sign of the foliage, festoons and 'cherubins' referred to above.

At a chapter meeting held the following month, on 30th July 1756, it was unanimously agreed that,

> their œconomist for the time-being shall pay for the space of seven years to come annually out of their oeconomy to the Bishop of Ossary for the time being the sum of thirty guineas towards beautifying the Choir in the cathedral provided the exigencies of the cathedral will admit it and that the first payment of thirty six guineas be immediately made to the Bishop of Ossary by the late Oeconomist.[47]

The dean and chapter did not refer again to the matter of building works for almost a year, at a meeting of 10th August 1757, when they unanimously approved 'the Plan for beautifying & adorning the Cathedral Church of St Canice Kilkenny', laid before them by the Bishop.[48] This followed extensive correspondence between

Pococke and Miller over the course of the year (the last letter in this collection being dated 12th December 1757), during which time the two had entered into the intricacies of style, practicalities and workmanship related to the needs of the Bishop.

One of the more interesting letters in the collection is that dated October 1756, following the bishop's meeting with Miller at his home in Radway, when the architect, as recorded in his diary entry for that day, 30th September 1756, had emerged from his sickbed to meet his guest.[49] In this communication, the bishop thanks his host for his 'favour at Radway', and proceeds to list the various alterations and additions he wishes to make to the architect's initial designs. His preference for Gothic taste is emphasised several times in this letter – for example, in his request for Gothic ornaments below the moveable pulpit, an iron gothic rail, and for the bishop's court to be 'done in the Gothic taste' so as to 'appear to greater advantage at the south end of the cross isle'. At the end of the letter (written from his family home in Newtown, Berkshire), and typical of his generosity, the bishop notes, 'I have taken the liberty to order half a hogshead [of port wine] to be sent to you, of wch. I beg the favour of your acceptance by which you will much oblige.'[50] The gift eventually arrived and was duly appreciated both by Miller and his wife – as recorded in a letter from London dated 17th February 1757 – which encouraged the bishop to offer another present, undoubtedly a copy of his Eastern book: 'I have ordered my book binder to prepare a work of one who has a very great regard for you & yours, & shall request the favour of you to let it have the honour of a place in your Library.'[51] In his next letter, dated 3rd November 1756, the bishop observes: 'I am sure the Choir will be most completely adorned with Gothic taste, & I wd. not have it defective upon account of sparing any reasonable expence, but would have it as perfect as can be, as a monument of your Genius.'[52] In his final letter from this collection, sent from Kilkenny on 12th December 1757 after a gap of six months in the correspondence, the bishop refers to Miller's failing health (delicately termed 'a little fall-back'), and states that he is glad the workman Cobb – the carver to be sent from England to execute the work – has not yet arrived, though he would be happy to receive him any time from March of the following year when there would be employment for him.[53]

That is the last we hear of the plans to ornament the cathedral in Gothic style according to Miller's designs,[54] and while this correspondence drew to a close, the chapter and dean moved on, concerning themselves with the details of other minor building operations in St Canice's, such as the construction of walls to the proper height between the churchyard and the 'Liberary' (in September 1757),[55] and later (March 1758) the slating of the 'Widow's Alms House in the Cathedral Church yard'. The cost of this latter work – thirty shillings, payable to Richard Coote – was being given as a 'Charity by the Revd Dean & Chapter, and not to be a precedent for the future repairs of said Alms House'.[56] At the same time, the bishop was petitioning to widen the gateway between the 'Church yard and the Pallace [sic], & put up Gates thereto, which are to be kept locked'. It was agreed, by the chapter and dean on 30th March 1758 that this should be done 'at his own Expence', as should his proposal to construct a 'coverd way from the North Door of the Cathedral to the Wall opposite thereto & make a door in said Wall upon condition that the same be always kept in proper repair...' [57] This latter feature came to be known as the 'colonnade', and is described by Graves and Prim (who mistakenly attribute the date at which permission was granted to May rather than March 1758), as:

> a handsome structure, in the Grecian Doric style [which] completely disfigures the gable of the north transept, very much concealing the fine door from view, and hiding the lower part of the windows by its roof; indeed Pococke, whether from want of funds to defray the cost of glazing them, or from want of taste to appreciate the beautiful proportions of the original design, shortened all the principal windows considerably.[58]

According to John O'Phelan, the bishop had planned to continue the colonnade through the garden to the back door of the palace, but was prevented from doing so by his appointment in 1765 to the See of Meath.[59]

Given the amount of detail entered into by Pococke in his correspondence with Miller, and the great attention paid by him to the need for conforming to Gothic taste, the resulting inclusion of adornments in purely Classical style is indeed curious. As again described by Graves and Prim, almost a century after these alterations: 'The episcopal throne, prebendal stalls, galleries, pews, &c., are all of a fine dark-grained oak, but, being carved in the Ionic style, there is a sad want of harmony between them and the architecture of the fabric.' [60] McCarthy attributes this 'disappointing' outcome to Pococke's difficulties in finding workmen proficient in Gothic design, noting the criticism of these works by J. Prim in a publication from 1844.[61] He also asserts that Graves and Prim had not passed any such 'harsh judgement' in their book published thirteen years later. However, a closer look at this work shows that they were not altogether positive, when they somewhat disparagingly exclaim

> On entering the choir, the feeling which predominates in the well-instructed mind is regret that so much good workmanship and fine old oak timber should be thrown away on the fittings erected by Bishop Pococke. That a man just returned from foreign travel, at the period when he lived, should prefer the Grecian architecture, of the Ionic style, to the Gothic, is, however, nothing wonderful, and, perhaps, we should be grateful that his active and liberal disposition did not lead that prelate to remodel the entire building in the former style.[62]

7 – View of St Canice's by Francis Grose
engraved by J Hooper in THE ANTIQUITIES OF IRELAND (vol. I, pl.43)

While other commentators praise such alterations (John O'Phelan, for example, notes that Pococke 'new modelled and elegantly finished the choir'),[63] a further criticism is of the 'repeated coatings of whitewash to which the carved work of these windows has been subjected', a criticism voiced more than a century earlier by Sir James Ware, who complains of the stupidity of the plastering and white-washing of the pillars in the nave, greatly injuring their beauty. He is informed, however, that the present bishop (Este) 'intends to restore them to their antient Condition'.[64] Clearly, however, this was not done (or at least if it was, it was then undone by Pococke), since the chapter and dean of 4th September 1762 ordered that 'the North-isle of the cathedral be whitewashed'.[65] Similarly, Richard Twiss, in his controversial account of Ireland in 1775, observes of Kilkenny: 'Here is an old castle, and near the cathedral a very high round-tower. The roof of this church is supported by eight large quadruple columns, of black marble, which are embellished, or spoilt, by being white-washed' (Plate 7).[66] Similarly, just four years later, Edward Ledwich refers to the fact that the pillars in the interior had been whitened by 'an absurd and ignorant economist'.[67]

In April 1762, the dean and chapter turn their attentions again to the bishop's more ornamental works – as opposed to the repairs with which they were also concerned – when they begin to pay the arrears due to him for 'beautifying the cathedral church'.[68] However, since their role is largely a financial one, they do not pass any comment on the style of the works eventually effected. Consequently, nowhere in the cathedral's own records is there any reference to the change in style adopted between the original plans, first discussed in June 1756, and the completion of the works and subsequent settling of accounts for these works six years later.

On 13 June 1765, shortly before his departure from Kilkenny, the dean and chapter of St Canice's Cathedral recorded the following declaration in gratitude of the bishop:

> Whereas our present worthy Bishop Doctor Richard Pocock [*sic*] is now to be translated to the See of Meath, we take this first opportunity of our meeting to transmit to posterity our just sense of his merits and of our great concern for losing so good a Prelate, to whom among many other things, we owe not only for ornamenting but almost the very being of our cathedral, for we unanimously order this declaration to be recorded in our books, giving this further testimony of our gratitude, and respect for his Lordship and request the Sub-Dean to send him the earliest opportunity a copy of this Act.[69]

This declaration was signed, among others, by the Reverend Mervyn Archdall, the bishop's domestic chaplain and close friend. It was to his rural parsonage in Attanagh, near Durrow, that Pococke frequently retired to write, and it is said that, while there, he 'framed' the narratives of his travels through Ireland and Scotland. Over two decades later, in recognition of the bishop's former patronage and friendship, Archdall observes in the introduction to his famous *Monasticon*[70] that the 'late learned Dr. Pococke ... frequently noticed the defects of our monastick history, and urged the necessity of its improvement'.[71]

However, Pococke's undoubted appreciation of and expertise in ecclesiastical architecture, whether of England, Scotland or Ireland (he was recognised by antiquaries, for example, as having first observed that the Gothic arch consisted of two Saxon arches intersecting) makes his switch to Classical ornamentation in St Canice's even more puzzling. Surprisingly, almost a century after these embellishments had been completed, they were removed during the next major phase of restoration and repair (under the architect Sir Thomas Deane), and the gallery of the choir, comprising the Classical fittings so criticised by the co-authors Graves and Prim, were subsequently installed in Ennisnag, county Kilkenny (Plate 8), built in 1815 by the Board of First Fruits. Ironically, the rector of this small parish church (described by Lewis as 'a neat modern structure')[72] was the same Revd James Graves, a native of Kilkenny and at the time an influential figure in St Canice's Cathedral, being treasurer of the chapter.[73] Revd Graves was appointed rector of this

9 – View of the Ionic portico of the gallery at Ennisnag church

parish in 1863, shortly before the major renovations at St Canice's Cathedral began.

What remains today is a small but elegant oak gallery which spans the width of the church and is supported by a portico consisting of a double pair of fluted oak Ionic columns, positioned one behind the other and flanked on either side by a plain, unfluted column of hollowed varnished oak, constructed in four vertical sections (Plates, 9, 10). As can be seen from plates 10 and 11, the joins of the fluted columns are more difficult to discern than the plain ones, which have widened substantially with age and wear (Plate 11). The most spectacular feature of the architecture, however, is of course the very ornate carving of the capitals and the entablature (Plate 12). The Ionic capitals, in parts now quite damaged and in need of repair, are striking, and reflect the designs of the entablature above, in particular the recurring egg-and-dart pattern and the swirling acanthus foliage, the latter of which forms the basis of several members, including the fillet, the frieze and part of the cornice. Other Classical carved motifs appearing in this work include dentils and florettes (Plate 13). Granted, the Classical designs were clearly not the work of Miller, and in the absence of any evidence of his dealings with other architects it is interesting to consider what might have inspired Pococke's considerable modifications to the decorative element of the choir in St Canice's Cathedral. Given that we will probably never know precisely why his plans changed midway, nor who executed the final creation, it is tempting to suggest that the bishop eventually consulted his own experiences of Classical architecture from his travels, and in particular the beautiful plates in his book, published to great acclaim only a decade before he was translated to the See of Ossory.

As discussed earlier, Pococke's original intention in writing these volumes was to provide his reader with accurate drawings of the buildings he had seen in the East, later being persuaded to add to these illustrations descriptive accounts. Though it is impossible to single out one particular plate as the source of his actual inspiration, there are several that point to a definite influence, producing in St Canice's Cathedral a mixture of Classical architectural styles and motifs symbolic of his experiences abroad, namely an Ionic portico surmounted by a more elaborate Corinthian entablature.

His only depictions of buildings of the Ionic order are from Athens (where he remained for only five days), specifically the 'Temple Erectheion' (Erectheum) (vol. II, pt. II, bk. III, pl. LXVIII, 163) and the Temple of Ceres with the Remains of an Aquaduct (*ibid.*, pl. LXXI, 167). Of the first building, depicted in Plate 13, and illustrating his obvious appreciation of this style, he observes:

> the building is of a very beautiful Ionic order fluted within eight inches of the capital, which space is carved with bass reliefs of flowers; the cushion of the base is fluted horizontally, as described in Caria; the pilasters at the end of

Ennisnag church

10 – Close-up of the Ionic portico and entablature

11 – Detail of unfluted column , illustrating the join

opposite

12 – Detail of fluted column bases

13 – Detail of carving from entablature

the wall appear is if they were Doric, but in reality are only the cornish [*sic*] between the pillars continued round the pilasters, and below it the relief of flowers is likewise continued on them (Plate 14).

His admiration for the 'floral' design, which in fact would be better described as foliage (reflected in his repetitive use of such patterns in the choir for the cathedral), can be seen again in his depiction of the Door of the Temple of Baalbeck, in Syria (vol. II, pt. I, bk. II, pl. XVI, 109), which he describes as 'one of the most beautiful pieces of antiquity that remains'. Of the door, he asserts, 'Nothing can be imagined more exquisite than the door case to the temple, represented in the sixteenth plate: Almost every member of it is adorned with the finest carvings of flowers and fruits, the frieze, particularly, with ears of corn, most beautifully executed...' He comments

15 – Drawing of the door of the Temple of Baalbeck in Syria
from POCOCKE'S TRAVELS
(vol. II, pt. I, bk. II, pl. XVI, 109)

opposite

14 – Drawing of 'Temple Erectheion' (Erectheum)
from POCOCKE'S TRAVELS *(vol. II, pt. II, bk. III, pl. LXVIII, 163)*

also on the 'exceedingly rich' entablatures of the temple, 'both within and without', and the foliage carved in the central panel of the carving around the door (Plate 15) is close in appearance to the swirling pattern of acanthus leaves dominating the frieze of the cathedral entablature.

Pococke depicts himself, this time in Western costume, observing the beauties of more swirling foliage and rosettes adorning the entablature of the Temple at Pola in Istria (Plate 17). Elsewhere in the book he devotes much attention to the orders, making a particular study of Egyptian pillars, columns, capitals, cornices and entablatures, for example (vol. I, pls LXVI-LXIX, 216-19), and Roman oval capitals (vol. II, pt. II, bk. II, pl. LII, 57) (Plate 16), and frequently highlighting details of the capitals of columns and pilasters by including an enlargement of this feature in the lower section of his drawings.

16 – Drawing of Roman oval capitals
POCOCKE'S TRAVELS *(vol. II, pt. II, bk. II, pl. LII, 57)*

Though surprise has already been expressed in the fact that Revd Graves, albeit so scathing of these features, transferred part of the Ionic gallery from St Canice's Cathedral to his own small parish church in Ennisnag, more surprising still is the inclusion in his own house of yet more of the bishop's ornamentations. As can be seen from Plate 18, neatly positioned in the entrance hall to the glebe house, built in 1821 by the Board of First Fruits, is a pair of oak pilasters decorated with two of the Pococke capitals, forming a simple archway.[74] At first glance it appears that these capitals were taken from the actual columns, having been adapted for their new use by being cut in half. However, on closer inspection it is clear that they are flat, rather than in the round, and therefore can be assumed to have originally formed part of a pilaster. The only surviving photograph of the Ionic columns in situ (reproduced in the second part of McCarthy's article)[75] does not indicate the presence of any pilasters, but the quality of the image is poor and it is not even possible to make out whether the few columns depicted to the right of the central arch and organ are fluted or plain. Sadly, the original sepia photograph from which this reproduction was taken is now missing from St Canice's, and, in the absence of any other contemporary photographs or drawings pre-restoration in 1866, the author has been unable to obtain a better view of this.

Ennisnag Church and the glebe house, however, were not the only beneficiaries of the Pococke pilasters. St Canice's Library, in the grounds of the cathedral, has a large bookshelf situated to the right of the door of the main room. Adorning the top of the shelves are four more pilasters with the same flat capitals as those found in Graves' home (Plates 19, 20).

17 – Drawing of a temple at Pola
from *POCOCKE'S TRAVELS (vol. II, pt. II, bk. V, pl. CII, no. 2, 264)*

18 – Pilaster adorning the hallway of the glebe house at Ennisnag, county Kilkenny
(courtesy Teresa and Mike Donoghue; photo David Kane)

How these oak fittings came to end up in the hands of Revd Graves is docu-mented in the Chapter Book, 1863-1865, whose minutes are devoted largely to the problem of raising funds for the Cathedral's major restoration under Sir Thomas Deane.[76] After much debate, it was eventually decided, at a meeting held on 2nd November 1863, to apply for an Act of Parliament to authorise the dean and chapter to raise this money.[77] The Act, which was established eight months later on 14th July 1864, cited the 'dangerous State of Decay' of the building, and noted, 'it is doubtful whether the Cathedral can be safely kept open to Worship unless the same is put in proper Repair.'[78] Even before the necessary funding had been secured, the dean and chapter were anxious to begin the work on the exterior of the cathedral, and made arrangements to adapt the library room to be 'fitting for the Celebration of Divine Service'.[79] A few days later, a proposal was recorded as follows:

> That as it is most desirable that the Cathedral be fitted for Divine Service
> with as little delay as possible and as in order to that end we should at once
> make up our minds as to whether the Choir or the Nave shall be fitted up for
> that purpose, And we cannot do this so long as the present fittings [i.e.

Pococke's columns, panelling, etc.] remain in the Choir, we hereby desire Mr Robertson our Clerk of Works to have these fittings removed and the Arches into the Side Chapels opened without delay.[80]

A month later it was proposed by the treasurer, Revd Graves, seconded by the Archdeacon, and resolved that

the Timber of the Fittings of the Cathedral be disposed of by Auction saving such proportion as may be selected for the fitting up of Ennisnag Church same to be sold at a valuation together with such of the Old Stalls and Panelling which may be adapted to the fitting of our new Chapter Room.[81]

A fortnight later, this time in the absence of the treasurer, it was agreed that 'the oak fittings for the Church of Ennisnag be sold to Revd James Graves for four pounds'.[82] Accordingly, the auction took place, and in a later minute book entitled Chapter Minutes, 1865-69, the various transactions are recorded.[83] Listed in a section entitled 'Kilkenny Cathedral Economy Fund Account up to 27th February 1868' are the following entries:

Oct. 26th 1864 – To cash received from Mr W.J. Douglas Auctioneer being the proceeds of first sale of old oak, and other building materials and fittings sold by auction at the Cathedral – 42 9 6

Dec. 16th [1864] – To cash from same being the proceeds of the second sale of old Building Materials sold by Auction at the Cathedral on 15 November last – 25 2 3

William Carrigan, in his extensive historical account of the diocese, is therefore incorrect in his dates when he claims that it was in 1868, four years later, that the 'old oak galleries and panellings put up a century before by Bishop Pococke were re-moved'.[84]

Two other sums of money are recorded as being the proceeds of a further two sales of timber and slates, one amounting to £40 14s 1d (23rd March 1865), and the other £34 31s 13d (May 1865). In addition, the sum of £2 14s 4.5d was received from the Archdeacon of Ossory 'for the glass &c of screen over organs'. The total sum raised by such sales, together with various loans and mortgages, produced in excess of £11,000 for Sir Thomas Deane's Cathedral renovations. As his bill amounted to only £10,000, the surplus was subsequently invested.

Clearly, as Revd Graves was the treasurer of the chapter, he was given (or allowed himself) first refusal of the Pococke fittings before the remainder went to auction three weeks later. Such exotic furnishings in the form of an Ionic portico and Corinthian entablature would have been a welcome and, at 'four pounds', an inexpensive addition to the otherwise plain and austere interior of his church, and

19 – Detail of capital of pilaster in St Canice's Cathedral library
(photo: Susan Proud)

20 – View of the Pococke bookshelf in St Canice's Cathedral library
(photo: Susan Proud)

opposite

21 – Detail of library book-shelves in the old Bishop's Palace
(courtesy Heritage Council of Ireland; photo David Kane)

would have brought him great acclaim in what would have been only his first or second year as rector of that parish. Perhaps, having used as much as he needed for such a small church and his residence, he then donated the remaining oak fittings to the Cathedral library – itself being fitted up as a place of worship during the restoration – as a testimony and lasting memory to their originator, Bishop Pococke.

Alternatively, Pococke himself may have ornamented the episcopal library in this way while carrying out the alterations to the Cathedral, this work failing to be documented in the records; likewise with the library of the Bishop's Palace. The Ionic bookcases (Plate 21), in particular the distinctive Pococke capitals, bear a striking resemblance to those in plates 19 and 20. It would make more sense to assume that Pococke had created this library[85] than to imagine that the Ionic fittings, originally part of the Cathedral, were added to the Palace during the Victorian renovations. The other decorative elements of the shelving, however, such as the elaborate swagging and the grotesque masks, appear to belong to a later period and are not in keeping with what we have seen of Bishop Pococke's taste.

Finally, it is thought that some of Pococke's fittings were acquired by the owners of Dunleckney Manor, Bagenalstown, county Carlow. This Tudor-Gothic style mansion, built c.1850, was designed by the Scottish architect Daniel Robertson, who came to Ireland in 1829 and died in Howth, bankrupt, twenty years

22 – View of Dunleckney Manor, Bagenalstown, county Carlow
(courtesy Helen and Derek Sheane; photo David Kane)

later (Plate 22).[86] The current owners, Derek and Helen Sheane, have been told – although there appears to be no supporting documentary evidence – that the following oak fittings in the house derived from St Canice's Cathedral: the cornice and panelling above the fireplace in the school room (Plate 23); the circular group of carved cherubs, said to have come from the ceiling of the Bishop's throne (Plate 24); the impressive oak fireplace, also in the entrance hall, believed to have been the organ case from the Cathedral (Plate 25); and the spectacular baldachino in the front entrance hall, with its unrivalled solomonic columns of bog-oak, once the Bishop's throne (Plate 26). As can be seen in plates 22, 23, 25 and 26, the general impression of these features, with their distinctive Classical motifs, does indeed correspond with some of the Pococke fittings already examined, and the capitals of a further two pilasters in the school room, surrounding the window, have similarities with those already discussed.

While the scope of this study does not permit a full examination of these claims (the author learned of these after completing this study), it is tempting to imagine a connection between the two Robertsons – Daniel, the architect of Dunleckney Manor, and 'Mr Robertson our Clerk of Works', referred to in the

Dunleckney Manor,
Bagenalstown

23 – Detail of cornice and
panelling in the school room,

24 – Circular group of
carved cherubs, said to have
come from the ceiling of the
Bishop's throne

overleaf

25 – Detail of the fireplace in
the entrance hall, believed to
have been the organ case
from the cathedral

26 – Detail of the
balchadino, with bog-oak
solomonic columns, in the
entrance hall

(courtesy Helen and Derek Sheane;
photo David Kane)

Cathedral sources.[87] As we have seen, much of the joinery, particularly the panelling from the stalls and the columns, was sold at auction, while other valuable materials were divided up privately between the more senior members of the clergy. The glass of the organ screen, for example, together with the wooden framework, went to the archdeacon, who paid 'four pence halfpenny per foot, his offer for it being the highest made'.[88] Although the records of the auction have not been traced, it is possible either that the owner of Dunleckney, Walter Newton (or his representative), purchased some or all of the above items, or that at some later date the items stored in the parish church were transferred by the clerk of works, Mr Robertson, to the house.

As to the identity of the latter Mr Robertson, we can assume that he is James George Robertson (1816-1899), who came to Ireland in about 1828 to join his relative William Robertson, a practising architect in Kilkenny. James remained in Kilkenny for sixty years, during which time he held the post of diocesan architect for the United Diocese of Ossory, Ferns and Leighlin until 1869, hence his involvement in the Cathedral renovations.[89] Furthermore, as a noted antiquary and an active member of the Kilkenny Archaeological Society, he would have been on very familiar terms with the founder of this society, the Revd James Graves, and therefore in a good position to acquire any of the salvaged material ensuing from Sir Thomas Deane's renovations.

———

EPILOGUE

Apart from the sentiments expressed on the Pococke Monument (Plate 5), the bishop's name endures, though less distinctively, in the immediate locality of Kilkenny, with housing estates, golf courses and other amenities recently having been named after him.

———

ACKNOWLEDGEMENTS

The author is grateful to the following: Professor Michael McCarthy, for reading an earlier draft of this work and for giving valuable advice; Right Revd Michael Burrows, Bishop of Cashel & Ossory, for permission to photograph and reproduce the portrait of Richard Pococke, Very Revd N.N. Lynas, Dean of St Canice's Cathedral, for permission to consult and reproduce material from the Cathedral archives; Revd J.P. Kavanagh, Rector of Ennisnag church, for permission to photograph the building; Dr Susan Hood, Assistant Librarian and Archivist/Publications Officer, Church of Ireland RCB Library, Dublin, for providing archival material; Susan and Malcolm Proud, of St Canice's Cottage, for assistance in consulting sources in the Cathedral library, photography, and for their kind hospitality; the Director and staff of the Irish Architectural Archive for their kind assistance; Lesley Caine, Archivist, Warwickshire County Record Office, for providing archival material and for arranging permission to publish the Sanderson-Miller correspondence; Michael Foight, Special Collections and Digital Library Co-ordinator, Villanova University, for arranging for the digitisation of Ware's *History of Ireland*, and for permission to reproduce the photograph of the ground plan of St Canice's Cathedral (Plate 6); Donal Sheridan, Ennisnag, for providing information about Ennisnag church; Teresa and Mike Donoghue, Glebe House, Ennisnag, for kind permission to photograph the Pococke archway in their home; Derek and Helen Sheane, Dunleckney Manor, for kind permission to photograph several features of their home; and my husband, David Kane, for the photographic work.

ENDNOTES

The following abbreviations are used:

Pococke's Travels	Richard Pococke, *A Description of the East and Some other Countries: Observations on Egypt* (1742); and *Observations on Palestine or the Holy Land, Syria, Mesopotamia, Cyprus and Candia* (1745)
CB, 1672-1758	Chapter Book, 1672-1758, from St Canice's Cathedral, Kilkenny
WCR	Warwickshire County Record Office
RCB Library	Representative Church Body Library, Dublin

[1] See Michael McCarthy, 'Eighteenth-Century Cathedral Restoration, Part II', *Studies*, IXVI, 261, 1977, 60ff. and n.59. See also Michael McCarthy, 'Eighteenth-Century Cathedral Restoration: Correspondence relating to St. Canice's Cathedral, Kilkenny, Part I', *Studies*, IXV, 260, 1976, 330-43.

[2] See Edward Ledwich, 'The History and Antiquities of Irishtown and Kilkenny' in C. Vallancey (ed.), *Collectanea de Rebus Hibernicis*, IX (Dublin, 1781) 453ff., and Peter Shee, *Epitaphs on the Tombs in the Cathedral Church of St Canice, Kilkenny, collected by John O'Phelan* (Dublin, 1813) 41-43.

[3] McCarthy, 'Cathedral Restoration, Part II', 60.

[4] Joseph Foster, *Alumni Oxonienses 1715-1886 (L-Z)* (1888) 1124

[5] See Richard Mant, *History of the Church of Ireland*, 2 vols (London, 1840) II, 198, where a letter from Archbishop King to Dr Swift (28th February 1708) is quoted, in which the author states, 'As to Dr. Milles's preferment, you will not expect from me any account how it relished here. Some say, if General Laureston had been primate, it would not have been so.' In another

letter, the archbishop (this time addressing Dr Charlet on 7th January 1720) says, 'He is one you sent us, and you must answer for him.' The archbishop's 'predilection' for men of Irish birth was well known (see *ibid.*, 561).

[6] British Library, ADD. MS 19939.

[7] John Ingamells, *A Dictionary of British and Irish Travellers in Italy, 1701-1800* (Yale, 1997) 779-80

[8] Robert Wood, *The Ruins of Palmyra otherwise Tedmor in the Desart* (London, 1753) and *The Ruins of Balbec otherwise Heliopolis in Coelosyria* (London, 1757). These two publications, the result of well-financed expeditions to the Middle East, were to have a phenomenal impact on Western culture, particularly in the development of neoclassical architecture and interior design.

[9] The subject of an article by this author in *Irish Architectural and Decorative Studies*, VIII (Dublin, 2005) 12-42, entitled 'The Classical taste of William Ponsonby, 2nd Earl of Bessborough (1703-97)'.

[10] Royal Society citation, EC/1741/15. Among his proposers was Martin Folkes, Inspector of Medals and Coins in the Egyptian Society, of which Pococke was also a founder member.

[11] *Pococke's Travels*, I, i.

[12] *ibid.*, iii. Michael McCarthy, in a lecture delivered at the National Gallery of Ireland (date uncertain), states that he has no difficulty in accepting the Egyptian drawings as the work of Pococke himself as they are amateur in character by comparison with the prints of the buildings at Athens, Pola and Mylasa. I am grateful to Professor McCarthy for providing me with the text of this lecture.

[13] Daniel William Kemp (ed.), *Tours in Scotland 1747, 1750, 1760 by Richard Pococke Bishop of Meath, from the original MS and drawings in the British Museum* (Edinburgh, 1887; reprinted by Heritage Books, Maryland, 2003).

[14] *ibid.*, xxix.

[15] See M.G. Sullivan's article on Samuel Wale in *The Dictionary of National Biography* (Oxford, 2004-08). See also *Bryan's Dictionary of Painters & Engravers*, 5 (1905) 328-29.

[16] See especially Book II, part II, chapter III, 277-78.

[17] For a full account of these two clubs, see R. Finnegan, 'The Divan Club, 1744-46', *Electronic Journal of Oriental Studies*, IX, 9, 2006, especially chapters 1 and 2.

[18] See Royal Irish Academy, MS 24 E 28.

[19] The minute book for this club is also in the Royal Irish Academy, MS 24 E 37. Pococke was one of the founder members of this organisation and was also one of its officers. For an interesting analysis of the club's minute book, see E. Charles Nelson, 'The Dublin Florists' Club in the Mid Eighteenth Century', *Garden History*, X, 2, 1982, 142-48.

[20] His collections were sold at auction in 1766 and 1777, the two sale catalogues providing detailed information on the nature and extent of his connoisseurship. See Mr Langford and Sons, *A Catalogue of a Curious Collection of Greek, Roman, and English Coins and Medals, of the Right Reverend Dr. Pococke, Lord Bishop of Meath, Collected by his Lordship, during his Travels* (London, May 1766), and Mr Gerard, *A Catalogue of a valuable Collection of Antient and Modern Coins and Medals containing very large and rich series, in Gold, Silver, and Copper, of Greek Kings, Cities, and People, Roman Families, and Imperial Coins, besides a considerable Number of Saxon, English, and other modern Coins and Medals...* (London, January 1777). Both sale catalogues are in the British Library.

21 Quoted in Kemp (ed.), *Tours in Scotland*, xlv-xlvi. The bishop referred to here is the contro-
    versial Robert Clayton (1695-1758), whose town mansion on St Stephen's Green (Clayton
    House, now Iveagh House) is said to have set the style for palatial town houses in Dublin dur-
    ing the period. Though Bishop Clayton's publications are largely of a theological nature, it is
    clear that Pococke refers to the prelate's latest book, *A Journal from Grand Cairo to Mount
    Sinai, and back again...* (London, 1753).

22 The Revd John Swinton (1703-77) was a noted oriental and Arabic scholar, and at the time of
    Pococke's letter was chaplain at Oxford Gaol. He married in the 1740s, some years after
    becoming involved in homosexual scandals involving the warden of Wadham, Robert
    Thistlethwayte, and his pupil George Baker. See article by E.I. Carlyle, 'Rev. Rictor Norton' in
    The Dictionary of National Biography (Oxford, 2004-08).

23 Mrs Delany moved to Dublin after her marriage to the dean in 1743, and much of her corre-
    spondence was published in 1861-62 (five volumes). An abridged version appeared in 1900
    entitled *Mrs Delany (Mary Granville) a Memoir 1700-1788* (New York and London, 1900).
    The comment quoted here is stated in a letter to XXX dated 2nd January 1761, and is repro-
    duced in many works, including Michael Quane, 'Pococke School, Kilkenny', *Journal of the
    Royal Society of Antiquaries of Ireland*, 80, 1950, 41.

24 As described in the catalogue of Liotard's collecton of pictures published in Paris in 1771. See
    *Jean-Etienne Liotard, 1702-1789: Masterpieces from the Musees d'Art et d'Histoire of Geneva
    and Swiss Private Collections* (Somogy Editions d'Art, Paris, 2006) 55.

25 See Michael McCarthy, ''The dullest man that ever travelled?' – A re-assessment of Richard
    Pococke and of his Portrait by J.-E. Liotard', *Apollo*, 143, 1996, 26 and n.14.

26 See W.B. Stanford and E.J. Finopoulos (eds), *The Travels of Lord Charlemont in Greece &
    Turkey 1749* (London, 1984) 163ff. For further discussion of Charlemont's travels, see also
    W.B. Stanford, 'The Manuscripts of Lord Charlemont's Eastern Travels', *Proceedings of the
    Royal Irish Academy*, section C, vol. 80, no. 5 (Dublin, 1980) 69-90, and Cynthia O'Connor,
    *The Pleasing Hours: The Grand Tour of James Caulfield, First Earl of Charlemont (1728-
    1799), Traveller, Connoisseur and Patron of the Arts* (Cork, 1999).

27 Thomas Shaw, *Travels, or Observations Relating to Several Parts of Barbary and the Levant*
    (Oxford, 1738) viii. A copy of the 1757 edition of this book is listed in the sale catalogue of his
    library collection, see *A Catalogue of the Library of the late Right Revd. Dr. Richard Pococke,
    Lord Bishop of Meath Deceased* (Dublin, 1766) 2. This suggests that Pococke did not own, and
    probably had not seen, Shaw's book before embarking on his own travels in the same year.
    This is substantiated in a passage from a letter to his mother, where he shows that he had sent
    to England for a copy of the book to be forwarded to Constantinople for him. However, the
    book never arrived, and he wrote to her again telling her that he had seen another copy and had
    found it no help. Michael McCarthy relates this incident on p.3 of the text of a lecture on
    Richard Pococke (date uncertain). The sale catalogue also lists, on p.8, the 'Supplement to
    Shaw's Travels' (Oxford, 1746), in which the author castigates Pococke for not having
    acknowledged his indebtedness to him. However, as shown above, clearly Pococke did not
    consider Shaw's book to have been particularly enlightening.

28 See Finnegan, 'The Divan Club', plates 5 (Lord Sandwich), 9 (Sir Francis Dashwood), 10
    (Lord Duncannon) and 13 (James Nelthorpe), all depicting members of these societies in orien-
    tal dress. It can be assumed that the donning of these costumes was part of the ritual of the
    Divan, and perhaps even the Egyptian Society (1741-43), of which Dr Pococke and his cousin

Revd Jeremiah Milles were founder members.

[29] For a detailed account of this institution, see M. Quane, 'Pococke School, Kilkenny', 36-72.

[30] From a diary published in 'Some Old Annals of the Stoney Family' by Major F.S. Stoney, 13. Quoted in James B. Leslie, *Ossory Clergy and Parishes: being an Account of the Clergy of the Church of Ireland in the Diocese of Ossory, from the Earliest Period, with Historical Notices of the several Parishes, Churches, &c.* (Enniskillen, 1933) 30.

[31] The entire transcript of his will (drawn up on 10th July 1763) and the codicil (dated 24th March 1765, only six months before his death) is given in Kemp (ed.), *Tours in Scotland*, lxiii-lxv.

[32] Samuel Lewis, *A Topographical Dictionary of Ireland*, 2 vols (1837) I, 282-84.

[33] See Mant, *History of the Church of Ireland*, II, 627. For references to Eastern plants, see *Pococke's Travels*, I, 281-44 and plates LXXII-LXXV. As already noted, these were designed and engraved by D.H. Ehret.

[34] WCR, 125B/798, reproduced as Letter 1 in McCarthy, 'Cathedral Restoration, Part II', 63. It has been held that the Bishop's Palace, erected on the foundations of the medieval palace, was actually built by Charles Este, Bishop of Ossory from 1736 to 1745; see, for example, Mark Bence-Jones, *A Guide to Irish Country Houses* (2nd revised edn., London, 1990) 167. However, Bishop Este merely enlarged and improved this residence, the error perhaps being attributed to Chetwood's description, in 1748, of the palace as being 'new built'. The most comprehensive account of this building is 'The Bishop's Palace, Kilkenny' in *Old Kilkenny Review* (Kilkenny, 2003) 30-53 by the Integrated Conservation Group.

[35] From the preface of Shee, *Epitaphs on the Tombs in the Cathedral Church of St Canice*, 5.

[36] CB, 1672-1758. This manuscript, which in fact continues much later than the date suggested in the title, is kept in St Canice's Cathedral, Kilkenny, and I am most grateful to Dean Norman Lynas for allowing me access to the records and for permission to quote them in this study.

[37] *ibid.*, 334.

[38] *ibid.*, 335.

[39] See table entitled, 'Benefactors for Adorning the Cathedral of St. Canice, 1756' in J. Graves and J.G.A. Prim, *The History, Architecture & Antiquities of the Cathedral Church of St. Canice, Kilkenny* (Dublin, 1857) 59.

[40] WCR, 125/B798. Lyttleton, a noted antiquary, knew Pococke through the Royal Society of Antiquaries, to which they had been elected fellows in the early 1740s. He was, at the time of his correspondence with the bishop, engaged in the restoration of Exeter Cathedral, and had two years previously (in 1754) written the building's first history, eventually published in 1797. A further connection Pococke had with Exeter was, of course, with his cousin Jeremiah Milles, whose preferrement to that cathedral had taken place almost a decade earlier, in 1747, when he was appointed precentor, prebendary and then canon residentiary, until succeeding Lyttelton as dean in 1762. For an excellent discussion of this building, see Sam Smiles, 'Data, Documentation and Display in Eighteenth-Century Investigations of Exeter Cathedral' in Dana Arnold and Stephen Bending (eds), *Tracing Architecture: the Aesthetics of Antiquarianism* (Wiley-Blackwell, 2003), 80-99.

[41] CB, 1672-1758, 330.

[42] See William Hawkes, 'Sanderson Miller of Radway, 1716-1780, Architect' (dissertation submitted for Diploma in Architecture at University of Cambridge, Jesus College, 1964) 65. I am grateful to Mrs Lesley Caine at Warwickshire County Record Office, for providing me with

relevant extracts of this dissertation.

43 Cited in William Hawkes (ed.), *The Diaries of Sanderson Miller of Radway, together with his Memoir of James Menteath*, Dugdale Society Publications, 41 (Dugdale Society, Stratford-upon-Avon, 2005) 35, 251.

44 The full title of the book is *The Whole works of Sir James Ware concerning Ireland revised and improved*, and was published in Dublin. Sir James Ware's dates were 1594-1666. However, Pococke had a copy of the 1705 edition, which is listed in the sale catalogue of his library, *A Catalogue of the Library of the late Right Revd. Dr. Richard Pococke*, op.cit,. 3.

45 *The Whole works of Sir James Ware*, 433.

46 *ibid.*, 434.

47 It was at this meeting that a John McCreary was appointed as beadle 'to attend the cathedral and take care of the churchyard at a yearly salary of forty shillings ... [and] be provided ... with a blue surtout coat turned up with red and that the same be badged with the seal of this body' (CB, 1672-1758, 337). However, the appointment was to be terminated six years later, in September 1762, when it was ordered that McCreary be 'turned out for the neglect of his duty and that a proper person be appointed in his room' (CB, 1672-1758, 369).

48 CB, 1672-1758, 341.

49 He records, 'In a violent sweat. Could not get up until near three o'clock. Mary read twelve Spectators. Wrote part of a letter to Mr Wright. Mr Hughes dined with us. Dr Pococke, Bishop of Ossory, came at 5 with letter from the Dean of Exeter [Dr Lyttleton]. Conversation with him about alteration in Kilkenny Cathedral. Very wet day. See Hawkes (ed.), The Diaries of Sanderson Miller, 275.

50 WCR, 125/B/799.

51 WCR, 125/B802. It would be interesting to know if he inscribed this with the words 'Donum Authoris', as he did with the copy donated to the library of King Edward's School, of which his father (also Richard Pococke) had been headmaster for nine years. See C.F. Russell, *A History of King Edward VI School Southampton* (privately printed, 1940) 206.

52 WCR, 125/B/800

53 WCR, 125/B/785.

54 The editor of Sanderson Miller's diaries conveniently summarises the extent of the architect's plans, as follows: 'the chancel was to be fitted out with new carved oak stalls, surmounted by the arms of the preceding seventy-five bishops. The arms were to be in stucco for economy and painted under Miller's direction. At the west end of the chancel, a gallery was to be formed with rosettes on the cornice. The lower part of the walls were to be wainscotted with clustered columns to give "a Gothick look". Above this, the walls were to be of stucco, and the existing ceiling remodelled, but keeping to original centre ornament of "foliage, festoons and cherubs", which Pococke considered "would suit very well with the Gothic work as there is nothing in it relating to the Orders". At the east end of the chancel, there was to be a bishop's seat on the south, with three cushions and a canopy above, a double communion rail in gothic, and a moveable pulpit with Gothic ornament.' Hawkes (ed.), *The Diaries of Sanderson Miller*, 276, n.9.

55 *ibid.*, 343.

56 *ibid.*, 345.

57 *ibid.*, 347.

58 Graves and Prim, *History, Architecture & Antiquities*, 57-58. McCarthy, 'Cathedral

Restoration, Part II', however, asserts that Bishop Williams blocked the windows in the 17th century, not Bishop Pococke (see n.64).

[59] See Shee, *Epitaphs on the Tombs in the Cathedral Church of St Canice*, 42.

[60] *ibid.*, 57.

[61] See McCarthy, 'Cathedral Restoration, Part II', 61.

[62] *ibid.*, 90-91.

[63] See Shee, *Epitaphs on the Tombs in the Cathedral Church of St Canice*, 42.

[64] Ware, *The Whole works of Sir James Ware, etc*, 434.

[65] CB, 1672-1758, 369.

[66] Richard Twiss, *A Tour in Ireland in 1775* (London, 1776) 141, and R. Finnegan (ed.) *A Tour in Ireland in 1775, Richard Twiss* (Dublin, 2008) 70.

[67] Francis Grose, *The Antquities of Ireland*, edited by Edward Ledwich, I (London, 1791) 34. This is taken directly from Ledwich's earlier work, see note 2, above.

[68] CB, 1672-1758, 368.

[69] *ibid.*, 393.

[70] Full title, *Monasticon Hibernicum: An History of the Abbeys, Priories and Other Religious Houses in Ireland, Interspersed with Memoirs of their Several Founders and Benefactors. Likewise an Account of the Manner in which the Possessions Belonging to These Foundations were Disposed of, the Present State of Their Ruins* (printed for RIA by Luke White, Dublin, 1786).

[71] Quoted in Mant, *History of the Church of Ireland*, II, 625-26.

[72] Lewis, *Topographical Dictionary of Ireland*, I, 607.

[73] It is maintained, too, by the editor of Pococke's Scottish tours, that this same 'learned antiquary' had in his possession the original manuscript of John O'Phelan's famous work on St Canice's tomb inscriptions. See Kemp (ed.), *Tours in Scotland*, xlix. As noted by his biographer, in 1849 Graves and his relative, James Prim (editor and subsequently proprietor of the *Kilkenny Moderator*) helped to establish the Kilkenny Archaeological Society for the preservation, examination and illustration of ancient monuments of Irish history, manners, customs, and arts, especially as connected with the county and city of Kilkenny. Twenty years later this society became the Royal Historical and Archaeological Association of Ireland, and Graves became editor of its journal. See article by J.T. Gilbert (rev. Marie-Louise Legg) in *The Dictionary of National Biography* (Oxford, 2004-08).

[74] This house was built at a total cost of £738 9d 3s. See Ecclesiastical Commissions (Ireland) Fourth Report, 1837, 160-61.

[75] McCarthy, 'Cathedral Restoration, Part II', 62.

[76] This source was originally thought to be in St Canice's Cathedral but turned out to be located in the Representative Church Body Library, Dublin, and I am grateful to Dr Susan Hood for finding this for me.

[77] RCB Library, Chapter Book, 1863-1865, 21.

[78] See RCB Library, MS C3/13/2/2.

[79] RCB Library, Chapter Book, 1863-1865, 57, meeting of 23rd August 1864. A reference is made, on p.65 of this manuscript, to another book which was to be purchased to keep a record of the proceedings of the 'continuation of the works of reparations', under a committee of the Entire Chapter appointed 'to watch the progress of the works', but sadly this book has not been located.

80   RCB Library, Chapter Book, 1863-1865, 59-60, meeting of 3rd September.

81   *ibid.*,64, meeting of 4th October 1864.

82   *ibid.*,65, meeting of 20th October 1864

83   There are no page references in this manuscript, which is located in St Canice's Cathedral.

84   *The History and Antiquities of the Diocese of Ossory*, III (Dublin, 1905) 148.

85   See the study on the Bishop's Palace by the Integrated Conservation Group (my note 34 above), where it is suggested that the library was created by Pococke (p.47).

86   See the biography of Daniel Robertson in Anne-Martha Rowan, *Dictionary of Irish Architects*, Irish Architectural Archive, www.dia.ie/architects/view/4570.

87   See my note 80, above.

88   RCB Library, Chapter Book 1863-1865, 62-63, meeting of 20th September 1864.

89   See biography of James George Robertson in Rowan, *Dictionary of Irish Architects*, www.dia.ie/architects/view/4573.

―――――

Hard times:
an episode in the life of the Belfast portrait painter Samuel Hawksett

EILEEN BLACK

ELDOM IN THE EARLIER ART HISTORY OF BELFAST DOES ONE COME ACROSS CORREspondence which sheds light on aspects of an artist's life, which adds flesh to the bones of a long-dead painter. One such collection of letters is to be found in the papers of the Royal Belfast Academical Institution, held in the Public Record Office Northern Ireland. Written by Samuel Hawksett (1801-1859), the correspondence reveals the difficulties he experienced in receiving payment from the school for a portrait he had painted for it, and tells of his subsequent straitened financial circumstances. A sorry saga, the letters point to duplicity and meanness of spirit on the part of the school's managers, and show them to have been surprisingly hardheaded in their business dealings.

The foremost portrait painter in Belfast during the first half of the nineteenth century, Hawksett was a native of Cookstown, county Tyrone.[1] Little is known of his early life or training except that he had received instruction in the drawing school of the Academical Institution, established in 1814.[2] His teacher there was the fiery Italian, Gaetano Fabbrini, drawing master from 1814 until his dismissal in 1820.[3] Hawksett first came to notice in 1824, when a copy he painted of *St Catherine of Alexandria*, by Federico Barocci, was exhibited in the town's Commercial Buildings, to great acclaim in the local press.[4] During the second half of the 1820s, he spent lengthy periods in London, fulfilling professional engagements in the capital.[5] An exhibitor at the Royal Hibernian Academy between 1826 and 1834, his sitters included prominent local figures such as the Marchioness of Donegall, Revd Dr William Bruce, and shipowner Robert Langtry (Plate 1).[6]

1 – Samuel Hawksett, ROBERT LANGTRY   c.1743, oil on canvas, 131.5 x 101 cm

(© Ulster Museum 2008; courtesy Trustees National Museums Northern Ireland)

As can be seen from the somewhat pedestrian quality of this latter work, Hawksett's abilities were limited and his sitters invariably have a stiff and rather lifeless appearance; they also had a rather unnatural look to their complexions. That his shortcomings were standard and not simply the result of 'off days' is clear from a decidedly scathing review in the *Belfast News-Letter* of 28th September 1838, worth quoting from at some length because of its relevance and insight:

> Mr. Hawksett has a good number of portraits in the present exhibition [the Belfast Association of Artists, 1838]. The likenesses are all pretty correct, and we will do him the justice to say that they are all carefully and minutely finished; on a close examination, we are convinced, they must be the result of immense patience and labour; at the same time, we think that Mr. H. deals rather too much in white, brown and red cheeks, which give his pictures the appearance of too much mannerism. When you see one portrait of Mr. H.'s you see them all, that is to say, the same style of colouring that suits the commoner will do for the king, or *vice versa*. Now we are of opinion that it should be the study of the portrait painter to transfer to canvas the *complexion* of his sitter as faithfully as the *features* … Perhaps Mr. Hawksett's most glaring fault lies in the attitudes; they are too stiff and formal.

Nevertheless, despite such shortcomings, Hawksett maintained a steady practice in Belfast until the mid-1840s.

During the 1830s he undertook two commissions for the Academical Institution (Plate 2), the foremost educational establishment in town at the time,

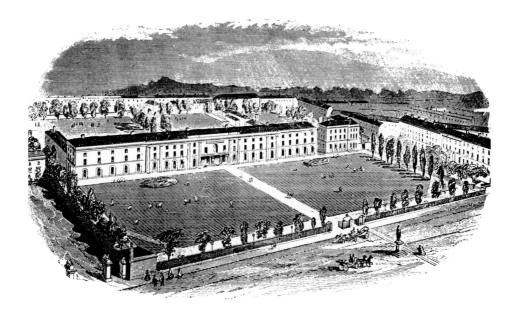

3 – Samuel Hawksett
JOSEPH STEVENSON
c.1837, oil on canvas, 129 x 102 cm
(© Ulster Museum, 2008; courtesy
the Trustees of National Museums
Northern Ireland)

opposite

2 – THE ROYAL BELFAST
ACADEMICAL INSTITUTION
from an engraving (c.1855) in
Joseph Fisher and John H. Robb,
THE BOOK OF THE ROYAL BELFAST
ACADEMICAL INSTITUTIONC
CENTENARY VOLUME 1810-1910
(Belfast, 1913) and on the cover
of John Jamieson, THE HISTORY OF
THE ROYAL BELFAST ACADEMICAL
INSTITUTION *1810-1960 (Belfast,*
1959)

namely, a portrait of King William IV (no longer at the school) and one of Joseph Stevenson, honorary secretary of the Institution.[7] The portrait of Stevenson (Plate 3), painted around 1836 and shown in the Belfast Association of Artists' exhibition of that year, displays all the stiffness of pose typical of Hawksett, and also the rather strange and unnaturalistic colouring referred to in the above *Belfast News-Letter* critique.[8] A version of the work, probably the prime original, is still at the school. Its commissioning and purchase by the Institution seems to have been a straightforward affair, unlike that of the portrait of the king.

IN THE WINTER OF 1831, THE BOARD OF MANAGERS AND BOARD OF VISITORS OF the Institution (the governing body, known as the Joint Boards), desiring William IV become patron of the school, requested Lord Belfast, Vice-Chamberlain of the Royal Household, to ask him if he would agree to this.[9] The king assented by mid-November, and commanded that the Institution add 'Royal' to its name.[10] The idea for the portrait – obviously intended to commemorate this kingly patronage – was most probably raised at a general meeting of the school's proprietors on 22nd November following, although this cannot be corroborated either through the school's records or by press reports.[11] What is certain is that the proposal to commission the work was made by 20th December, as a letter from Lord Belfast to the Joint Boards makes clear. According to the noble lord,

> he had taken the first opportunity to request his Majesty to allow his Portrait to be taken to be hung up in the Institution and that his Majesty had been graciously pleased to permit Mr. Hogshea [Hawksett] to copy the best of his Portraits for the Institution but his Majesty had not time to sit for that purpose.[12]

At a meeting of the Joint Boards in early January 1832, Hawksett was 'appointed to go to London to draw a Portrait of His Majesty and that his expense be paid by private subscription from the Members of the Board and others, not to exceed Sixty pounds'.[13]

By 27th May 1836 the portrait was almost finished, and Hawksett thereupon presented his bill to the Joint Boards. His somewhat lengthy letter of explanation makes interesting reading for the light it sheds on his own financial situation:

> In placing my account before you, I think it right to present the reasons which have obliged me to go beyond the sum suggested by Dr. McDonnell [£60] as being the amount you were disposed to give for a portrait of His Majesty. I need not say that I have anxiously endeavoured to make the picture good, as I have spared neither time nor labour with that view, and as to expense, the following statement will speak for itself.
>
> When I went first [to London] in 1832 for the purpose of painting the King's picture, I took of my own, ten pounds – £10.0.0 and borrowed from Dr. McDonnell – £20.13.0. When this sum was exhausted I returned home, untill [sic] I should be able to realize another supply three years afterwards, accordingly I set out with twentytwo pds. – £22.0.0. This having proved insufficient to enable me to produce a picture worthy of my commission and the facilities His Majesty was graciously pleased to grant me, I had recourse to a remittance of £15.0.0 more, through Mr. Molloy, this enabled me to produce the picture in your possession which has cost me as you may perceive in mean outlay sixtyseven pounds thirteen £67.13.0.
>
> Therefore Gentlemen I am induced to hope you will consider it good value for one hundred pounds – £100.0.0.[14]

If Hawksett had hoped for a speedy settlement of his bill, he was to be sadly mistaken. After waiting another few months, his patience appears to have worn thin, and on 18th July 1836 he wrote again:

I beg leave most respectfully and earnestly to call your attention to my request of the 27th of May, believing that notwithstanding the multiplicity of your public business of late, you would have condescended to take some favourable notice of it before this, if you had for a moment imagined that my promises and arrangements for some time past with those to whom I am in debt, were made on the faith of that generous promptitude which character-ized you towards Mr. Silo [the framer of the portrait], and which I am quite unconscious of having rendered myself undeserving of by any misconduct, on the contrary I am persuaded that the good feeling of the Gentlemen com-posing the Boards only requires to be touched by the information which I am unwillingly obliged to communicate. The truth is, I am this very week greatly pressed for money, and must cast myself entirely on your consideration...[15]

Unfortunately, payment was not to be forthcoming, despite the emotional overtones of this appeal. Nonetheless, despite his obvious disgruntlement with the situation, Hawksett exhibited the king's portrait, with that of Stevenson, at the Belfast Association of Artists' show later in the year.

The winter of 1837 saw him applying yet again for redress. However, the response from a meeting of the Joint Boards on 21st November was anything but hopeful: 'Resolved That the order for the Painting having been given not by the Joint Boards, but by certain individuals on their own Account – The Joint Boards can only refer Mr. Hawksett to the Persons by whom the Painting was ordered.'[16]

Not surprisingly, the matter continued to rumble on, with the next letter from Hawksett to the Boards being dated 17th July 1838:

I take the liberty of addressing you again on the subject of His late Majesty's Picture, for which I have not been able to obtain a settlement. Upon the receipt of your letter of Nov 22nd [the Joint Boards' response of 1837 above], with a copy of the Resolution of your Boards, I felt rather annoyed at the determination therein expressed, but upon reflection conceiving myself to have a just cause, I thought if I could only manage to submit the subject to your view in the same light as I was impressed by it myself, I would have every chance of being successful, as you would then see my reasons which would in some degree excuse my importunity.

At your request I waited on Doctor McDonnell the only *Surviving Member* of the *Board* from *whom* I received the order to paint the Picture, Doctors Tennent and McCleery, and William Tennent Esq being now deceased, and showed him your Resolution, at which he said, 'That although the Picture had not been ordered by the Board, with a condition that they should pay for it out of the Public money, yet, it was so *perfectly understood* to be a *transaction undertaken* for the advantage and *honour* of the

Institution, he could not suppose the Boards would ultimately fail in contriving some means of reimbursing [?] me, and he advised me to repeat my application, when he was sure my claim would at once be recognised.'

The plain statement of my case, is, that in 1832, the *then* Managers of your Royal Institution ... came forward and signed *their names* as a requisition to His Majesty, that I might obtain permission to paint *for them* His portrait. [There is no mention of this petition for the picture in the Joint Boards' minutes.] The liberty was granted in the most gracious and condescending manner, and the picture in Belfast in 1835, when I was requested ... to have it ready for *the* Lord Lieutenant's inspection in October. A suitable frame was ordered, and before His arrival punctually paid for, *both* were *shown to him* as the *Public property*, and no other idea was then entertained by any person. Some months after, I sent in my account, so low, that the most fastidious could not object, a Gentleman was appointed to receive the various Subscriptions, by whose order I recd 29£ of Subscriptions on the 28th Feby, 1836. Since which time I have made several respectful applications without effect, to the last of which I recd a Resolution the Boards or a few of them had come to [that of 21st November 1837], referring me to the 'person or persons who gave the order on their own account'. This greatly astonished me, the King being dead, and some of those most desirous of having it also deceased, believing as I did, that a succession of Managers did not imply the overthrow of all the wishes of their honourable predecessors, which this Resolution so far as it went effectually did. Supposing some mistake to exist, I now respectfully appeal to the good sense, and common justice, of the Joint Boards, for a speedy redress of my grievances on this subject. Trusting this appeal may not share the fate of my former applications.[17]

As a result of this, two members of the Joint Boards (James McCleery and Maurice Cross) were deputed to obtain information as to who had authorised the commissioning of the portrait.[18] The result of their enquiry, recorded in the Joint Boards' minutes of 21st August 1838, found that 'the order was not given by the Boards of the Institution; but by several Individuals in their private capacity'.[19] These findings must have caused Hawksett considerable dismay.

The situation must have pricked a few consciences, for in the following month a sum of money was collected and given to Hawksett.[20] The exact amount remains unknown; however, it was obviously not the £71 outstanding (he had already received £29 of the £100), as he continued to push for settlement.

In 1839 he tried a different approach, and placed his case before the proprietors of the school at their annual meeting on 2nd July. Though his letter of appeal is missing, a report of the proceedings in the local press contains a useful summary of the meeting, and sheds light on what became of the painting:

> Dr. Cooke [Revd Dr Henry Cooke, one of Hawksett's champions] ... read a
> letter from Mr. S. Hawksett, the artist, complaining, in terms apparently
> prompted by a keen sense of injury, that a picture of his late Majesty, Wm.
> IV, which he had been engaged to paint for the Institution, and in executing
> which he had incurred much expense, by a visit to London, etc., had been left
> on his hands for some years, and that his account remained unsettled.[21]

Clearly, he had reclaimed the portrait at some point, although it is not known when.
It was certainly still at the school in early 1837 when the *Belfast Commercial
Chronicle* of 1st March commented upon it being there.

A long discussion then ensued amongst the proprietors as to whether the
Joint Boards were liable for payment or not. The conclusion reached concurred with
the Boards' findings of 1837 and 1838:

> that highly respected friends of the Institution, some of whom were since
> dead, had designed the picture as a present ... and that the order had emanated
> from them. Under these circumstances, it was conceded, on all hands, that the
> Boards were not called on to settle Mr. Hawksett's claim out of the public
> funds; but, it was also admitted, that he had not been treated in fairness, and a
> subscription was opened, in the Hall [the school's Common Hall], to liqui-
> date the amount due to him (about £100), to which almost every one present
> willingly contributed, though several felt themselves called on publicly to
> deny an assertion in Mr. Hawksett's letter, – that payment had been withheld
> by the Boards, because he had voted for Mr. Emerson Tennent [Conservative
> MP for Belfast], at the last election![22]

This last charge, which smacks of paranoia on Hawksett's part, appears to have
been met with some surprise, and led 'three or four of the leading officers of the
Institution' to declare that 'they were, until then, totally ignorant of Mr. Hawksett's
politics.'[23] (Hawksett is aluding to the fact that he had voted for James Emerson
Tennent in the 1837 general election and not for the Liberal candidate James
Gibson, a member of the Joint Boards. He seems to have thought that this preju-
diced the Boards against him). The discussion of the subject ended at this point.
Unfortunately, the sum of money collected in the Hall remains unknown.

In 1840, Hawksett approached the proprietors yet again, at their annual meeting on 7th July. As with 1839, his letter of appeal is missing. From newspaper coverage of the event, however, it would seem that after the meeting of 1839, W.J.C.
Allen, a member of the Joint Boards, was 'pressed to set about collecting subscriptions; but, on going through the town, he found that people were unwilling to subscribe, until Mr. Hawksett should retract his offensive charges.'[24] What these

additional claims were is not recorded in the press coverage of the 1839 meeting, Hawksett's only reported accusation being that concerning Emerson Tennent.[25]

The proceedings of the meeting of 1840 make somewhat comical reading, as the discussion around the 'pictorial question' (to quote Revd Dr Henry Cooke) degenerated into a verbal sparring match between Cooke and Revd John Scott Porter, the school's honorary secretary.[26] Cooke, prior to reading Hawksett's letter, explained that he had altered some expressions in it and stated that

> if any remained that might appear harsh, he ... would not hold himself accountable for them; but he hoped, the Proprietors would take into consideration that a person not accustomed to composition, was liable to use expressions that might imply more than was intended.[27]

Whatever about the intemperate tone of Hawksett's letter, his accusations were certainly thought-provoking. After recounting events surrounding the execution of the work, he claimed that the Joint Boards' loyalty to the king had declined after his death. He also complained of the shabby treatment he had received from the school, charged the Boards with breach of agreement, and threatened legal action if the picture was not paid for. For Cooke's part, he thought the money should be paid whether Hawksett had a legal claim or not, and expressed his willingness to subscribe another ten shillings.

A discussion then ensued on the history of the portrait's commissioning and the extent of the Boards' liability. In Porter's opinion, the Boards had nothing whatever to do with the matter. Cooke, however, declared that he understood there was in existence a 'memorial from [them], praying his Majesty to permit Mr. Hawksett to be permitted to take his portrait'.[28] Porter, however, denied that the Boards had ever made any such application and said he could find no trace of it in the records. Cooke then stated that he believed the money would have been paid if the king had lived longer. Porter responded by stating that when the king was alive, the Boards' answer was the same as it was now: 'that they were not liable for the price of the picture, and that they had never employed Mr. Hawksett to paint it.'[29] Cooke thereupon repeated his belief that the money would have been paid if the king had lived. By this stage, the atmosphere appears to have become quite heated, judging by Porter's rejoinder:

> The Boards had certainly considered the picture as the property of the Institution, as it had been received as a present; but they never had paid, nor engaged to pay, one penny for it. Mr. Hawksett had shewn [sic] himself a very pertinacious and abusive individual. He had, moreover, contrived, under one pretence or other, to carry off the picture from the Institution; and it would be a more proper proceeding, if the Boards were to send a Constable

to look after him for having carried off their property, than that he should bring charges against them. For his ... part, he was not disposed to subscribe a penny to pay Mr. Hawksett.[30]

Cooke then suggested that the matter be submitted to a lawyer chosen by both sides, an idea which was quickly dropped because of the expense involved. Eventually, he undertook to have Hawksett 'withdraw his offensive letters of this year and last year, so that they might not be an obstruction to a subscription', and the subject was closed.[31] Hawksett agreed to this course of action in early August, and must surely have felt that the end was in sight.[32]

It was not to be. On 3rd August 1841, a full year after his hopes had been raised, he placed yet another letter before the proprietors at their annual meeting on that day. The content should come as no surprise:

Gentlemen,

It is first my duty to thank you which I do most cordially for the resolutions passed in my favour in 1839 and 1840 [not quite the case, as the Boards still denied liability], in consequence of my applications to you for the price of His Majesty's picture which I painted for the Royal Belfast Academical Institution in 1835. [Hawksett's memory is clearly shakey on this point, as the picture was commenced in 1832 and completed in 1836.]

But in the next place, in as much as no benefit has resulted to me, I am obliged once more to solicit your favourable consideration of the injury which such a delay of payment inflicts upon me.

When I learned that the letters which had been laid before you for me were withdrawn to make way for a settlement, I communicated to the Joint Boards my acquiescence in that measure respectfully expressing my desire to learn at what time the settlement consequent thereupon might be hoped for, as I believed that it was their duty to give effect to your determination.

I have received no reply from any quarter, no intimation that the measures which were to follow the withdrawment of my letters have been adopted, and I am therefore reluctantly compelled once more to place my claim for payment before you.[33]

As a result of this, W.J.C. Allen and another member of the Joint Boards, James Standfield, resolved at a Board meeting on 5th October following to try to raise more subscriptions.[34]

This further attempt was also unsuccessful, so Standfield reported to the proprietors' annual meeting of 5th July 1842.[35] This same meeting saw yet another letter from Hawksett read to the company. Though not reported in the press, the content was apparently the same as ever: when might he expect payment for the portrait? Needless to say, the response was also the same as ever:

> it was explained, that neither the Court [of proprietors] nor Boards had any-
> thing to do with the matter. Some individuals had interested themselves in it,
> and Mr. Hawksett had both the picture and part payment; and the Boards or
> Court were in no way responsible to him.' [36]

With that, the matter was finally closed, as far as the school was concerned.

Though there was no further reference to the painting in the school's records, this was not the last to be heard of it. In June 1859, notices appeared in the *Northern Whig*, stating that the picture was to be raffled on 18th July at 52 Fountain Street for the benefit of Hawksett's widow, with 150 tickets at £1 each.[37] That Mrs Hawksett was anxious to sell seems clear from one of the pieces, which stated that the king had sat to Hawksett at St James's Palace – a claim at variance with Lord Belfast's statement of December 1831, which had explained that the king had no time to sit.[38] Whether such 'puffing up' of the portrait was successful or not remains a mystery, as does the current location of the work.

NOT ONLY IS THE WHEREABOUTS OF THE PAINTING UNKNOWN, WHAT IT ACTUALLY looked like is something of a puzzle. Described in one of the above-mentioned *Northern Whig* raffle notices as being full-length and 9 x 6 feet (274.5 x 183 cm), press comments at the time of its showing at the Belfast Association of Artists in 1836 are somewhat confusing.[39] According to the *Belfast News-Letter* of 13th September, the work was 'a successful imitation of Lawrence. The head is well painted, and placed on the shoulders with an air of great dignity. The draperies fall gracefully, and into rich folds – every thing is done with an eye to the best effect. It is in every respect a pleasing picture.' However, the *Northern Whig* of a few days later was less specific, and described the painting as being 'chiefly after Sir Thomas Lawrence'.[40] That the 'draperies' were actually a cloak of some kind is made plain by an amusing piece in the *Belfast Commercial Chronicle* around the same time. Written in stage Irish, supposedly by one Darby Fegan of county Armagh to his wife Molly after a visit to the exhibition, his recollections went thus:

> ...a bit beyont him [a portrait of a black slave in chains by Arthur Joy] –
> would you believe it, Molly – there stood King William the Fourth, blessings
> on his good-natured countenance, as clever a lookin gentleman as you'd see
> of a summer's day, and mighty clane dressed – he'd a cloak upon him would
> make our Jenny [his daughter] and you cloaks a-piece, and somethin over.
> Bill [the guide in the exhibition] tould me ... how the King sat for his picture,

4 – Sir Thomas Lawrence
WILLIAM IV WHEN DUKE OF
CLARENCE
c.1827, oil on canvas,
253.5 x 162 cm

overleaf

5 – Sir David Wilkie
WILLIAM IV
1832, oil on canvas,
270.5 x 177 cm

6 – Sir Martin Archer Shee
WILLIAM IV
1833, oil on canvas,
270.5 x 178 cm

(all The Royal Collection © 2008
Her Majesty Queen Elizabeth II)

till a handy little Belfast man drew him out in Lonnon. I suppose he ris when he was done ... I am tould here, his image is for the big school-house, in town ... where there's the best of learnin to be had...[41]

As if the above descriptions were not confusing enough, to add to the puzzle, Lawrence's portrait of the king in the Royal Collection shows him wearing a three-quarter-length coat and not in a cloak of any kind. Painted around 1827, the work depicts him not as monarch, but as Duke of Clarence (Plate 4).[42] However, two other full-length portraits in the Royal Collection show him both as king and in grandiose draperies: that by Sir David Wilkie of 1832 (Plate 5) and one by Sir Martin Archer Shee of 1833 (Plate 6).[43] Hawksett may have seen the Wilkie in 1832; he could certainly have seen both works at Windsor Castle on his second visit to London in

1835. He may perhaps have taken the pose and background of the Lawrence portrait and added the draperies of the Shee (the figure in which is closer to the Lawrence than that of the Wilkie). Though conjecture, this seems not impossible given that the portrait appears to have been something of a hybrid, judging from its description in the press.

INTERESTINGLY, IN 1837 THE SCHOOL ACQUIRED ANOTHER PORTRAIT, THAT OF THE Lord Lieutenant of Ireland, the Earl of Mulgrave, whose visit Hawksett referred to in his letter of 17th July 1838. The artist was the young Dublin portrait and subject painter Nicholas Joseph Crowley (1819-1857), who had been living in Belfast in 1835 and 1836. That the painting was an 'official' commission is clear from press reports of the Belfast Association of Artists' show of 1837, in which the portrait was included. The *Belfast Commercial Chronicle* was loud in its praise: 'we must admit that the proprietors of the Institution have every reason to congratulate themselves on the manner in which Mr. Crowley has fulfilled the honourable commission entrusted to him,' whilst the *Northern Whig* declared: 'The portrait of Earl Mulgrave displays great skill ... the painting is intended for the Royal Belfast Institution...' [44] Full length and showing the earl in the costume of Governor-General of Jamaica, standing in a landscape, the picture clearly had considerable merit. Unfortunately, the work is no longer at the school, which knows nothing of its whereabouts. [45] Whatever about the location of the painting – the fate of which is a somewhat bizarre parallel to that of the Hawksett portrait – a young artist in the early stages of his career might have been expected to charge for such a work. This Crowley declined to do, as is obvious from a letter he addressed to the Joint Boards on 19th December 1837:

> Gentlemen,
>
> In compliance with the request of Sixty Proprietors of the Institution, his Excellency the Lord Lieutenant has honoured me by sitting to me for his Portrait.
>
> The picture is now finished. May I beg of you to accept it, as a proof of my high appreciation of the honour done me by soliciting me on this occasion...[46]

So delighted were the Joint Boards with the donation that they arranged for the chairman, secretary and treasurer to form a deputation to wait on Crowley and present him with a letter of thanks. [47]

Whilst Crowley's admiration for the school was probably genuine and his altruism wholly sincere, there may have been another factor behind his generosity. He and Hawksett almost certainly knew each other well, for both had served on the committee of the Belfast Association of Artists in 1836 – Crowley as secretary, Hawksett as treasurer. By the winter of 1837, Hawksett's problems in obtaining payment for the king's portrait – which he had certainly regarded as a commission – had become obvious. He may well have regaled Crowley with details of the situation. Crowley, wishing to avoid any possible unpleasantness, may have decided to take the easier option and present the portrait to the school. Whilst this is simply speculation, the thought is worth considering.

———

ACKNOWLEDGEMENTS

I am grateful to the Royal Belfast Academical Institution and the Public Record Office Northern Ireland for permission to quote from the school's records. My thanks also to the Royal Collection for the use of images, and to Lucie Strnadova for her assistance with this matter.

ENDNOTES

The following abbreviations are used:

BCC	Belfast Commercial Chronicle
BNL	Belfast News-Letter
NW	Northern Whig
PRONI	Public Record Office Northern Ireland

[1] According to the Burial Register of the New Burying Ground of the Belfast Charitable Society, Hawksett was born in Cookstown, county Tyrone, and was aged fifty-eight on his death on 9th February 1859. W.G. Strickland's Dictionary of Irish Artists (Dublin and London, 1913) incorrectly records his dates as 1776-1851. The name Hawksett is not known in the Cookstown area and may have been altered to Hogshaw, Hockshaw or Hockset, all of which were current in the region in the nineteenth and twentieth centuries.

[2] BNL, 9th December 1828. For information on early drawing schools in Belfast, see Eileen Black, Art in Belfast 1760-1888: Art lovers or Philistines? (Dublin and Portland, OR, 2006) 15-21.

[3] *BNL*, 27th January 1824.

[4] *ibid.*, 13th and 27th January 1824.

[5] He is known to have been in London from late 1824 until the spring of 1825 (*BNL*, 5th November 1824) and from late 1828 to early 1829 (*ibid.*, 4th November 1828).

[6] The portrait of the Marchioness of Donegall was exhibited at the RHA in 1826 (39). Langtry was the father-in-law of the famous actress and sometime mistress of Edward VII, Lillie Langtry. See Eileen Black, *A Catalogue of the Permanent Collection: 4: Irish Oil Paintings, 1831-1900* (Ulster Museum, Belfast, 1997) 27-29, for further details on Hawksett.

[7] For information on the school, see Joseph R. Fisher and John H. Robb, *The Book of the Royal Belfast Academical Institution: Centenary Volume 1810-1910* (Belfast, 1913) and John Jamieson, *The History of the Royal Belfast Academical Institution 1810-1960* (Belfast, 1959).

[8] There are three versions of the portrait – one in the school, one in the Ulster Museum and one in a private collection. Stevenson was honorary secretary from 1808 until his death on 13th January 1837.

[9] PRONI, SCH 524/3A/1/4, Joint Boards' meeting of 15th November 1831. Lord Belfast was Vice-Chamberlain of the Royal Household from 1830 to 1834 and 1838 to 1841.

[10] *ibid.*

[11] There is no mention of the idea for the portrait in press coverage of the general meeting of proprietors on 22nd November 1831, namely, in the *BNL*, 25th November 1831, and *NW*, 24th November 1831. Those who subscribed five guineas to the school were known as proprietors and had the right to elect the administrative officers from amongst themselves. The Board of Managers and Board of Visitors were elected from proprietors who subscribed twenty guineas. For the administrative structure of the school, see Jamieson, *History of the Royal Belfast Academical Institution*.

[12] PRONI, SCH 524/3A/1/4, Joint Boards' meeting of 20th December 1831.

[13] *ibid.*, Joint Boards' meeting of 3rd January 1832.

[14] PRONI, SCH 524/7B/73/1. The author first saw Hawksett's letters in PRONI in 1978 and made transcripts of them. However, on rechecking them in 2008, the letter of 26th May 1836 had apparently gone missing. The quoted letter is therefore from a transcript. Regarding persons mentioned, Dr James McDonnell was a member of the Joint Boards. Joseph Molloy was drawing master at the Institution from 1830 to 1870, and is best known for his illustrations of the seats of local nobility and gentry, engraved and published by E.K. Proctor in his *Belfast Scenery in Thirty Views* (Belfast, 1832).

[15] PRONI, SCH 524/7B/73/2. Modesto Silo & Sons, a local firm of carvers, gilders and picture frame-makers, supplied the frame for the portrait.

[16] PRONI, SCH 524/3A/1/5, Joint Boards' meeting of 21st November 1837.

[17] PRONI, SCH 524/7B/73/3. Dr Robert Tennent and Dr James McCleery were members of the Board of Managers. William Tennent was one of the proprietors.

[18] PRONI, SCH 524/3A/1/5, Joint Boards' meeting of 17th July 1838.

[19] *ibid.*, Joint Boards' meeting of 21st August 1838.

[20] *ibid.*, Joint Boards' meeting of 4th September 1838. The collection of this unspecified amount was made by Robert James Tennent.

[21] *NW*, 4th July 1839.

[22] *ibid.* James Emerson Tennent (1804-1869), politician and traveller, was elected Conservative MP for Belfast in December 1832. He and George Dunbar were defeated as Conservative can-

didates for the town in the general election of August 1837 by the Liberals James Gibson and the Earl of Belfast. Gibson and the earl were unseated on petition in March 1838, and Emerson Tennent and Dunbar declared elected. Emerson Tennent was re-elected in 1841 but was unseated on petition. He regained his seat in 1842, and remained a member of the House of Commons until July 1845, when he received a knighthood. See B.M. Walker (ed.), *Parliamentary Election Results in Ireland, 1801-1922* (Dublin, 1978) and *Oxford Dictionary of National Biography* (Oxford, 2004).

23 *NW*, 4th July 1839.
24 *ibid.*, 9th July 1840. W.J.C. Allen was honorary secretary of the Institution from 1844 to 1877.
25 *BNL*, 5th July 1839; *NW*, 4th July 1839.
26 Revd John Scott Porter was honorary secretary of the Institution from 1837 to 1840.
27 *NW*, 9th July 1840.
28 *ibid.*
29 *ibid.*
30 *ibid.*
31 *ibid.*
32 PRONI, SCH 524/7B/34/21, letter of 4th August 1840.
33 PRONI, SCH 524/7B/35/32, letter of 3rd August 1841. (This letter has an incorrect reference in the SCH 524 calendar, being catalogued as SCH 524/7B/35/31.)
34 PRONI, SCH 524/3A/1/5, Joint Boards' meeting of 5th October 1841.
35 *ibid.*, annual meeting of proprietors, 5th July 1842.
36 *NW*, 7th July 1842.
37 *ibid.*, 9th and 10th June 1859. Hawksett married twice: Rachel, who died of cholera on 15th July 1849, and Mary Anne, who died of consumption on 25th April 1866 (Burial Register of the New Burying Ground of the Belfast Charitable Society).
38 *ibid.*, 10th June 1859.
39 *NW*, 9th June 1859 gives the dimensions of the portrait.
40 *ibid.*, 15th September 1836.
41 *BCC*, 17th September 1836.
42 Oliver Millar, *Later Georgian Pictures in the Royal Collection* (London, 1969) 62 (cat. no. 877), pl. 229.
43 ibid., 143 (cat. no. 1185), pl. 276 (Wilkie); 116 (cat.no. 1084), pl. 301 (Shee).
44 *BCC*, 20th September 1837; *NW*, 21st September 1837. The portrait was no. 22 in the Belfast Association of Artists' exhibition. According to the *BCC* of 1st March 1837, the earl was sitting to Crowley at that time.
45 Correspondence from Christopher Maitland, Royal Belfast Academical Institution (letter of 7th February 2008). The portrait was certainly at the school in 1888, when it was exhibited in the Belfast Free Public Library Opening Art Exhibition (13).
46 PRONI, SCH 524/7B/31/87. In 1838 the Joint Boards paid Crowley £32 10 0 for a frame for the Mulgrave portrait and other expenses relating to the picture; PRONI, SCH 524/3A/1/5, Joint Boards' meeting of 5 June 1838. Crowley may have ordered a new and better frame for the work since presenting it in 1837.
47 PRONI, SCH 524/3A/1/5, Joint Boards' meeting of 19th December 1837.

'Doing Everything of Marble wch can be Done with it': some descriptive accounts of the Kilkenny Marble Works

TONY HAND

A T SOME TIME DURING THE EARLY 1740S, A VISITOR TO MADDOXTOWN, COUNTY Kilkenny, examined what he called a 'Curious piece of Mechanicall Art' situated on the banks of the River Nore, a few miles south-east of Kilkenny city. He suggested that, with the proper encouragement, this machinery would prove 'a Valuable Manufactory to this place [Kilkenny] and to the Whole Kingdom In Generall'.[1] These comments, along with a detailed report of this 'Mechanicall Art', are contained in the papers of the Physico-Historical Society, held in Armagh Public Library. This society was established in 1744, and its purpose was to record the antiquities, natural history, geography, economy and society of the whole of Ireland. Its papers were based on topographical and statistical returns sent to Walter Harris, a founder of the society, from selected persons representing each county, the respondent for county Kilkenny being one Hugh Dawson (Plate 2).[2] The machinery that Dawson witnessed was the innovative and highly developed equipment involved in the cutting and polishing of the renowned black marble of Kilkenny. Dawson informed Walter Harris that the inventor of this wonderful industry, known as the Kilkenny Marble Works, was 'Mr William Colles a Native of this Kingdom' (Plate 1). Colles' enterprise was open for all to see, and it appears that no visit to Kilkenny was complete without visiting the Black Quarry, the source of the marble, and the Marble Works. This article will examine some of the more enlightening reports of the quarry and the marble mills to reveal how William Colles transformed the mar-

1 – S. Whitmore, WILLIAM COLLES (1702-1770) *oil on canvas, 75 x 62 cm (Rothe House, Kilkenny)*
(courtesy Kilkenny Archaeological Society; all photos by the author unless otherwise stated)

2 – An account of the Black Quarry from the Physico-Historical Society Papers
(courtesy the Governors and Guardians of Armagh Public Library)

ble industry in Kilkenny and how his endeavours influenced this industry, not only at local and national levels, but at an international level also.[3]

William Colles (1702-1770) was the second son of William Colles, a surgeon, of Kilcollan and the city of Kilkenny, and his second wife Hannah. At an early age William was adopted by his aunt, Mrs Elizabeth Berry. She had been married and widowed three times but only had one child from these marriages; this child died in infancy, hence her adoption of William. William's father passed away in 1719 and declared in his will that his son was so amply provided for by his aunt that all he was to receive was £100 and a family heirloom of a silver hilted sword. William senior appears to have been a fairly wealthy man, having bought lands in Kilcollan and Lisnafunchin from Kilkenny Corporation in the 1690s. He built a number of houses on the west side of St Stephen's Green, Dublin, in 1716, in one of which his eldest son Barry died in 1785.[4] It transpired that the young William was not amply provided for by his aunt, as she became embroiled in a dispute over property in Spain associated with her first husband, and, arising from this, all that she left to William was 'the satisfaction of burying her at his own charge'.[5]

It appears from this that William had to learn the art of self-reliance at an early age. Nothing is known of his education, and not being inclined to follow in his late-father's medical footsteps, he 'depended on his own exertions', becoming 'a man of universal talent, pre-eminent as a mathematician and mechanician'.[6] By

1742 William was earning over £300 per annum from his marble business, the fruit of his inquisitive and inventive mind.[7] Colles may have been something of a mathematician and inventor, but he also displayed a very keen business sense.

It was, in fact, Colles himself who first brought his inventions to public attention. In February 1732 he wrote to the recently formed Dublin Society informing them of improvements he had carried out in Kilkenny regarding the exploitation of marble. In his letter he mentioned a quarry on the outskirts of Kilkenny city, formed of 'Excellent black Marble, beautifully Veind, with great Variety of White'.[8] He also mentions that he had just secured an interest in this quarry on foot of successful experiments carried out on cutting and polishing the marble, using machinery driven by water power. This feat was the first of its kind in this country and in Britain, and the quarry Colles described was the famed Black Quarry of Kilkenny.

Colles recognised that the traditional way of sawing and polishing marble was laborious and costly;

> ye tedious & expensive Methods of sawing, & polishing which, in the comon Way renderd the Trade for the said Marble less extensive than it might be, if wrought by a more expeditious Manner, induced me to try some Experiments in relation to sawing the same by an Engine, wch appearing practicable, I obtained an Interest in the Quarry, & some Mills, on the River ... where I have now ten Saws, wch are mov'd by Water, & going Night and Day, and saw the Marble more true, and expeditious, than it can otherwise be done.[9]

Sawing marble in the 'comon Way' was indeed a laborious affair. The basic technique for sawing stone was that a mixture of water and sand was fed between a flat toothless metal blade and this was moved back and forth along the stone. The blade ground the sand against the surface of the stone, slowly wearing a narrow channel in the stone. Pliny, writing in the first century AD, gave an account of this method of sawing stone from Roman Antiquity. He stated that 'This division [sawing], though apparently effected by the aid of iron, is in reality effected by sand; the saw acting only by pressing upon the sand, within a very fine cleft in the stone as it is moved to and fro.' [10] Little seems to have changed in this method of cutting stone up to the seventeenth century, as revealed in an entry in the diary Samuel Pepys, dated 24th February 1664. Pepys was observing a stonecutter sawing marble at Somerset House and recorded how 'He told me ... how he could not saw above 4 inches of the stone in a day, and of a greater [amount] not above one or two [more inches] ... Their saws have no teeth, but it is the sand only which the saw rubs up and down that doth the thing.' [11]

Not only had Colles set up ten water-driven saws to cut the marble, but he had also constructed another machine to grind the marble with sand so as to enable it to be polished by hand. He employed upwards of thirty men to polish and finish

3 – Mr Stern Tighe's house on Usher's Quay
It is now demolished. The downpipe on the right was
made from marble, eight inches square and in lengths
of three feet (courtesy Irish Architectural Archive)

4 – Piece of marble water pipe
Note the countersunk top to allow pipes to fit neatly
without leaking.

marble chimney pieces, tables, cisterns, mortars and tombstones 'wch I sell at more reasonable Rates, than heretofore they were Sold'.[12] The success of the initial experiments led Colles to take things one step further. He developed a system enabling him to bore 'Pipes of the sd Marble, wch I have brought to such Perfection, that I can bore Pipes of any reasonable Length from 2 to 10 inches Diam fit for conveying water underground, or from the tops of Houses'. Colles sounded very confident indeed that his products were top quality and fit for their purpose, and as if to quell any doubts Society members may have had about the said items, he concluded his letter by stating that the pipes could be witnessed carrying out their task 'at Mr Stern Tighs Mercht on Ushers Quay' (Plates 3, 4).[13]

In November 1734, the following advertisement appeared in *Faulkner's Dublin Journal*:

> Just arriv'd from Kilkenny, and are to be sold at the Kilkenny Marble Ware-house in Batchelor's-Lane, the lower End of the Batchelor's Walk, Marble Chimney Pieces, Tables and other Marble Furniture of the best kinds and newest Fashions; As also, a large Parcel of Flags, the best and cheapest, for flooring of any Flags hitherto brought to this City. At which Place, as also at the Marble Mills near Kilkenny, all Kind of

5 – George Miller, MR. COLLES MARBLE MILLS, MILLMOUNT
detail of early nineteenth-century watercolour
(courtesy Royal Society of Antiquaries of Ireland: Miller-Robertson Collection)

Marble Work is made and sold at reasonable Rates, by Mr. William Collis.[14]

This advertisement displays the business acumen of William Colles. Just a few years after informing the Dublin Society of his marble cutting and polishing ventures in Kilkenny, he is firmly established as a marble dealer in Dublin, selling his own products. He was using a natural resource to craft items that were not only practical but fashionable also, appealing to a clientele that was busy in the construction of town houses at this time. Colles was now bringing to fruition the ideals contained in his letter to the Dublin Society. He was providing marble more expeditiously than ever before by a process never before seen in this country, resulting in the price being more reasonable for a quality product, and, ironically, rather than machinery replacing men, it was creating much employment locally.

Two anonymous English gentlemen, on visiting Kilkenny in the late 1740s, were suitably impressed by the 'Invention & Contrivance' they witnessed at the Marble Works. They wrote in their book *A Tour through Ireland...*[15] that the mills were worked by 'the finest Piece of Mechanism our Eyes ever beheld'. The visitors were of the opinion that a statue 'cut by the Chisel of a Praxitelles' should be erected to the 'Inventor, Mr. Collis'. The mills, situated 'in a delightful Bottom, the Passage to it through a pleasant Grove ... do their marvellous Work by the Help of the River; and are so wonderfully contrived, that they saw, bore, and polish at the same time' (Plate 5). Colles appears to have had a production line in operation at the mills: the machinery was 'perpetually at Work, by Night as well as by Day, and required little Attendance'. This concurs with Colles's statement above that the operation was 'going Night and Day'. The Englishmen felt that the Marble Mills were beyond compare: 'Had I not seen any thing worthy of notice in the Kingdom, but this one, I should think all my Labours fully paid.' They sounded suitably impressed, to say the least.

Alongside the marble mills, the gentlemen stated, were warehouses in which were stored chimney pieces, cisterns (Plate 6), buffets, vases, punch bowls, mugs of different dimensions, frames for mirrors and pictures. The visitors also mentioned the quality of the marble: 'It is full as durable, and bears as fine a Polish as any brought from Italy.' Unfortunately the authors are very economic with their description of the workings at the quarry. Blocks of marble weighing several tons were removed from the quarry, 'yet the Method the Contriver has used to lift them, draw them out, and convey them to the Mill, without any other than manual Operation, adds still more to the Surprize'.[16] This tantalisingly brief summary of the quarrying methods being carried out indicates that no machinery was being used in the quarrying of the marble.

6 – A fine example of a carved Kilkenny Marble cistern
(photo courtesy Knight of Glin)

The Black Quarry had been the source of quality stone in Kilkenny for architectural and decorative purposes since medieval times, but now Colles was exploiting this natural resource more efficiently than at any other time in the quarry's history. The quarry lies in the great expanse of carboniferous limestone that stretches across central Ireland. The age of the marble has been estimated to be about 300 million years old.[17] Over this time the marble was laid down in the form of beds. These beds inclined from the river, to appear near the surface in the area of the quarry. Situated on a sweeping bend of the River Nore in the Archersgrove area, the quarry had been used by the people of Kilkenny as and when they needed it. The marble was used by local sculptors for many monuments and memorials found in Kilkenny and the surrounding area, a splendid example being the Rothe monument, carved in 1637 by Patrick Kerin, in St Mary's church. (Plate 7).

In an article by the Revd James Graves and John Prim written in 1858, there is an account of marble quarries in Kilkenny written in the seventeenth century and attributed to Bishop David Rothe. This account mentions two quarries, one to the east of the city, the other lying to the north.[18] The marble from the northern quarry was of a rough grain, prepared in large quantities and dressed for building purposes. The inhabitants of Kilkenny were 'distinguished above most others of the realm by their propensity to erect structures of marble of a large and more splendid class'. The quarry to the east is most certainly the Black Quarry, as the marble was described as 'cerulean, black, white, or variegated with divers hues', and was 'exported to a distance, or else stored at home for building purposes'.[19] Whether the marble was exported a distance from Kilkenny or a distance from Ireland is unclear from this account, but the fact that the marble was 'exported' from the region proves the estimable quality of the stone. We do know that in 1664 the Duke of Ormonde instructed John Morton to raise marble from the 'Quarry near Kilkenny' for a chimney piece, and that it be 'sent forthwith to Waterford that so it may be sent in the Spring on the first ship' to the Lord Chancellor of England, the Earl of Clarendon.[20] In 1652 Dr Gerard Boate stated that marble was to be found in many places around the country, but 'more about Kilkenny, where not only many houses are built of the same, but whole streets are paved with it'.[21] It would appear from this statement that Boate was suggesting that the marble was being put to better use here than anywhere else in the country at that time. He also suggested that the quarry 'belongeth to nobody in particular, lying in common for all the townsmen, who at anytime may fetch as much out of it ... without paying anything for it'.[22]

Thomas Dineley, believed to have visited Kilkenny in 1680/81, described the recent addition to Kilkenny Castle – the water house. This structure, adjoining the bowling green, had a summer banqueting room attached, 'floor'd and lin'd with white and black marble, which abounds here'.[23] James Beeverell is regarded to have visited Kilkenny in 1707. In the Irish volume of his *Les Delices de la Grande-*

Bretagne he noted the following:

> The quarry from which the inhabitants get their marble is only two or three
> hundred paces from the town and belongs to no-one in particular, so that any-
> one may take as much as he wants. The marble found there is greyish in
> colour when newly cut from its bed, but receives a fine polish and takes on a
> dark blue colour.[24]

The quarry had been in the hands of Kilkenny Corporation at this time, but early in
the eighteenth century it became a private concern, and by 1730 Colles was its
leaseholder. For a clearer view on how William Colles transformed the operation of
the quarry, we must return to Hugh Dawson.

Dawson had emphasised the quarry's reputation, its marble 'which being a
Black Ground with good Variety of White figures Is Justly famous for Its Beauty;
Solidity & ye High Polish It Takes & Retains'.[25] The white particles were assumed
to be broken shells of several types of sea creatures, and they stood proud of the surface of the stone by a quarter to half an inch. The vocabulary used by the author is
interesting. He suggested that, at some stage, the marble was a 'Soft Blew Slab of
Clay', and at a period of, perhaps, 'ye Deluge', it was mixed with broken shells and
on the 'Withdrawing of the Waters or by Some Power In Nature to us as yet
Undiscovered' this mixture became solidified. The possibility was then considered
that the white particles were never shells in the first instance, and were formed in
the stone at 'the Creation of All things'. These comments display an enquiring mind
trying to reason the formation of the fossilised marble in relation to Biblical
accounts of the Creation and the Great Flood.[26]

Dawson's next descriptions are physical rather than hypothetical, and display
a first-hand knowledge of the quarry. A layer of about twenty feet of clay and loose
limestone covered the uppermost part of the quarry. This rested upon another thirty
feet of inferior stone which was used for walls. At this time, he says, the quarry was
being worked to a depth of about seventy feet from the surface. This is a considerable depth, and indicates that the quarry had been producing stone over a long period of time. Dawson goes on to state that the quarry was opened originally from the
river and gradually worked into the rising ground, following the limestone beds.

The means by which the stone was quarried in the past were regarded as
somewhat primitive by Dawson. As the stone was only being used randomly for
building or monumental purposes, those using the quarry 'had not the Art of Sawing
It for Marbles', nor did they use gunpowder, resulting in 'those Beds wch were
Difficult to Raise' being left behind. Most likely these beds were of valuable stone,
but were rendered inaccessible due to the piecemeal quarrying being carried out.

---

7 – Patrick Kerin, Rothe Memorial (1637), St Mary's church, Kilkenny

The current quarrymen used the modern method of clearing the upper levels with gunpowder, which they 'Ram with Dry Clay Into Holes bored In the Solid Stone'. This was the standard method of quarrying, and upon reaching the superior beds, all blasting ceased. He goes on to say that the quality stone was then raised with 'Very long Crows[bars] and by Driving Iron Wedges under the Blocks of Marble & In the Back Joynts'(27), a method known as 'plugs and feathers'.[28] Blocks had been raised that were over twenty feet long and weighing over twenty tons. This concurs roughly with Richard Pococke's comments when he visited the quarry in 1752 where he witnessed 'entire pillars and jaumes of doors of one stone' being raised, up to a length of fourteen feet.[29] Dawson informs us that the quarry 'Is the Estate of Warden fflood Esq and Mr Richard Jacob', and was at that time in the occupation of Mr William Colles. Pococke also provided a description of the marble and its products during his visit in 1752. He said that there were two or three kinds of marble in the quarry, 'the white being made by petrified shells, but there is a sort called the feather marble from some resemblance of feathers'. The machinery 'turned by water for sawing and polishing ... made punch bowls, tea dishes, saucers and frames of pictures'.[30]

Dawson's account above of the quarrying of marble at the Black Quarry does not tell us how the marble was loaded and taken away. The normal series of stages in removing and transporting blocks of stone were that once the required block was removed from the quarry face, it would have been lowered carefully to the quarry floor. Some remedial work may have been carried out at the quarry prior to its delivery to the marble mills. Whether preliminary work was required or not, the block would be placed on horse- or ox-drawn carts and then transported to the mills, but as the Black Quarry was very close to the Nore, it was possible that some of it may have been loaded on to barges and brought down the river to the Marble Works just a few miles away. There was a quay on the Nore at the Black Quarry, and Colles laid a wager with a gentleman by the name of Godfrey Cooksey as to the possibility of bringing up a load weighing forty tons on a boat from the quay at the Black Quarry to the new quay at John's Bridge in the city in 1762,[31] a formidable task, indeed, to haul such a weight against the current. Whether Colles won his bet or not was never recorded.

In the seventeenth century, the whereabouts of the marble being exported was not revealed, except for Clarendon's chimney piece, but in the eighteenth century the two English gentlemen informed their readers that 'this ingenious Gentleman sends yearly several Ship Loads to England'. They also felt that their fellow countrymen were 'often better in improving than inventing, but here ... their Industry must fail' when compared to the innovations Colles had carried out at the Marble Works.[32]

It was not only English visitors that recorded their visits to Kilkenny; a French traveller, Aubry de la Mottraye, visiting in 1729, commented that Kilkenny was a 'large City, one of the most magnificently built on account of the Marble

Quarries'.[33] A fellow countryman, Charles Etienne Coquebert de Montbret, was less impressed when visiting Kilkenny in 1790. In his travel recollections, *Carnets de Voyage*, he remarked that the streets were 'badly paved, without footpaths or lamp-posts'. However, he does portray the quarry in better light. The structure of the quarry was soil, gravel and several beds of limestone, which lie upon 'seven or eight bands of non-conchiferous marble two or three feet wide and then return to the black stone'. The marble was worked at a depth of thirty or forty feet and was 'exploited from top to bottom entirely in the open air'.[34] Hugh Dawson stated the marble was being worked at a depth of seventy feet from surface in his description from about fifty years earlier, so we may assume that the Frenchman's measurement of thirty or forty feet was the thickness of the quality stone deposited below at least thirty feet or more of inferior material. This may appear that not much marble had been quarried during this period, but it should be remembered that a quarry will advance in both vertical and horizontal directions in order to access the more lucra-tive beds of stone, and in the Black Quarry the most lucrative beds were the black marble beds containing the fossilised remains of once-living sea organisms.

In 1757, Emanuel Mendes da Costa gave an account of the fossilised stones and marbles that were known at that time. He stated that black marble could often contain coralloids, remnants of coral, composed of a whitish opaque spar, and when polished could result in a beautiful finish, and 'Sometimes this marble has also many white sparry casts of shells, both turbinated and bivalve; but this is not com-mon, and is only observable in the sort dug at Kilkenny.'[35] He describes the Black Quarry, which 'is about half a mile from Kilkenny in Ireland; the quarry is vast, having been workt many years'. The ground above the quarry consists of small masses or 'nodules of this same marble, no wise different from what is found in strata in the quarry' which was used to pave the streets of the city.

It was not only male visitors that wrote of the quality of the Black Quarry. Anne Plumptre, writing in 1817, noted that the 'marble quarries are not above a quarter of a mile from the town; they are very extensive'. She stated that all the rock was composed of course and fine marble. The finer marble slabs were 'reserved to be polished and used for the purposes of chimney-pieces and the like', and the course marble was 'employed in all the most ordinary uses ... with this refuse the town is paved'.[36] She also recorded that some of the 'poorest houses in the town are in like manner built of marble, the roads are mended with marble, and some of the inclosures are fenced with marble'.[37]

William Colles was very adept at self-promotion and relaying the benefits of his machinery, but appeared very coy in explaining how this machinery actually car-ried out its work. In 1743 Colles wrote a letter to the Revd John Perry in Dublin.[38] In this correspondence he enlightened Perry on how his own business was developing as he informed the good reverend that he was 'always on new Inventions for Doing

Everything of Marble wch can be Done with it', and that he had 'Contrived a very Light Cheap and Expeditious Handmill of stone for grinding apples for cyder'. This invention would result in greater volumes of cider produced. and would also 'grind them without leaving any part unground'. Colles also described another new product he had brought to fruition, this being 'picture frames of marble for Prints and small paintings wch Look light & neat'. These were obviously the same frames the English gentlemen and Richard Pococke were to observe on their later visits. The last item mentioned regarding the Marble Works was the new method he had invented for 'giving many Kinds of mouldings in the marble by water without ye help of a stone cutter'. Colles does not elaborate any further, so once again we must turn to Hugh Dawson for some idea on how the machinery performed its tasks.

Dawson described how Colles had 'Erected Mills on the River Nore for Manufacturing the said Marble where by Iron Saws moved by two Waterwheels It Is Sawed with Much more Expedition and Truer than by Mens Hands'.[39] After this initial process, the marble is then 'Ground to Bring It Truly out of Winding by a Waterwheel fixed Horizontaly which Is moved by a Current Passing by One Side of the Wheel while the Rest Wades in an Eddy'. To take the stone 'out of Winding' or 'out of twist' was, and still is, a process to create a flat plane surface which, up to this, was always done by hand.[40] Once this flat surface was achieved, the other surfaces could be squared and measured from it. Placed above this horizontal waterwheel

> is a Circular Bed of the Saw'd Marble of 27 feet In Diameter Laid Levell and Bedded In Sand on wch are laid a parcelle of Marble Slabbs…wch by an arm Passing from the Shaft are Moved Round over the Bed and by a Small wheel fixed on said arm are so Shifted to and from the Center That they Every round change their Possision so as to Make no Hollows In ye Bed.[41]

It is difficult to picture this process, but it appears that there were three waterwheels in action – two vertical wheels and one horizontal wheel. It does state that the smaller slabs of marble were rubbed over and back along the large circular piece, and that, most likely, sand was used as an abrasive in this process. It is also not clear whether the circular bed was a standard twenty-seven feet in diameter or how such a large piece was cut into a circular shape. The thickness of this piece is not mentioned and we are not informed as to whether it had to be replaced, or how often it may have been replaced when worn. It would have to have been cut by hand, as Colles would surely have mentioned if he had invented a machine for cutting blocks into circular shapes. Was it one whole piece of marble or was it constructed from a number of pieces to form a circle? Even the quarrying of such a large piece, if it was one piece, is a mystery.

This description of the horizontal wheel is very likely a variation, or adaptation, of the horizontal-wheeled flour mill which had been widely used in this country since early medieval times. A mill of this kind consisted of a small two-storey wooden building, or stone in this case. The lower compartment, where the wheel was situated, straddled the millrace, the water entering through a chute at one end and flowing out the other, which was open. The millstones were placed in the upper compartment where the grinding was carried out. This would appear to be the basic mechanics of Colles' wheel. Whatever the case may have been, the time taken to complete this rubbing process is indicated in the following:

> the Bed Stones take a fortnight or 3 weeks to Rubb Sufficiently but the Uper Stones wch are always In Motion are Rub'd twice In a Day Here the Marble after being Rub'd on the fface Is alsoe Rub'd on the Edges wch Makes It as True as if Chiselled and free from Gapps.

This appears to suggest that the circular bed was stationary, as it was bedded in sand, but after a fortnight or three weeks would seem to have done its job, while the smaller slabs were moved by an arm attached to a shaft being powered by the horizontal waterwheel. The following stage in the process involved the marble being placed in another mill,

> where 3 or 4 Peices [sic] being Laid Side by Side there and fixed on Each of Them a piece of a Kind Greet [grit] Stone Called Black Hone…which being moved by ye Mills Backwards and forward the whole Length of the Marble Slabb Takes out ye Tracks of the Sand & Leaves the Marble Smooth Skin'd and Black:

This would indicate that the marks left by the sand during the rubbing process were then removed by the honing process. This was the last mechanical process prior to the marble being worked on by the stonecutters into chimney pieces, tables and other items, before being returned to another mill for the finishing touch:

> It Is again Laid In a Mill like the last mentioned over the Sawmill & Moved by one of the wheels wch move ye Saws where the fflat part Is Polished with Emery & Putty & Entirely ffinished; no hand being able to give It a Higher Gloss than this do's.

It is evident from this description that one of the waterwheels was powering the cutting and the polishing of the marble. Alongside the waterwheel used in the honing process, Colles had constructed a machine which was capable of producing some rather diverse objects, including the marble water pipes as mentioned earlier. This machine was used for

> Making Pumps for all wch uses they are Excellent He alsoe Turns & Polishes Marble Punch bowls, by the Same Mills. and Has thereby Made Engines for

Extinguishing fires…wch Is a Valuable Improvement of these Kinds of Engines being Less In Bulk more Durable Incapable of Rusting & Subject to fewer Repairs.

Dawson concluded by stating that the marble mills were Colles' 'own Invention & Contrivance', a fact reiterated at the end of the eighteenth century in a survey by William Tighe, confirming that the marble mills were still being worked by the Colles family and that they were the 'invention of Alderman Colles, grand-father of the present proprietor'.[42]

William Colles had already stated seventy years previously that he had carried out experiments to ensure the machinery would function as he intended it to, but did not elaborate any further on these experiments. Tighe, on the other hand, informs us that Colles tried out models of the machinery in a small stream, and when satisfied that the machinery would work at full scale, 'he applied his marble to the construction of a vast variety of articles'. So amazed were the local people by Colles' creations that 'to this day his feats are proverbial among them, and they speak of him as a necromancer'.[43]

Tighe stated that some coarse work on the marble was carried out at the Black Quarry, indicating that the quarry was still the source of the marble, and 'a few blocks are split in the town by handsaw; where a little of the polished work is also done.'[44] The main work was carried out at the marble mill 'which is on the left bank of the river, near two miles from Kilkenny, to arrive at which blocks must be drawn across the bridge' (Plate 8). Tighe recorded that the mill 'is admirable for the simplicity of its structure, and for the power it exerts'. At this stage there was only one waterwheel in operation. This wheel was ten feet in diameter, which had 'twelve floats or ladles', and moved a 'crank at one end of its axis, to a frame containing twelve saws, which do the work of about twenty men'. A second crank, positioned at the other end, moved a frame consisting of five polishers. This polishing frame had recently been fitted underneath with another frame containing eight saws. From this description we can see that one waterwheel, centrally positioned to operate the cranks, was powering three separate pieces of equipment for cutting and polishing the marble. Although the waterwheel moved these frames, they did not reduce the waterwheel's power output, 'the power of the machine fully equal' to its task.[45] According to Tighe, the means by which the wheel was constructed ensured it was not dependent on a strong flow of water: 'The strength of the stream has some effect upon the working of the wheel, but not much', and, in any case, 'water is never wanting'. The operation 'may fairly be said to do the constant work of forty-two men daily'.[46]

Due to the mill's method of construction, it was stopped only for necessary repair work during the day, but at night the operation was completely shut down so

8 – Bridge at the ruins of the Marble Mills, Maddoxtown, county Kilkenny

that sand could be supplied to the saws and work could be carried out on the polish-ers. It certainly appears at this time that the mills were not in operation twenty-four hours a day, as in the past, and only one waterwheel was being used compared to three in William's time. Richard Colles, William's grandson, appears to have streamlined the operation and concentrated more on manufacturing chimney pieces, as Tighe enlightens us a little, stating that 'The working of these smaller articles [vases, punch bowls, frames, etc] is now abandoned, as well as many of the con-trivances of the inventor'.[47] Richard was 'extremely attentive to the business, which seems in a very thriving state'. Due to the efficiency of the mills, the marble was easily worked, resulting in it being sold at moderate prices, with a middle-sized chimney piece costing about two or three guineas, and the price of 'the common ones, usually made, varies from twenty five shillings to four guineas' (Plate 9).[48]

An interesting point Tighe made was that at the time of his survey there was a duty to be paid on marble in a finished state entering into England and Scotland. The cost of two shillings per cubic foot appears to have deterred the export of fin-ished marble products such as chimney pieces, etc, and any marble exported across the Irish Sea was in 'the rude block'.[49] The aforementioned chimney pieces were obviously for the home market, but there is also the possibility that some of these chimney pieces were destined for the North American market (Plate 10).[50] In all, Tighe estimated that the Kilkenny Marble Works exported about fifty tons of marble

9 – Kilkenny marble chimney piece, Castlefield House, county Kilkenny

10 – Kilkenny marble chimney piece in the home of Colonel Samuel Washington,
Harewood, West Virginia (photo courtesy Knight of Glin)

annually. This figure would seem to have increased greatly if we are to believe Mr and Mrs S.C. Hall, who stated that around a hundred tons of marble was exported to England by the 1840s, and that 'one waterwheel, by machinery, saws and polishes slabs with the par of 40 men'.[51]

Tighe tells us that the saws were made of a soft iron, and lasted about a week. There was a constant supply of water and sand provided for the saws, the sand being taken from the Nore, 'well washed and riddled until nothing remains but very fine and pure siliceous particles'.[52] The rate of cutting at Kilkenny by water power was, according to Tighe, ten inches per day, twelve inches when the flow of water was stronger, this being equivalent to two men cutting with a handsaw, which is comparable to Pepys' earlier account above. After the cutting process, the marble was then taken from the mill and polished with cove stones. Tighe tells us that this cove stone was a brown sandstone, or grit, and was imported from Chester. The marble was now ready to be polished by the hone stone, 'found in the hills between Kilkenny and Freshford'.[53] After this, the marble was returned to the mills where it received its final polish with rags and putty. The main processes were the same as they were seventy years earlier when William first invented them.

Tighe informs us that between forty and fifty men were employed at the quarry and the mills, indicating that the Colles family was still a good employer. The price for raising and squaring marble at the quarry was 9s 9d per week, and overall the wages varied from eight to twenty shillings per week.[54]

Land carriage was problematic for the Marble Works. Tighe stated that the weighty marble being sent to Dublin had to be transported on cars as far as the Barrow at Leighlin-bridge, and from there to the Grand Canal. The marble for export was sent to Waterford, and 'goes by land at least as far as Thomastown'.[55] Richard Colles echoed the sentiments of his grandfather when he estimated that over six shillings per ton could be saved on the carriage to Waterford if a canal was constructed to the tidewater at Inistioge. In addition to the savings, he felt that demand for the marble would increase also.

Marble in 'the rude block' was exported through the port of Waterford and mainly shipped to Liverpool and Glasgow at this time. Tighe states that, on occasion, Colles would take white Carrara marble from Liverpool, 'which he works up at Kilkenny into handsome and high priced chimney pieces, generally inlaid with coloured stones, and adorned with sculptures in relief'.[56] It would appear that Italian marble had been worked at Kilkenny for a number of years prior to Tighe's survey, as the following newspaper advertisement from 1785 show: 'Marble Mills near Kilkenny. For sale, a large assortment of Kilkenny Marble Chimney Pieces of the newest kinds of Italian and Kilkenny Marble finished in the best manner, which will be sold on the very lowest terms.'[57]

The Kilkenny Marble Works was the seen as the standard by which all other marble industries should be encouraged to attain. In Scotland it was regarded as the best example by which that country's marble industry could and should be developed. The description of the Marble Works given in *A Tour through Ireland...* was used to show how such an account could be used to encourage the government to develop Scotland's natural resources. John Knox, writing in 1789, stated that the north of Scotland 'abounds in marble of curious colours and qualities, [and] it may be proper to employ certain qualified persons to examine into the different veins, and make a report of their observations to government.' [58] The author then used the account of the Marble Works by the two Englishmen to portray how the 'expediency and utility of such information', such as that from Kilkenny, could assist in the exploitation of the marble and the creation of much employment in these areas.[59]

In the nineteenth century, Samuel Lewis was another individual who regarded the Black Quarry as still the most important quarry in the entire area. The 'jet black specimens' of marble were the most valuable of all.[60] The blocks of marble were transported to the marble mill, 'a very elegant combination of simplicity of structure with powers of execution'. Lewis then paraphrases William Tighe as he states that the mills perform the work of 'forty-two men daily. Water never fails, and from the excellence of its construction it is scarcely ever stopped on account of repairs.' [61]

William Colles' ingenious endeavours were seen as a pivotal point in the development of sawing and polishing marble. The Middlebury Historical Society of Vermont, USA, saw Colles as reinventing saws driven by water power in the cutting of marble. His use of water-powered machinery to polish marble was regarded as most innovative. The Middlebury Historical Society was formed in 1843, and decided to research and publish a history of marble quarrying in the New England area of the United States in 1885.[62] Professor Henry Seely, a prominent member of the Society, gave an account of the development of tools and machinery involved in the marble trade in chronological order. He began with the mallet, chisel and drill, used from earliest times. Hand-saws were next, Seely using Pliny as the authority for this (as already noted above), with the saws being fed sand and water by hand from 350 BC. Ausonius was the authority on the fact that saw mills for cutting stone, driven by water power, were used in Germany in the fourth century AD. The intervening centuries saw long toothless saws, up to twenty-three feet in length, in operation in the Pyrenees, and a design by Leonardo da Vinci for two or more saws stretched on a frame, known as 'gang saws', used from the sixteenth century. After such illustrious figures Seely placed William Colles. Seely noted that not since the fourth century in Germany had saws been driven by waterpower, but this process had been 'reinvented by William Colles, Kilkenny, Ireland, 1730'. Polishing and boring marble was 'done at the same place ... and by the same power'.[63] Seely enhanced his essay by quoting from William Tighe and *A Tour through Ireland...*, supplied through correspondence with Richard Colles and Revd James Graves of Kilkenny. More than 150 years after his key inventions brought sweeping changes to the marble industry in Ireland and Britain, William Colles' contribution to the industry was given international credit by the greatest marble-producing area of nineteenth-century America, and still one the largest today.

William Colles suffered from gout for most of his life, and he finally succumbed to an attack of this affliction in March 1770. His body was interred in the family vault in St Mary's church in Kilkenny city. On the exterior of the west wall of the south transept of the church stands a monument to his memory (Plate 11). Colles' involvement in the civic life of the city, his role in the linen and flour industries, his promotion of the ill-fated Nore navigation, and his part in transforming public and private architecture of the time are subjects for future discussion. He will be remembered forever as the man who harnessed the power of nature to create artistic marvels from nature. His memorial, carved from Kilkenny marble, is inscribed with the following words from the pen of his nephew-in-law, Dr Arthur Jacob, Archdeacon of Armagh:

Inventas aut qui vitam excoluere per artis
[Who ennobled life by arts discovered]
To the Memory
Of
ALDERMAN WILLIAM COLLES
Whose steady attention to all Religious and Civic duties
Gained him the love of his fellow citizens
And
Whose ingenuity
Procured him the admiration of Strangers.
By an uncommon genius he discovered
And
By unwearied application he perfected
The Art
Of sawing, boreing [sic] and polishing marble by water mills
Which
By lowering the price of that valuable manufacture
Rendered it more extensive.
His whole life was employed in works beneficial to society.
His manner was inoffensive and his conduct always upright.
He died the 8th day of March, 1770, in the 68th year of his age.

Within a week of Colles' death, the following advertisement appeared in *Finn's Leinster Journal*: 'The business formerly carried on at the Marble Mills, and the

11 – Memorial to Alderman William Colles, St Mary's church, Kilkenny

opposite 12 – Ruins of the Marble Mills, Maddoxtown, county Kilkenny

Flour Mills near Kilkenny, by the late Alderman William Colles, is now carried on by his son William Colles.' [64] Even with the sad loss of William Colles it was business as usual at the Marble Mills. Not even Death could stop the water flowing and the wheels from turning, as they carried out their respective tasks. As for the Black Quarry, the following notice appeared in the next edition of the newspaper: 'To be let and entered on immediately, the famous black marble Quarry near Kilkenny, lately in the possession of Alderman William Colles, deceased. Proposals to be sent to Henry Flood, Esq; at Farmley near Kilkenny.' [65]

The Black Quarry was filled in a number of years ago, and a petrol station now occupies part of the site on the Bennetsbridge Road on the outskirts of Kilkenny. A rock face is still visible today, but this gives no indication as to the size of the excavation that lies below the surface. The Marble Mills now lie in ruin on the banks of the Nore at Maddoxtown (Plate 12). The Colles family finally ended their association with Kilkenny and the Marble Works in the 1920s after a period of almost two hundred years. Thankfully we are blessed with countless marble chimney pieces and other assorted marble items, scattered throughout Ireland and abroad, as testaments to the craftsmanship of the employees of the Kilkenny Marble Works and to the genius of its creator, Alderman William Colles.

———

ACKNOWLEDGEMENTS

I would like to thank Desmond Guinness and Desmond FitzGerald, Knight of Glin, for their hospitality and enormous generosity. A debt of gratitude is owed to Dr Edward McParland for his support and constant encouragement. Thanks are also due to the staff of the following: Armagh Public Library, Irish Architectural Archive, Royal Society of Antiquaries of Ireland, and Kilkenny Archaeological Society, especially Cóilín Ó Drisceoil and Emma Devine, for their courtesy and permission to reproduce images. The assistance of the following individuals is gratefully appreciated: Mary Kelleher at the Royal Dublin Society; Sinéad Mahony and Melosina Lenox-Conyngham, Lavistown, Kilkenny; Seamus and Caroline Corballis at Castlefield House, Kilkenny; and the late Ted Nevill, Cork. A special word of thanks to George Sherwood senior for access to St Mary's church, Kilkenny. I am also very grateful to Donal McDonald and Jim Harling, the Kilkenny branch of An Taisce, and Clara Heritage Society, Kilkenny. Finally, thanks to my colleagues Livia Hurley, Patricia McCarthy, Conor Lucey and Kevin Mulligan, always on the look out and prepared to pass on any mention of Kilkenny marble.

ENDNOTES

[1]   Armagh Public Library, Topographical and Statistical Returns from Various Respondents sent to Walter Harris and the Physico-Historical Society of Ireland, circa 1745. This citation is worded as requested by Armagh Public Library.

[2]   For a detailed account of the Physico-Historical Society, see Eoin Magennis, 'A Land of Milk and Honey: the Physico-Historical Society, improvement and the surveys of mid-eighteenth-century Ireland', *Proceedings of the Royal Irish Academy*, 102C, no. 6, 2002. The account of the Kilkenny Marble Works in Armagh is undated, but would have been compiled in the period given in this article. The account of the Marble Works in the Physico-Historical Society's papers was the basis of a paper delivered at the Royal Irish Academy Committee for the History of Irish Science meeting, Trinity College Dublin, 14th March 2008.

[3]   William Colles was an alderman and treasurer with Kilkenny Corporation. He also served as Mayor of Kilkenny in 1755. He was influential in the Nore navigation scheme and the flour and flax industries in the city. He was involved in house construction, in both town and country, and barracks and bridge construction. Colles worked with Francis Bindon, and arranged for his nephew Christopher Colles to work under Davis Dukart. He was also the grandfather of the noted surgeon Abraham Colles, he of the 'Colles Fracture' fame. This article is only concerned with his interests in the marble business. The stone was actually limestone but was referred to as marble due to its ability to take a polish.

[4]   *Records of Eighteenth-Century Domestic Architecture and Decoration in Ireland*, 5 vols (Irish Georgian Society, Dublin, 1909-13; reprint 1969) II, 106.

[5]   National Archives, Dublin, Prim Papers, M.86a, Notes on the Colles Family.

[6]   *ibid.*

[7]   *ibid.*, M.87. In a letter from John Blunden to John Lloyd, October 1742, regarding William's proposal of marriage to Peggy Lloyd, Blunden states he has no objection to the marriage of his cousin to Colles. 'Mr Colles is a widower with one daughter, his fortune is of his own making.' This marriage did not take place.

8 This letter was read and ordered to be registered at the Dublin Society's meeting dated 3rd February 1732. It was entered into the minutes of the meeting, which are filed in the records of the Royal Dublin Society.

9 *ibid.*

10 John Bostock and H.T. Riley, *The Natural History of Pliny, Book XXXVI* (London, 1857) 325-26.

11 Robert Latham and William Matthews (eds), *The Diary of Samuel Pepys*, V, 1664 (London, 1970) 63.

12 Letter to the Dublin Society.

13 *ibid.*

14 *Faulkner's Dublin Journal*, 903, Saturday, 23rd November, to Tuesday, 26th November 1734. This same advertisement appeared in many subsequent issues. Some eighteenth-century documents use 'i' rather than 'e' when spelling Colles. For the purpose of this article, 'i' will be used in direct quotations only.

15 Anonymous, *A Tour through Ireland in several entertaining letters ... by two English gentlemen* (London, 1748) 191.

16 *ibid.*, 192.

17 Ted Nevill, 'Kilkenny Bird's Eye Marble', *Old Kilkenny Review* (Kilkenny, 1988) 502.

18 Revd James Graves and John G.A. Prim, 'The History, Architecture and Antiquities of the City of Kilkenny', *Journal of the Kilkenny and South-East of Ireland Archaeological Society*, II, 1858-59. The authors provide evidence to suggest that this account was written after 1624 and prior to the rebellion of 1641. Rothe was Bishop of Ossory from 1618 to 1650.

19 *ibid.*, 324.

20 Bodleian Library, Oxford, Carte MS 145, f.86, Duke of Ormonde to Mr Morton, 31st December 1664. The Lord Chancellor was building Clarendon House in Picadilly, London, at this time. Ormonde enclosed a design for a chimney piece made from Kilkenny marble, but sadly this no longer exists with the letter. Clarendon's house was demolished in 1683. See Rolf Loeber, *A Biographical Dictionary of Architects in Ireland 1600-1720* (London, 1981) 78.

21 Gerard Boate, 'Ireland's Naturall History', *A Collection of Tracts and Treatises Illustrative of the Natural History, Antiquities, and the Political and Social State of Ireland* (Dublin, 1860) 122.

22 *ibid.*

23 Evelyn Philip Shirley, 'Extracts from the Journal of Thomas Dineley, Esquire, giving some Account of his Visit to Ireland in the Reign of Charles II', *Journal of the Kilkenny and South-East of Ireland Archaeological Society*, IV, 1862-63, 106.

24 R.W. Lightbown, 'Some Eighteenth and Early Nineteenth Century Visitors to Kilkenny, Part 1', *Old Kilkenny Review*, III, i, 1984, 4.

25 Armagh Public Library, Physico-Historical Society Papers.

26 The use of Biblical references tends to indicate that Hugh Dawson was actually the Revd Hugh Dawson of Kilkenny mentioned in a deed in which Dawson had taken a house from William Colles in Coal Market, Kilkenny city. Registry of Deeds, Dublin, 271/18/173106.

27 Armagh Public Library, Physico-Historical Society Papers.

28 See Patrick McAfee, *Stone Buildings* (Dublin, 1998) 104-5, for a concise account of this method of quarrying.

29 George T. Stokes (ed.), *Pococke's Tour in Ireland in 1752* (Dublin, 1891) 129.

30   *ibid.*, 127-28.

31   National Archives, Dublin, Prim Papers, M.87. Letter dated 12th September 1762; addressee not stated.

32   Anonymous, *A Tour through Ireland...*, 191-92.

33   R.W. Lightbown, 'Some Eighteenth and Early Nineteenth Century Visitors to Kilkenny, Part I', *Old Kilkenny Review*, III, i, 1984, 5.

34   Síle Ní Chinnéide, 'A View of Kilkenny, city and county, in 1790', *Journal of the Royal Society of Antiquaries of Ireland*, 104, 1974, 29-31.

35   Emanuel Mendes da Costa, *A Natural History of Fossils* (London, 1757) 232. Mendes da Costa was a fellow of the Royal and Antiquarian Societies of London and a member of the Imperial Academy of Germany.

36   Anne Plumptre, *Narrative of a Residence in Ireland During the Summer of 1814, and that of 1815* (London, 1817) 226.

37   *ibid.*

38   National Archives, Dublin, Prim Papers, M.87. Letter dated 15th November 1743. As can be seen from the quotes from this letter, Colles remained very vague as to the actual designs of his inventions. No drawings or plans are known to exist for any of his designs, and it does seem strange that he never expanded on how his machinery worked. Perhaps seeing as how the machinery was open for anyone to see, its workings were easily understood when viewed.

39   Armagh Public Library, Physico-Historical Society Papers.

40   McAfee, *Stone Buildings*, 72-74.

41   Armagh Public Library, Physico-Historical Society Papers. All passages quoted are from these papers.

42   William Tighe, *Statistical Observations Relative to the County of Kilkenny, made in the years 1800 & 1801* (Dublin, 1802; reprinted Kilkenny, 1998) 105. William's grandson Richard was now running the operation.

43   *ibid.*

44   *ibid.*, 103.

45   *ibid.*

46   *ibid.*

47   *ibid.*, 106.

48   *ibid.*, 104.

49   *ibid.*

50   Thomas M. Truxes, *Irish-American Trade, 1660-1783* (Cambridge, 1988) 75. Truxes mentions that a Dublin merchant, William Alexander, one of the leading exporters of Irish linen to British America during the 1760s and 1770s, sometimes supplied Kilkenny marble to colonial buyers. It is possible that Colles knew Alexander through the linen trade. The chimney piece in Plate 10, is in Harewood, West Virginia, in the house built by Samuel Washington, brother of George, in 1771.

51   Mr and Mrs S.C. Hall, *Ireland; its Scenery and Character*, 3 vols (London, 1842) II, 41.

52   Tighe, *Statistical Observations Relative to the County of Kilkenny*. See also Clara Heritage Society's *A Social History of the Parish of Clara in County Kilkenny* (Kilkenny, 2006) 80. One of the occupations mentioned at the Marble Works was 'sand risers', indicating that it was a specific, specialised job to take the sand from the river and render it fine and pure enough to be used for sawing and polishing the marble.

[53] Tighe, *Statistical Observations Relative to the County of Kilkenny*, 104.

[54] *ibid.*, 102.

[55] *ibid.*

[56] *ibid.*, 103. It certainly appears that Richard Colles was making chimney pieces to cater for any size of purse. This is very evident from the variety of styles of pieces that are still in existence.

[57] *Finn's Leinster Journal*, 29th January 1785.

[58] John Knox, *A View of the British Empire, more especially Scotland; with some proposals for the improvement of that country* (London, 1789) 465.

[59] *ibid.*, 466.

[60] Samuel Lewis, *Topographical Dictionary of Ireland* (London, 1837) 107.

[61] *ibid.*

[62] See Zadock Thompson, *History of Vermont, Natural, Civil, and Statistical* (Burlington, VT, 1842) 114-15. Thompson states that the first marble quarry opened in the United States was in Vermont in about 1800, and marble was discovered in Middlebury in 1804. In 1810, 20,000 feet of marble slabs were sawn here. At the time of publication in 1885, over 6,000 men were employed in the marble industry in the New England states, and Vermont alone accounted for about $2.5 worth of marble.

[63] Henry Seely, 'The Marble Fields and Marble Industry of Western New England', *The Marble Border of Western New England: Papers and Proceedings of the Middlebury Historical Society*, I, part 2, 1885, appendix. Prof. Seely was formerly secretary of the Vermont State Board of Agriculture, and at the time of this publication was attached to the Chemistry and Mineralogy Department at Middlebury College.

[64] *Finn's Leinster Journal*, Wednesday, 14th March, to Saturday, 17th March. William Colles continued to run his late-father's business until his untimely death in 1779, aged only 34.

[65] *ibid.*, Saturday, 17th March, to Wednesday, 21st March.

———

A 'good figure': the story of George Cockburn (1764-1847) as revealed through contemporary letters and papers

JANE MEREDITH

B UT FOR DR EDWARD MCPARLAND'S INTEREST IN ANDREW CALDWELL (1733-1808), this article, or the thesis on which it is based, would probably never have been written, or at least not by this writer. Caldwell (Plate 1), the owner of the Newgrange estate, county Meath, was a barrister and fine arts connoisseur with a special interest in architecture. McParland was of the opinion that, writing under the pseudonym 'L', he was probably the author of the important series of 'essays' published in the *Freeman's Journal* between 27th December 1768 and 7th February 1769 (the time of the Royal Exchange competition). These critical essays were considered by McParland to be 'the most explicit recommendation of neo-classicism to be published in Ireland in the eighteenth century'.[1] An article written by Luisa Vertova in the *Burlington Magazine* in July 1995, entitled 'A late renaissance view of Rome',[2] reinforced the belief that Caldwell had a special interest in architecture. It concerned the discovery in an English private collection of a previously unpublished late-sixteenth-century pen-and-ink drawing entitled *View of the Campidoglio, 1598-1603* (Plate 2). Inscribed on the back of the drawing was an annotation reading: 'sent from Rome to Andrew Caldwell by his uncle Colonel Heywood 1776'. It turned out that not only was the private collection owned by a descendant of the Caldwell family, but that another family member, living in Suffolk, owned a considerable archive of Caldwell Papers, which included nine bound volumes entitled *Caldwell of Newgrange*. These proved to be a veritable trea-

1 – Martin Ferdinand Quadel, ANDREW CALDWELL (1733-1808)
c.1779, oil on canvas (private collection)

101

2 – VIEW OF THE CAMPIDOGLIO
sent from Rome to Andrew Caldwell by his uncle, Col. Nathaniel Heywood, in 1776
1598-1603, pen and ink, 37 x 107 cm (detail) (private collection)

sure trove, and their discovery heralded, for this writer, the beginning of a year of excitement and discovery which involved a (temporary) move to England.

The beautiful cabinet containing the archive (Plates 3, 4) was specially commissioned in 1869 by Captain Charles Benjamin Caldwell (1809-1896). This Caldwell was at that time the owner of the Newgrange estate, having inherited it from his father, Charles Andrew Caldwell, in 1859. For many years, he continued living at his London home in Clarges Street, Mayfair, but some years before he died he moved, with his wife Sophia Frances (Cust), to Bray, county Wicklow. It was he who organised the collection, assembly and binding of the Caldwell Papers, employing John Tuckett (Plate 5) to do the job, and also to compile the family pedigree. In April 1942, Sotheby & Co, of 34-35 New Bond Street, London, in their valuation of heirlooms under the will of C.H.B. Caldwell (Charles Henry Bulwer, who inherited the Newgrange estate from his uncle Charles Benjamin in 1896),[3] specified that 'The family letters, papers, accounts, deeds, medals and orders contained in nine volumes, three drawers and two small cupboards in a metal bound cabinet'[4] were among the heirlooms. The majority of correspondence in the nine bound volumes in the cabinet concern Andrew Caldwell (sixty-eight letters written by him to family members, and 353 to him), as well as a considerable number of letters written between various family members and friends. Numbered among his relatives, friends and correspondents were Lord Charlemont, the antiquarian Joseph Cooper Walker, the Shakespearian scholar Edmund Malone, the founder of the Linnean Society James Smith, the artists Conrad Gessner and John Warren, Lord Bessborough, Brian Lawless (later to become Lord Cloncurry), Coquebert de

Montbret, the Bishop of Dromore, Frederick Hamilton (brother of Sir William), Lord Mountjoy, Thomas Pennant (Welsh naturalist and antiquary), Lady Eleonor Butler and Sarah Ponsonby (the 'Ladies of Llangollen'), his special friends Frederick Trench and the collector and bibliophile Alexander Mangin, to name but a few. Of the sixty-eight letters written by Andrew Caldwell, thirty were to his father (many describing his life at Glasgow University, where Adam Smith was one of his teachers) and twenty to his nephew and ward George Cockburn, the subject of this article. Of the 353 letters received by him, only six were from Cockburn. As Cockburn was not the subject of the thesis being researched, no effort was made during the year in England to trace further correspondence between him and his uncle. However, on returning to Dublin (and again tipped off by McParland) I attended a lecture given by Dr Ray Astbury who, because of his interest in the classical marble artefacts collected by Cockburn on his travels (many of which are exhibited in the UCD Classical museum), had discovered that the National Army Museum in London held a considerable number of letters exchanged between Cockburn and his uncle, Andrew Caldwell. Painstakingly, from a microfilm, Astbury had transcribed nearly all of them. We then did a swap, and found, to our

3, 4 – Cabinet (1869) especially made to house the Caldwell papers, bound in nine volumes

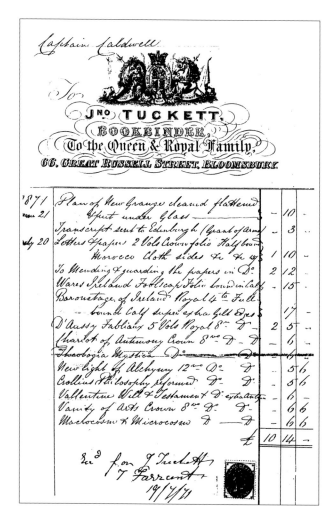

5 – *Letterhead and account (detail) from John Tuckett, who bound the Caldwell papers*

opposite

6 – *Robert Hunter*
MRS COCKBURN *c.1761-69, oil on canvas, 74 x 61 cm (private collection)*

great satisfaction, that several of the Caldwell letters were in answer to Cockburn's, and vice versa. It is therefore on these two sets of papers, together with further material found in the British Library, that this article is based.

In his early years, Cockburn (hence to be called George) led a happy and uncomplicated life. He was the only child of Dublin merchant and army agent George Cockburn senior (1712-1775) and his wife Ann (1734-1769), Caldwell's sister. At some time after their marriage in 1761, Ann's portrait was painted by Robert Hunter (Plate 6),[5] and a break in the story is called for here in view of new information in the Caldwell Papers concerning this artist.

Until now, the exact year of Robert Hunter's death has not been known, although he was generally thought (by Strickland, among others)[6] to have died in or after 1803. As Anne Crookshank points out in her article in the *Irish Arts Review* on

Robert Hunter,[7] Hunter's name continued to appear annually in the *Dublin Directory* until 1803, although Crookshank does not think that he painted much after the sale of his paintings in 1792. She suggests that, like many people who don't change names in the telephone directory, he simply forgot to take it out, but assumes that he died in 1803 or shortly afterwards. The new material would seem to confirm that, in fact, he died in January or February 1801. Andrew Caldwell knew him and regretted his death. In a letter to Edmund Malone dated 5th February 1802 he wrote:

> It is strange how soon with most people minute circumstances are forgotten, I had occasion to call the other day on old Mrs. Hunter, she is bedridden & her memory failing, Hunter is dead just 12 months, & the Grandaughter could not recollect the date or day on which he died, poor Hunter is a great loss to one, he was full of Anecdote of Painters, Engravers and other ingenious

Artists that were either of this country or ever came into the Country, he knew them all, he had been long consider'd as the Senior of the Profession.[8]

To return to Ann, she was never in the best of health, and early in 1763 became dangerously ill. She recovered and was taken to convalesce at Bristol Hott Wells. In June 1763 her husband wrote to his mother-in-law, Eliza Caldwell:

> Ann recovers wonderfully, has a vast appitite ... She drinks asses milk half a pint between five & six, rises at seven, at the Wells before Eight, drinks three glass of watter 30 Minuts between each glass when she exercises in the post chase (for we are obliged to keep on) comes home to Brekfast, on horseback by ten, rides on the Downs for two houres, to the Well half after twelve, takes another Glass Watter, Dinnes at two, at four drinks the Watter again, home to tea, then to the rooms, at nine she craves some light thing for supper (a Rabitt or so) & in bed by ten. This method pursued will make her well & strong in a short time, that I hope to be at home by the beginning of August.[9]

Ann must have been pregnant at the time of their return as George was born in February 1764.[10] The family lived in considerable comfort in their house in Cavendish Street (now 7 Parnell Square), an inventory of the entire contents of which Cockburn senior compiled in 1763. The original of this inventory was discovered recently in the British Library,[11] and what a relief it was to find it. The inventory had been available before this (held by the Irish Architectural Archive),[12] but was only a copy of a copy of the original. This was made, in a school notebook, by C.P. Curran, in his very difficult to read spidery handwriting. He wrote that it was 'made by me from a copy lent me by Mr. Naylor of Liffey Street and made by him from the original in his possession. He purchased it at the Hamilton Rowan sale at Shanganagh Castle.' The beautiful clear handwriting of the original inventory is shown in Plate 7, and it lists every detail of the contents of the furniture and equipment of the house, room by room, down, for instance, to the last chair, piece of kitchen equipment, item of jewellery ('a Brilliant Diamond Ring 1 stone 15 grams £113 15s 0d'), chair cover, ring 'for pulling out the window shutters', picture, etc. The pictures (it is not made clear whether they are paintings or prints) are not separately listed but are included in the inventory for each room, and there are 140 of them altogether, of which only twenty are attributed, excluding twenty-four Dixon flower-and-bird pictures. The estimated value of the pictures ranges from £1 0s 0d to £56 17s 6d ('A picture sent from Rome by Col. Forester'), and there is a preponderance of attributions to sixteenth-century Netherlandish painters – Ferdinand Bol, Jan Fyt, Jan Wyck, David Teniers the Younger, Franz Hals, Adriaen Brouwer, Rembrandt van Ryn, Swanenburgh and Jan Both. Two Irish painters are listed, Butts and Samuel Dixon, and the English landscape painter Richard Wilson is represented twice. The French painter Jean-Baptiste Jouvenet contributed one of the most highly valued pictures, *Eneas & Venus*, at £25. The line-up of painters is impressive, but it is important to keep in mind that mistaken or wishful attributions were common in the eighteenth century, as, indeed, they can still be to this day. However, this original record of the entire contents of a mid-eighteenth-century Dublin gentleman's house is an important find, and awaits further study.

The family was not to enjoy its peaceful existence for long because, on 20th April 1769, Ann died tragically young, and George, only five years old, was left motherless. While Cockburn senior grieved for his young wife, Charles and Eliza Caldwell mourned the loss of their eldest daughter. On 26th August 1769 Charles wrote to his wife: 'My ever dearest, ... I rejoyce at the account you give of little George and hope he will be spared to make some amends for our dear Nancy [their pet name for Ann] that is gone.' [13] Although later to become a boarder at Dr William Darby's school at Bally Gall, near Portarlington, at first the young George continued to live at home in Cavendish Street with his father, fondly supervised by his maternal grandparents and two maiden aunts, Francis (Fanny) and Henrietta, who all still lived a short distance away in their family home in Henry Street. On Sundays, the two families (including George's uncle Andrew Caldwell) would meet in the Strand Street Presbyterian Meeting House, their regular contributions to which are recorded in the Strand Street subscription books. [14]

With his father's death in May 1765, any kind of order and security that had been established in the eleven-year-old George's life after the death of his mother was disrupted. His father had appointed Andrew Caldwell as his guardian, and there's no doubt that this responsibility totally disrupted Caldwell's life as well. He was a forty-one-year-old barrister, a bachelor, with little experience of children, who almost overnight was required to assume responsibility for George and his affairs. As the Caldwell Papers show, he took this responsibility very seriously, moving into Cavendish Street and keeping meticulous accounts tying up Cockburn senior's affairs and relating to household expenses and George's needs. [15] At the time of his father's death, George was home from boarding school recovering from measles, and for attendance on him Caldwell recorded that Dr Cleghorn was paid £11 7s 6d. His education features largely in the accounts, including such items as:

To Dr. Darby's fees for the year ending 25 October 1775: £27 8s 6d; Latin master: £1 2s 9d; Writing master: 11s 4d; Drawing master: 11s 4d; Paid yourself going to school: 2s.8d; Coachman for bringing you to school: 1s 1d; Expenses on the road to & from Portarlington: £1 15s 10d; Butter, Bread, Sugar & Chaise Hire to Ballygall: 2s 2d; the Drawing Master 6 months ending this day: £4 18s 2d; Hudson for cleaning your teeth: 2s 2d; You and Master Cleghorn going to the Play: 6s 6d; You for Toys & Presents: 14s 0d;

Street Parlour

	£	s	d
Blue English Paper	4	14	
73½ Yards of Guilding	6	13	10
A Javandole & Two Jaquerd Sockets	4	14	
A Looking Glass	25		
Ten Chairs & Two Arm Chairs	18	16	
A Shaveing Chair	1		
A Mahogany Cestern & Stand	1	10	
A Mahogany Side Boards	3	8	3
A Mahogany Cooper for Bottles	1	1	8
A Mahogany Breakfast Table	1	10	
A Mahogany writing Desk & Drawers cost in Lond 20/-	11	7	6
Twentien Pictures	68		
A Steel Grate & Fire Irons	4	11	
A Marble Italian Chimney Piece w th Guilt decorations	16		
A Fire Screen gulding	2		
A Carpet Bought from Lawless	8	5	
Two Marine Window Curtains 13 Yards in Each at 3/4	5	18	8
Two Italian Shades for the Windows	4		
Foure Jaquerd Rings for Pulling out the Wind Shutters		8	
Foure Jaquerd Pins for the Window Curtains 10 Each		3	4
One of Deeys best Locks for the door going into the Hall	1		
One D° for the door going into the back Parlour	1		
One Willton Carpet & 2/6 makeing 56 ½ yds at 6/6	18	5	7½
A View of the Rehine by Swaneenburghy	1	4	1½
A Sleeping Bours D°	1	6	6
A Dying Saint at D°		6	6
Carried to Opposite Side	213	14	

7 – *Inventory of household furniture, Cavendish Street House, 1st January 1763*
(detail, p.21; original in the British Library)

the Fencing Master: £2 5s 6d.; the Riding Master: £2 5s 6d.; for Barley Sugar to you: 2s 8d; You for Pocket Money etc. in Easter Hollidays: 5s 5d; Maintaining Shoeing etc. your little horse 14 months: £14 0s 0d; Mrs. Caldwell on your account: £26 0s 0d.

The frequent mention of Mrs Caldwell (Plate 8) in the accounts is significant as, from the beginning, she was a constant presence in Cavendish Street, and on the death of her husband Charles in March 1776, she and her two daughters moved there permanently, leaving Alicia Caldwell (Charles's sister, her nephews' and nieces' much loved 'Aunt Ally') in Henry Street. This must have lifted an enormous weight from Andrew Caldwell's shoulders, although their presence did not always please him, as we learn from a letter George (now in the army) wrote to him from Florence in March 1783: 'I feel much for your present situation in Cavendish Row, as you are obliged to see the fireside & 3 old women every morning & which you seem to dislike so much'.[16] There can be no doubt that George was upset by all the sadness and upheaval in his young life and that this was reflected in his behaviour is suggested in Dr. Darby's letter to Andrew Caldwell dated 3 April 1776. It reads:

> Sir, ... Believe me I do not wish yr little Ward to leave me either at Easter or Whitsuntide – At this Season I give but 5 days & at Whitsuntide but two; Very few Boys leave me at either time, those only who have their Parents in Town – I shall with Pleasure keep him the two long Vacations, for I know he will be very troublesome to you & good Mrs Caldwell. I am with great Esteem Dr Sir Yr most Obedt Humble Servt Wm. Darby.[17]

It seems that, even though he only came home for occasional holidays, the responsibility of looking after George weighed heavily on Caldwell and his mother, and the summer of 1777 found Caldwell in London, staying with Lord Bessborough (for whose Irish estate he was the agent and his friend, Peter Walsh, the manager) and looking for a suitable boarding school for George. In a letter to his mother dated 26th July 1777 Caldwell wrote:

> I had conversation upon the subject [a school for George] with Mr. Eustace, poor Cockburn's great friend, he is a man of much Wisdom and Experience, he is strongly against our sending George so far away from us, and advises to get a tutor to stay with him in the vacations that would be a constant companion and never leave him to the servants or improper company, but this you know is utterly impracticable nor have we room for such a Person'. Referring to one possible school Caldwell continues: 'the terms are pretty high, but then our little fellow would be taken the best care of possible and Canning thinks there are no vacations allowed.[18]

8 – Martin Ferdinand Quadel, ELIZABETH HEYWOOD, WIFE OF CHARLES CALDWELL ESQ. OF DUBLIN
c.1779, oil on canvas, 91 x 79 cm (detail)   (private collection)

It is obvious that Caldwell has no wish to take heed of Mr Eustace's wise and kind advice and that, as far as he is concerned, one of the advantages of the school under discussion is that there are 'no vacations allowed'! This becomes even clearer in a subsequent letter to his mother when, the first school having fallen through, Caldwell writes, on 7th August: 'I really don't know what to do, every place I have enquired about there is the same objection, & the Masters & their families constantly go away in the Vacations, thinking it necessary after the laborious life they lead.'[19] He also notes that nowhere has he found anything that can compare with the Quakers at Ballitore. At last, on 25th August 1777, Caldwell writes that he has found a suitable school at Chiswick, and that the master, Mr Rose, keeps eight or nine boys with him during the vacations, for which 'some additional consideration is paid'.[20] Caldwell urges his mother to get George despatched as soon as possible and to try to find 'some kind person' who will undertake to accompany him on the journey. He tells her that Mr and Mrs Rose will not expect George to be 'completely well rigg'd' and have undertaken to purchase any 'cloaths' he may need, and Mr Rose has requested that George should bring with him a copy of Robertson's 'History of America' unbound, which can be purchased at Wilsons on Dame Street. In a letter to his mother dated 29th August 1777 Caldwell writes: '...your Account of George is very unpleasant, I am the more confirm'd in my determination not to stir from this 'till I see him fairly settled here. I plainly perceive there is not an hour to be lost ... contrive any way in the World or any Expence to send George over.'[21] On 31st August 1777 Mrs Caldwell wrote to her son:

> this morn I have parted with our Darling Child nothing but absolute necessity could have reconciled me to it, there is a good prospect of his getting safe to you I believe he will land tonight he went in the Clermont Packet, and there was a Genteel young Gentleman a Captain Doyn that Fanny addressed, when she told her name he said he knew her family very well that he was going to London & woud with pleasure take all the care he could of the Child ... I gave George 14 Gns he declared he would not go if he did not get all the mony. I persuaded him to put 10 Gns in the trunk & [illegible word] enough he put it in one of his shoes & 4 Gns & sum silver in his pocket he went away in great health & spirits. I went for him on Friday and by talking to Darby I found out the reason he was so very desirous to leave the school, he was the Ringleader & Contriver of a Baring out & vowed he would shoot [illegible word] if he broke into the Room & George told me he certainly would have fired at him but not with Balls, and that Darby never was so fond of him since & gave him harder lessons and Darby told me if you had consulted him he would have advised to do what you have done, for he did not think he would ever have come to much good if he was kept here. I would

advise you to acquaint the man he is going to as much as you can of his Temper he can't bear Contradictions, and is very resolute in accomplishing his on schemes, and he openly declares he hats the Book, if the man should press him or forse him too much in that respect I am apt to fear he will run away or do some desperate thing ... he says he will go into the Army ... he has a great dale of sense and if he can be managed may make a Good Figure, he must be kept in aw & yet I don't believe he would bear severity – I don't know but that one whipping might do him good tho he always says let me see the man that durst do it don't let him see this letter he would never forgive it.[22]

Fanny Caldwell wrote to her brother at the same time: 'Be sure tell the Gentleman what a queer indulged child he has been ever since he was born & that his manners are to be attended to as much as the improvement of his mind & to make him hold up his Head – Oh how I long to have him safe with you.'[23]

And so, the young George, now thirteen years of age, embarked on the next stage of his life in high spirits. He enjoyed the adventure of the journey, and soon settled down into his new school, which was not the one Caldwell had originally chosen for him. On 4th September 1777 Caldwell wrote to his mother:

he is not to go to Mr. Rose's, but to Mr. Crawfords in the same Neighbourhood, after I had almost determined on the other, I got an intimation ... that at Rose's school the living was too poor & wretched and would not answer for a Gentleman's child ...the appearances [of the new school] are delightful, beyond Hackney, the House magnificent, charming Gardens, and every thing in a fine stile, the Master is a Clergyman ... Mr. Crawford tells me the whole expence including every possible charge, will be about a hundred and ten or twenty pounds pr ann, I think that nothing in a case of this importance, and as he is to remain in the Vacations of which there are but two, it is rather cheap.[24]

We hear no more of George until, in a letter to Caldwell dated 7th May 1781, his friend William Cleghorn writes:

I have had the pleasure of seeing Mr. George frequently & find him much improved. He really has acquired a justness & propriety of thinking on a variety of subjects above his years. His taste for painting is very considerable, & his judgement better than that of many, who have seen many more paintings. His understanding is excellent and am sure under your direction it will be well cultivated.[25]

There was to be little opportunity for Caldwell to 'direct' his ward (although, as we shall see, George continued to cultivate his taste in painting independently of his uncle) because in a letter, also written on 7th May 1781, George dropped a bomb-shell: he had joined the army. This is an important letter, and as it heralds the beginning of his life career in the army, it is transcribed in full below:

From George Cockburn, London, 7 May 1781, to his uncle Andrew Caldwell at Cavendish Row, Dublin.

Dear Uncle

I wrote to you the day before yesterday to tell you that I got a Commission in the 1st Regt of Guards; Mr. Forbes advanced the money, & you will be so good as to send over £1300 to pay him. It is not likely I shall be sent abroad, but if it should happen so I must not hear of any objection from Ireland, for I will go. I should be obliged for my own honour. I should have no objection to go abroad, but as I know you would not like it, I hope it may not happen, indeed there is no likelihood of it, but if it should happen so, you must be content, for I would go. I am now satisfied (you will say for the first time in my life) & my friends must be satisfied, for I am resolved to stay in the Army. Perhaps they think I will quit in 4 or 5 years, but they will find themselves much mistaken. I shall stick to the Guards.

I sent you a Catalogue of the Exhibition.[26] It is thought a very bad one.

I want 12 Shirts & stocks imediately. I have but the 8 which I got in Dublin, they must be made & sent directly. I must get half a dozen here for I have not enough to have a clean one every day. If I cant have them in 3 weeks time, don't have them made, but let me know & I will then get them here. I could not do without for a longer time.

As to money it will cost £100 to fit me out & I must have £200 a year beside pay & £100 at setting out – that is the least that any of the officers have. You will write to Mr. Forbes about it & also desire him to pay for the Cloaths I mentioned to you.

The Commission cost £1100.

I shall take proper care of myself here, you may depend. As to boarding with anybody, or any of that sort of thing, I would not do it, or anything of the kind upon any account. I told you my Plan, beside there is a regular dinner at the Tilt, where the officers go if they chuse it, & are charged so much a head, & when they don't dine pay nothing of course.

Col. Heywood [George's great-uncle, his grandmother's brother, who was for 30 years equerry to the Duke of Gloucester] has been very civil to me. I shall follow his advise & yours but shant trouble myself about anybody else's for I know that the People in Dublin know no more about the Guards than the Pen I am writing with. Now the whole thing is settled you need give yourself no further trouble, as you may depend on my acting always like a Gentleman. I suppose I shall be pestered with letters of advice, I shall always be glad of yours, but will not pay the least attention to others. I hope to hear from you soon & am your Affectionate Nephew G. Cockburn. My love & respects to all my friends, I shall always be glad to hear from them, but if their letters are filled with nonsense (you will be ruined) and all that kind of thing I will instantly throw them into the fire (Plate 9).[27]

As it turned out, George was to leave England sooner than he had anticipated, and on 20th August 1782 he informed his uncle that he was to set sail from Portsmouth for Gibralter almost immediately with Lord Howe's fleet. He wrote:

I like the Army and ought therefore to learn my duty & Gibralter is the place for making a soldier ... one thing I beg is that if you should disapprove of it, you will not make any work about it or show it, as it could not be of the least use now, & I hope you will excuse me when I say that it would make you appear ridiculous.[28]

His presence in Gibralter, while it was under siege, was George's only experience of military war service throughout his long army career. During his time there he acted as aide-de-camp to General Elliot, and from there he began the correspondence with

9 – Detail from George Cockburn's letter to Andrew Caldwell, dated 7th May 1781, informing him that he had joined the army (private collection)

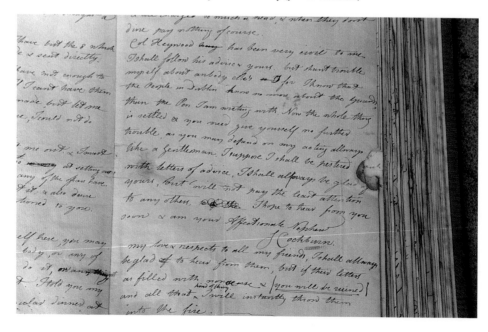

his uncle that was to continue throughout his several European tours as he availed of all the opportunities the army offered him for travel abroad. No young man could have grasped this opportunity more eagerly, and sadly space will only allow for a small selection of his experiences – taken from the sixty-six letters exchanged between Caldwell and George – to be mentioned.

George was not long in Gibralter. He arrived on 12th October 1782, and barely three weeks later was writing to his uncle that he was planning to return to England shortly as Gibralter was 'well fortify'd by nature, & a vast deal by art & the Spaniards seem at last to give up all thoughts of taking it'.[29] He considered that being an aide-de-camp was only a civility, and 'to say the truth tho anyone would think an Aid Camp to Gen. Elliott must have a vast deal to do, they have just nothing at all. In military business he does every thing himself; & in respect to attendance he requires none.'[30]

And so, in November 1782, armed with route advice and some very important introductory 'proper letters' from General Elliot, George, aged only eighteen, set off on his own mini-Grand Tour, which was to end in London just six months later in May 1783. His tour started in Italy, in Leghorn (Livorno today), which he reached after a terrible six-week voyage when his ship ran aground on the rocks off the coast and was nearly lost. In spite of his alarming storm-tossed journey, he still managed to write to Caldwell from the ship, and stressed, as he was constantly to do thereafter, that whatever his uncle wanted in the way of books, pictures, drawings or 'anything' he would do his best to acquire them and promised to take great care of them. His journey from Leghorn continued, via Pisa, to Florence (twice), Rome (twice), Naples, Turin, Geneva, Lyons, Lausanne and Paris. Italy did not impress him and he wrote to his uncle from Florence on 1st January 1783:

> In truth I am not much in love with Italy ... The Travelling machines worse than a Dublin car, & tho I believe you think the Irish more addicted to theft, and cheating than any other nation, I assure you that the Lower People here are infinitely worse (money they say is in their blood) but you meet with more civility, & a willingness to oblige from the Gentlemen than in England. I saw the famous [Uffizi] Gallery yesterday. A vast collection of Pictures, Statues, & Antiques, but like all other great collections, would take up a great deal of time to examine well. I shall see it two or three times more.[31]

He moved on to Rome, about which he wrote in a letter from his next port of call, Naples, that in the five weeks he was there he had become 'well acquainted with every thing remarkable',[32] but nevertheless felt the need to see most things again. It was during this, his first visit to Rome, that he had his portrait painted by Hugh Douglas Hamilton (Plate 10).[33]

The 15th February 1783 finds George writing to his uncle from Naples,

10 – Hugh Douglas Hamilton, GEORGE COCKBURN (1764-1847)
c.1783, oil on canvas, 25 x 20 cm (whereabouts unknown)
(cat. 46, TRICORNS AND TURBANS, exhibition of British portraits, 1987, Martyn Gregory Gallery, London)

where his 'proper letters' from General Elliot held him in good stead as he met the governor, General Acton, and England's ambassador to Naples, Sir William Hamilton, whose marriage to Emma still lay in the future. George informed Caldwell of the terrible earthquake that had occurred on 5th February 1783 in Calabria, in the toe of Italy, where it was estimated that 'near a hundred thousand people [had been] lost'.[34] No circumstantial account was available, but the frigate that had brought the news was 'to sail the first wind to the relief of the poor persons who have survived, but at present the wind is contrary, & the weather bad so that it may be some time before she gets there'.[35]

Having visited Rome for a second time, George himself suffered 'contrary' winds during his voyage from there back to Leghorn to collect some baggage, from where, on 20th March 1783, he wrote of his uncomfortable journey:

> The Danish ship I came over in was bad indeed, I had the whole Cabin the dimensions was about six feet square & 5 high, so you may imagine how pleasant the time was. The Captain was a very honest good fellow, & done all in his power to make his devil of a Vessel agreeable; there were only 8 people captain sailors passangers & all.[36]

In the same letter, commenting on his second, shorter visit to Rome, he writes: 'You mention'd in a letter ... Pope Julio's palace [which today, known as the Villa Guilia, houses one of the world's premier collections of Etruscan artefacts], & I found it out, but no one resides there, & it is difficult to get in being all shut up. I hear there is some good architecture about it but it is nothing in Rome.' Later, from Florence, he wrote that although he considered he had seen 'everything' in Rome, to describe it would take up too much paper and he would wait until he saw his uncle to tell him about it. He did, however, inform him that he had acquired 'Volpati's [Giovanni Battista Volpati, 1633-1706] fine prints of Raphael's Rooms in the Vatican',[37] which he considered very cheap 'at about four pounds',[38] and offered to send to Rome for a set for Caldwell if he so wished. He was so impressed with Rome that he assured him that should he (Caldwell) ever go there, he would never return!

Moving on, and travelling via Bologne (where he saw many fine pictures which, unfortunately, he did not have the space to elaborate on) and Modena, George arrived in Turin at the beginning of April. He wrote:

> I think myself now at home, as the people here are civilized. Such a race as the Romans I never saw, no one law to keep the common people in order. They seem (tho that is the case in Florence & Naples) never happy but when cover'd with dirt, & I assure you that I never saw in the worst part of Ireland, so much misery, dirt, & impudence as in Italy, & all the Foreigners I have seen are of the same opinion.[39]

Early April saw George in Lausanne, whence he writes:

> I arrived here this morning from Geneva, where I stay'd 3 days. I shall return tomorrow & the next day set out for Paris. I had fine weather for my journey over the Alps, & the passage is in fact nothing. Some people are fond of making difficulty's of the most trifling things. I had my carriage taken in pieces at the other side of Mount Cenis, cross'd over it (16 miles) & had the carriage ready again with trunks & every thing in 8 hours. This is a poor & dirty town, but in a most charming situation near the Lake of Geneva. The country about it very rich & the people good natured & obliging. Such fellows as the Italians I never saw & hope never to see again. They are much worse than the Savages of America, but the Frenchmen & Swiss I like much.[40]

Nearing the end of his tour, on 20th April, George began his month's visit to Paris, which he thought would, like London, require half a year to know well. Politically it was an exciting time to be there as Benjamin Franklin and David Hartly (a member of the British parliament who represented the British monarch, King George III, at the signing of the Treaty of Paris on 3rd September 1783) were both in town. George writes: 'The English in general visit Dr. Franklin, and the Irish never omit I am told. I have not seen him, as having a Commission it would be improper as yet. I am told he is very cunning, & will take in Mr. Hartly who is at present here treating with the Americans.'[41]

Finally, on 30th May 1783, having been abroad for less than eight months, George arrived back in England, having sailed from Calais to Dover. On that day he wrote a disgruntled letter to his uncle telling him that:

> I am in no humour to write tonight, I had some things which I put in my Great Coat Pocket to escape the Custom house officers, & some lace for Mrs. Riall [his future mother-in-law]. I got them safe to the Door, & Davy's thick head forgot to take them out of the chaise, however as the Postillions of this country are honest I hope to get them, & Davy shall walk tomorrow to Dartford – 16 miles – for them, so I hope a march of 32 miles will put some memory into him.[42]

For the next two years the correspondence dries up, but we learn from other sources that George was promoted to captain-lieutenant in the 105th regiment in 1784, and transferred in 1785 to the 65th regiment, then quartered in Dublin. This regiment was sent to Canada in 1785, but its colonel, the Earl of Harrington, seeing George's great potential, kept him behind for recruiting duties and to study the Prussian autumn manoeuvres. So, on 9th September 1785, we find George once more abroad on army business, this time in Brussels, having begun what was to be a lightening tour, as he is back in London in November, only two-and-a-half months later. He covered a lot of ground during this short time (visiting Belgium, Holland and Germany for the first time, and France for the second) carrying out his military duties, satisfying his curiosity about countries and people new to him, and seeing as much art and architecture as he could, remembering all the while to report conscientiously back to his uncle.

In Ghent he had bought some pictures and was most anxious to hear from Caldwell, who had a large collection of his own, that he approved of his choice. He wrote: 'Mr. Loridon de Ghellinck at Ghent is disposing of his cabinet. I bought 8 for Fifty-one Guineas. I dare say you will think I have been taken in, however wait till you see them.'[43] As we shall see later, Caldwell's approval of his purchases, which heralded the beginning of George's own collection, confirmed that, young as he was, he had already developed a discerning taste for painting. He had also seen 'Mr. Dannoots the bankers' cabinet, which he considered to be very good.

By 27th September 1785 he was in Cologne, having travelled through Belgium, visiting Namur, which he found delightful, Liege, which he considered to be 'a vile place, & full as dirty as Naas',[44] Spa, which equally failed to please, and Verviers, which he thought to be a pretty town. Once into Germany, he stayed in Aix-la-Chappelle for six days, not because he liked it – he considered it to be as bad as Spa – but because he met up with some officers there and then passed through what he considered to be the well-fortified town of Juliers. It comes as no surprise that he didn't like Cologne either, considering it to be 'very large, very ugly, badly built, dirty, narrow ill paved streets; but for all that looks well at a distance'.[45] After a quick dash to Bonn, he planned to set off for Dusseldorf, 'from which place I shall go to Wesel to see 12 Thousand Prussians'.[46] This trip was, of course, connected with his military commitments, which, because of the nature of this journal, have been played down, but a notebook kept by him confirms that, throughout his travels, he was concerned with 'the organization and administration of the British army and those of Germany, Austria, Holland, Spain and France'.[47]

Wesel impressed him greatly, and now in Antwerp, which he had reached via Maastricht, Louvain, Brussels and Malines, he wrote, on 28th October 1785: 'I was very lucky as the next day after my arrival was the Garrison review, a Capt. civily lent me a horse, & I was greatly entertained. It was the best review I ever saw. There was 8 Thousand men in the field.'[48] Antwerp pleased him, although its hours and climate did not: 'I dine some times at the table D'Hote (that is I dine at their supper). Their hours do not suit me. I am up every morning at six, breakfast at eleven, dine at six, and as the opera is over by eight, go to bed at nine. The weather has been constantly as bad as possible since I left England.'[49] He informs Caldwell in this letter that, when he was in Dusseldorf, he had bought himself a set of prints 'from Rembrandt's pictures', and had also purchased a set as a gift for his uncle. In a later letter, learning that Caldwell already owns this set, George asks him to present them to 'Mr. Mangan' (Alexander Mangin, Caldwell's great friend, who owned a large print collection).[50]

No one was happier than George's grandmother, Eliza Caldwell, when his tour was over. She wrote:

> I sincerely congratulate you on your safe return to England it was true joy to me, after many fears & anxious thoughts about you, I hope you have Don with the Continent for I believe you have seen every spot in it, & by your own Acct. you went thro much fatigue & had great Escapes & I cant help bleaming you for putting your health & strength to such unnecessary trialls, but so far it has given proof of a good Constitution, but you had better not repate it too often for fear of an unfortunate Nick.[51]

His uncle, too, was glad to see him home, and had good reports of the paintings George had bought in Ghent. He wrote:

> The Pictures are extremely well for the money, which in the article of Tableaux was a meer nothing, they are all of a convenient size and we can easily hang them up, but at present they remain in the St. Parlour for me to look at – the Frost Piece is the best and a pretty little Picture, the next is the Table Hill & the Dutch India Man, but it is crack'd thro' in coming over, I expect it was join'd formerly, the Frost prevents its being glew'd but shall Doctor it up soon & glew Canvas behind the crack will not be very visible, this picture seems to have been rub'd in the Cleaning. The Van Goyen seems to have been much repainted, the De Oliegar[52] very well but he is not a very capital hand, the old Peasant probably a fine copy, for you never would have got a real Teniers for that Price. The Boors in the Cottage very pretty, I suspect my large Piece of the Wedding [*A Dutch Wedding by Ostade*][53] is by the same hand, the two little moonlights exceeding cheap and pretty, I never heard the name before, Smeester, & suppose he may be some modern Artist, Hunter the Painter lik'd them all extremely well.[54]

For a while George divided his time between England and Ireland, spending some time at the home of his aunt, Catherine Riall, in Clonmel, and courting his first cousin, Eliza Riall, whom he planned to marry. However, in August 1888, he was on the Continent again, this time in Holland, trying hard to understand Dutch politics:

> This town [The Hague], the Windsor of Holland is all for the Prince ... from what I can find out the entire of the middling People are Patriots, The Cannaille as they call them here, & the courtiers (which you will perhaps reckon Canaille) are for the Stadtholder... Every person from the highest to

the lowest is forced to wear orange cockades, indeed men & women are cover'd with orange ornaments. Such are the changes; for ten months ago, that colour was so disliked that they dare not bring Carrots to Market ... I saw all the Court at the Play last night, & was at a review by the Stadtholder in the morning; he is the image of Lord Corhampton, but not so clever I fancy.[55]

Of Rotterdam, as of so many towns and cities he visited, George had little good to say:

Rotterdam is certainly situated with every possible advantage for Trade, and a bank which was at the entrance of the river, was swept away by the Ice in 1784 which has been of great service for large ships but I confess I never was more disappointed in the appearance of a Town. I had heard much of it, & think it a vile, nasty stinking Town as ever I saw, the houses all hang over, many of them as much as the Tower at Pisa. The Quay is destroyd by the Trees, which are very proper & desirable in the country, but of no use in a Town; but darkens the houses & prevents the circulation of the air.[56]

He liked the Dutch better than their towns, however, and considered them to be 'a good natured, quiet, honest people'.[57]

Somehow or other, in spite of his being constantly on the move, George's mail always seemed to catch up with him, and there was a letter awaiting him from his uncle when he arrived in Hanover in mid-October 1788. As well as containing family news, Caldwell informed him of the death of Gainsborough:

Stewart the Painter has resolved to go directly to London the Death of poor Gainsborough leaves such a prospect open, that Stewarts Head is fairly turn'd with the Expectation, I can't get a sight of him, he is always in the Country, I want to get home your Picture, I did intend to have the Madames [presumably his mother and sister] by him & perhaps my own, but I suppose he will not undertake them now.[58]

From this it would seem that Caldwell was acquainted with Gilbert Stuart, and that George's portrait had already been painted by him, but there was no further mention of it in the correspondence, and although it is shown in Lawrence Park's book on Stuart (Plate 11),[59] its present whereabouts is unknown.

Although Stuart returned to London at least twice,[60] he finally settled in Dublin, painting numerous commissions until his departure for what had become the United States in 1793. In fact, he did 'undertake' a portrait of Caldwell, and this is also listed in Sotheby's 'Valuation of heirlooms under the will of C.H.B.Caldwell dec'd',[61] where it is valued at £40. On 19th November 1969, by order of the trustees of the Caldwell estate, Sotheby's sold the portrait, describing it as a 'Portrait of

Andrew Caldwell of Dublin (1733-1808), half length, in black coat, striped silk waistcoat and white lace cravat, in a painted oval. 27in by 24in.' This portrait has now been traced to America and is the property of the United Missouri Bank of St Louis, Missouri, who have given permission for its reproduction here (Plate 12).

In this same letter, Caldwell also urged George to 'be sure to see the fine jet d'eau at the Gardens of Herrenhausen at Hanover the highest in Europe, I believe 100 ft, but there should be a very calm day.' [62] Later, George recounted that he had been unable to see the jet, not because the gardener had been ordered not to play from 1st October, not because he was only to play it in the summer on Sundays (the Tip (or bribe), he explained, was above all orders in Germany and would have easily overcome these obstacles), but because the pipes had been filled and covered with horse dung to prevent the cold from spoiling them!

When he arrived in Brunswick a month later there were two more letters from Caldwell waiting for him, to which he replied at some length. His letters of introduction had once more stood him in good stead, and he wrote that he had found the duke and duchess (Karl Wilhelm Ferdinand, Duke of Brunswick-Wolfenbuttel, and his wife Princess Augusta Charlotte) 'as polite as possible to the English, a great deal more so than they deserve, as they have been guilty of every excess. One fellow not long ago, had the impudence to piss from the boxes on to the Parterre, in the middle of the Opera, however he was well trounced for it he took his beating very quietly.' [63] George reported that although the Duke and Duchess were in great distress because of the recent death of their daughter, Auguste Caroline Friederike, there was 'not the slightest appearance of it. I believe Great People take things very cooly.' [64] George thought little of the palace of Wolfen-Buttel, which, in spite of its fine library, he considered to be not worth the time it took to pass through the Rooms: 'Such an execrable collection of Daubs I never saw, the walls are cover'd.' [65] The duke was an experienced campaigner and a master of modern warfare in the mid-eighteenth century, so was very a useful contact for George, who was invited to dine with him throughout his stay in Brunswick. The duke was not able to help him during his quick trip to Magdeburgh, though, as 'the Commanding Officer positively refused to let me see the fortifications, however, the Tip is superior to orders, even in Prussia. The poor man might have saved himself the trouble of refusing, for I saw every thing.' [66]

Back in Hanover, George wrote a long 'Military disertation' to his uncle detailing his observations of the activities of the Prussian army, feeling that as he had seen 'Seven days great manoevres at Berlin & Potsdam, & for 2 months in detail', [67] he was as well qualified as anyone else to give an opinion, but his next letter, written from Hesse-Cassel, was more concerned with domestic details. On his twenty-sixth birthday the following year, George was to become legally responsible for his own affairs, which had been managed by his uncle since his father's death in

11 – Gilbert Stuart,
CAPTAIN GEORGE COCKBURN
(1764-1787)

c.1788, oil on canvas, 76 x 64 cm
(detail) (whereabouts unknown)
(from GILBERT STUART, AN
ILLUSTRATED DESCRIPTIVE LIST OF
HIS WORKS, 4 vols, compiled by L.
Park (New York, 1926) III, 106)

12 – Gilbert Stuart, ANDREW
CALDWELL (1733-1808)

c.1790, oil on canvas, 69 x 61 cm
(detail) (courtesy UMB Financial
Corporation, Kansas City, MO)

1775. Some time thereafter he was planning to marry Eliza Riall, and therefore asked Caldwell to begin to look for a house of his own for himself, his mother and Fanny (Harriet having since died), and vacate the Cockburn house in Cavendish Street, if possible some time during the following summer. He went on to say that he liked Hesse-Cassel, which was a fine town in a beautiful situation. The Landgrave had a good collection of pictures and there was a handsome square in which was a museum. The front of the museum he considered to be 'very like that of the New hall in Dublin College where Dr Baldwins monument is ... There is a Circus not so large, or near as handsome as that at Bath.' [68]

George was to stay on the Continent for some time longer, finally arriving in Paris in February 1789, having visited Frankfurt, Mons, Valenciennes, Cambray and Peronne. A 'venerable yew tree' in the cloister of Peronne's 'very handsome church' reminded him of Mucross Abbey, but the 'French are not however as super-stitious as the Killarnians, as they have cut off several branches; it is still very hand-some and large.' [69] In a long letter to his uncle, written from Paris on 16th March 1789, George explained why he had decided to spend more time abroad rather than return to Dublin in April and propose to Eliza Riall as he had originally planned. He wished to act honourably and felt that as he would not be in a position to make a settlement on Eliza until he came into his estate on his twenty-sixth birthday, he might as well, 'having now seen almost every country except the south of France and Spain', rectify that situation and, in the process, 'encounter the Pyranees'. [70] Anxious to learn Spanish, George decided to base himself in Barcelona, where he stayed several weeks learning the language from an excellent Spanish master. With his usual enthusiasm he continued his sightseeing, and described his visit to Mt Serrat, which was

> certainly a most extraordinary mountain. There is a Convent of Benedictines on it, & they are tolerably hospitable. I went as the Paddys would say to the very tip top. I may say I slept two nights in the Clouds. The path up the mountain as far as the Convent is very narrow and dangerous, something like that to the top of the waterfall at Powerscourt. The Convent is halfway to the top. I was near three hours going to the convent, & half a day to see the Hermitage on the mountain above the Convent. It is very high, & going up I fancied myself in a Balloon, as the hills & villages below just appear as a lit-tle unevenness or spot on the regions below. I came down by the other side of the mountain, so that I saw it completely. [71]

He also enthused about the colourful torchlight Corpus Christi religious procession, with its bands, embroidered banners, marching monks of different orders, and the balconies of all the houses on the route filled with people dressed in their best, with ornaments and flags hanging from the windows.

Although he was later posted to Guernsey, this was to be the last letter that George sent to his uncle from the Continent, probably because travel in Europe was made difficult by the French Revolution and then the Napoleonic Wars, and by the time the army sent him abroad again (to Sicily in 1810), Caldwell was dead. Still only twenty-five years old, he had embraced every opportunity offered him throughout his three mini-Grand Tours. His collection of classical artefacts did not start until later, when he went to Sicily, but, as we know, he had taken every opportunity to look at paintings, having trusted in his own judgement enough to buy the Ghent paintings and the Volpati and Rembrandt prints, as well as carrying out 'commissions' for Caldwell.

No doubt because he always had plenty of varied news for his uncle, and because his paper space was limited, he seldom had an opportunity to describe in detail the many 'good collections' of pictures he had seen, which must have been frustrating for Caldwell; similarly with collections he had not liked, as with the 'execrable Daubs' on the walls of the palace of Wolfen-Buttel. No doubt, again because of limited space, his descriptions of the architecture of the cities and towns he visited was limited, although perhaps his youth showed in his often negative ('nasty, dirty, stinking') choice of vocabulary for what he had seen. Nevertheless, his few mentions of fine architecture were often tempered by his opinion that it did not always measure up to that of England or Dublin; for instance, his opinion that although he considered Hesse-Cassel (whose Landgrave he reported also had a good collection of pictures) to be a fine town in a beautiful situation, with a museum very like the new hall in Dublin College (William Chambers' Examination Hall), its Circus was neither as large or as handsome as that of Bath. He carried Ireland in his head wherever he went, comparing, for example, the steepness of the picturesque climb to the top of Mt Serat with the narrow and dangerous path to the top of the Powerscourt waterfall, and the cloister adjoining an old church in Pironne with Muckross Abbey.

The next time we hear from George is in the summer of 1794. Since we last heard from him he had married Eliza Riall (in March 1790), fathered three children (Catherine, in January 1791, George in January 1792, and Elizabeth in February 1793), and settled into his house in what had now been renamed 7 Rutland Square East, his uncle having bought a house further up the street, number 12 (which, until a few years ago, housed the Ierne Ballroom). The 11th August 1794 finds George in Southampton, aboard ship and about to sail with his regiment for Guernsey. He complains of the chaos at Southampton: 'Such bustle, misconduct, hurry & confusion as there is here you can have no idea of. Regiments embarking that have neither Arms Officers or cloathes – one would imagine were not likely to conquer Les Sans Culottes, but such is the system.' [72] In his reply to this letter, Caldwell hopes that George and his regiment will not be sent further than Guernsey, which he

believed 'the sans culottes [do not] have any intention of attacking, & therefore no occasion to have well appointed steady Troops for its Defence'.[73] George was to stay in Guernsey until the spring of 1795, and was not happy there. Several members of his regiment had died, having travelled from Southampton in ships 'which were but lately arrived from the West Indies, & with a contagious fever on board'.[74] There was a shortage of food, and the men were half-starved, but 'Oceans of Jin to be had for almost nothing, & in consequence the paddy's are very frequently what they call Hearty. It is altogether the worst place I know to send a young Regt. to.' [75] The redeeming feature of the island, in George's opinion, was the wealth of beautiful plant life, which, knowing his uncle's interest in botany, he described in some detail.

From the time he arrived home from Guernsey in the spring of 1795 until 1806, when he left to take up a command on the English staff in Hull, Sunderland and Chelmsford, George spent most of his time in Ireland, and it was during this time that his last three children were born (Phineas in November 1795, Ann in May 1797, and Mary in August 1805) and he acquired his country estate, Shanganagh Castle in Shankill, county Dublin. It must also have been during these years, some time after Hugh Douglas Hamilton's return to Dublin from Italy in 1791, that George retained him to paint a portrait of his wife Eliza and two of their children (Plate 13), but it is not clear which two. A label affixed to the painting reads, 'Lady Cockburn and her two children. H. Hamilton. RHA'. As Hamilton died in 1808 and George was not knighted until 1831, this can't be right, and one must assume that whoever labelled the painting was unaware of the date of George's knighthood. There was no mention of Hamilton, or either of the portraits, found anywhere in the correspondence studied.

The land Cockburn leased comprised just over a hundred acres and was bought in three lots, two in June 1800, and one in

---

13 – Hugh Douglas Hamilton, LADY COCKBURN AND HER TWO CHILDREN, oil on canvas, 150 x 150 cm

This portrait must have been painted some time after Hamiltonís return to Dublin in 1791. He died in 1804 and George Cockburn was not knighted until 1841. It must be assumed that whoever labelled the portrait was unaware of the date of his knighthood. (private collection; photo Michael Gray)

May 1801.[76] Part of this land had been leased to Joseph Kathrens in 1759,[77] whose widow completed building the house he had started, and, in 1769, sold her interest to George Roth, who named the house Fairview.[78] The house was subsequently let to a succession of tenants, the name of one of them, (Sydenham) Snow, appearing beside it on Taylor & Skinner's *Maps of the Roads of Ireland*.[79] By October 1780 we learn from a letter from his uncle, written from London, that George has settled into his country home and is very taken up with farming. Caldwell writes:

> The Poultry etc. I shall remember, the Admiral [George's uncle, Benjamin Caldwell, who commanded the Agamemnon before Nelson] roars at sending Turkeys to Ireland, but tho' we are pretty well off, yet there are curious improv'd breeds, & this is the place to procure every thing that the world affords.[80]

Over the next two decades, George was to enlarge and remodel his house to provide suitable accommodation for his growing family and visiting friends and relations, and for his considerable collection of books, paintings and classical marbles. A letter from Caldwell in July 1804 suggests that by then the work was well under way: a 'gentleman' he had met at a large dinner had 'expressed his surprise at what was doing at Shanganagh, he imagined you had got enough before.' [81] In fact, he had hardly started. George had engaged the architect Richard Morrison to carry out the work, and the Irish Architectural Archive's publication *The Architecture of Richard Morrison and William Vitruvius Morrison* records two visits to Shanganagh by Bryan Bolger, his measurer, one dated 1805.[82] In 1954 the exciting discovery was made by workmen carrying out alterations to Shanganagh Castle for the Office of Public Works of a letter written by George in 1818, enclosed in a bottle and sealed into the chimney turret for his picture gallery, which was under construction using the remains of a former tower on the site. Not only do we learn from this letter that new building was still underway, but also George's thoughts and opinions, as a fifty-four-year-old man, on religion and the politics of the day, and following the discovery of two cannon shot in the demolished tower, his 'take' on how they came to be there.

By the time the work was finished, the original house would hardly have been recognisable. It had been extended, and a profusion of battlements and turrets added to the exterior (Plate 14). Brewer wrote that at Shanganagh, Morrison had 'confined to the outward portion of the building all allusions to the gorgeous but rude manners of times long past' while adapting the interior 'to the habits of refined life – to the customs of society intent on intellectual pleasure as well as hospitable entertainment'.[83] George wished the future owners of the house as much pleasure and enjoyment as he had had in it, and hoped that 'as I am at all events the Improver and chief builder of it ... they will do me The favour to Drink to my memory a

14 – Drawing of Shanganagh Castle, 1857 (artist unknown)
(private collection)

Bumper of Good Claret.'[84]

He was not to enjoy his country life for long, and 1806 finds him back in England at the start of his tour of duty there. Meanwhile, Caldwell was happy to move in to Shanganagh (which he called 'The Shan') in a caretaking capacity, and spent much of the rest of his life there, learning about farming and enjoying the company of visiting family members. One such member was his nephew Charles Andrew Caldwell, only son of his brother Benjamin, who had come to Ireland to visit the Newgrange estate, which, in the fullness of time, he was to inherit. He was not used to Irish hospitality, and wrote to his mother:

> The host in Ireland can never say to his Guests 'Well you do not seem inclined to drink any more wine, will you go to the drawing room?' Such a speech would be an insupportable breach of hospitality. The Master of the house sits till his company gradually drops off, & if one is a toper, there he must stay. Give me (at least in this instance) the inhospitality of the other side of the water.[8]

During Caldwell's time at Shanganagh, a tragedy happened on the estate. In August

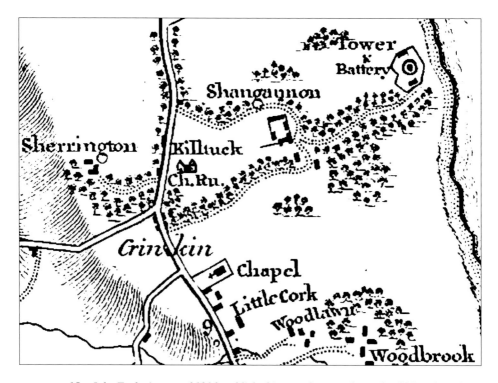

opposite 15 – John Taylor's map of 1816, published in two sheets at the scale of 2" to the mile
detail showing 'Shangannon' and the Martello Tower and Battery.
(Thanks to Andrew Bonar Law for locating and copying this detail.)

1807 his friend Peter Walsh wrote:

> It can be only by very blameable Neglect or great Ignorance in the Persons
> directing the Work that so fatal & awful an event should occur as that which
> you mention to have happened in the Well sinking for the Martello Tower at
> Shanganna [Plate 15], as it is always easy to ascertain the State of the Air in a
> Well before Men descend into it, by lowering a lighting Candle in a
> Lanthern.[86]

Fortunately this was the only tragedy occurring at Shanganagh before Caldwell's
death there on 2nd July 1808. At this point, of course, the correspondence between
uncle and nephew ceases, but we know from Astbury's article in *Classics Ireland*[87]
that in April 1810 George was put in command of a division of the army of occupation in Sicily, which position he had to resign in November 1810, having been
awarded the rank of lieutenant-general. He now had the leisure to pursue his interest
in classical architecture and artefacts, and although this part of his life is not record-

16 – Ferdinando Cavalleri, GEN. SIR GEORGE COCKBURN
oil on canvas, 84 x 69 cm (detail) (private collection)

131

ed in the correspondence studied, we learn from Astbury that before returning home the following year, he travelled widely in Sicily, no doubt building up his collection as he went.[88]

An unknown contributor to the Caldwell Papers wrote of George's life after his return from abroad in 1811:

> [he] was not afterwards employed [by the army], probably owing to extravagant opinions in religion and politics. He attained the rank of General in 1821. He was made a Knight Commander of the Hanoverian Guelphic Order, by George the 4th on his visit to Hanover in 1821 and received the Grand Cross of that Order from King William 4th, by whom he was Knighted at Brighton in 1831.[89]

At some time subsequent to his knighthood, the Italian painter Ferdinando Cavalleri (1794-1865) painted his portrait (Plate 16). We know that on his return, George settled down in Shanganagh, running his estate, becoming a magistrate for the counties of Dublin and Wicklow, pursuing his interest in Irish and English politics, writing and publishing numerous pamphlets and letters and, in 1815, publishing a work in two volumes, entitled *A Voyage to Cadiz and Gibraltar, up the Mediterranean to Sicily and Malta*, in 1810 and 1811.

Apart from one letter written by George to his cousin Charles Caldwell on the death of his (Charles') father Admiral Benjamin Caldwell in November 1820, we hear little of him in the archive correspondence until November 1835. Much of his 1820 letter is taken up with his anxieties about his daughter Eliza's forthcoming marriage to Augustus Heyman, and reminds us of his own concerns when planning to propose marriage to his cousin Eliza Riall. This letter is important, and therefore the relevant passage is transcribed in detail:

> Now as to the other point, Eliza's marriage ... The Gentleman is about 27 years old, & a Lieut in the Scotch Grey, by name Heyman. No young man can have higher character – we have known him intimately above a year, & he appears to be as amiable as you or I could desire – But Fortune my Dear Charley there is the rub I do not think great riches at all necessary to happiness, but a certain quantity is, for I am of the old opinion that when Poverty comes in, love is apt to fly out & in these times, what may do extremely well for a man & even a wife, without children, becomes a struggle, with a large family, & which generally comes in proportion to want of means – The young man is a favourite of mine, & yet for the above reason, I in truth, threw all the cold water I could on the match, but it is now determined on – His fortune is 20 Thousand Pounds & his Commission – but it is all in the funds, & you know I have a very bad opinion of the good old Lady in

Threadneedle Street – moreover eight thsd. of it belongs or rather the interest, to his Mother for her life, & she is not aged – so that with Eliza's fortune the utmost they will have during the Mother's life will be £800 a year – & I confess I think this is too little for Ladies or Gentlemen to Embark in Matrimony upon – He has consented to take from the old Lady (i.e. funds) & invest in Mortgage by Trustees, as much as will secure Eliza a [illegible word] of £400 a year, otherwise I would not have consented.[90]

The next two letters from George are to his first cousin Charles Andrew Caldwell, and concern their grandmother's portrait (Plate 8). In the first, dated 30th November 1835, he writes: 'I am glad to find that there is at least one of the Family anxious to preserve a most Capital Likeness of one of the best of women that I now in my old age, & remembering from almost infancy, declare to be in my opinion almost unequalled for every good quality possible to human nature',[91] and in the second:

as to Grand Mother's picture I should be happy to oblige you, but you ask what I would not give to mortal, or will ever part with during my Existence. I have left it to you at my death, but till then, would not give it to St. Peter & half a dozen more Saints if they came down from Heaven to beg it, unless by a command from God; & Lady C- should she outlive me, will not like to part with it. After she & yourself are under the sod, no person in the World (Geo Caldwell excepted) would give Ten Pounds for it, tho admirably painted by Quadal, & never was there a better likeness taken.[92]

Happily, this beautiful sensitive portrait still remains in the family, as does that of her son Andrew Caldwell (Plate 1), painted at the same time. The Moravian animal painter Martin Ferdinand Quadel (1736-1793) was known to be in Dublin in 1779, and also to have painted portraits, but these two are the only Irish ones that have so far come to light.

Although he was not to die until two years later, in his letter to his nephew Revd George Caldwell (his brother Charles' son) in May 1845, George clearly felt that he was coming to the end of his life. He was suffering with an enlarged prostate gland and was in considerable pain. The 'medicals' had told him that chances were against his recovery, and he anticipated that he would soon be joining twelve of his 'most intimate friends' who had died in the last twelve months. In the meantime, he busily got on with preparations for his departure: 'I am ... having my coffin ready a handsome mahogany – & a pretty Tomb & small Vault as they tell me in the Dublin Pere La Chaise [Harold's Cross cemetery] – so I take matters philosophically.'[93] Only the day before he had written to Nicholas Ellis about this tomb, which was to hold nine bodies and measure inside 'seven feet in length, seven feet in breadth, nine feet six inches in heigth' (Plates 17, 18).[94]

133

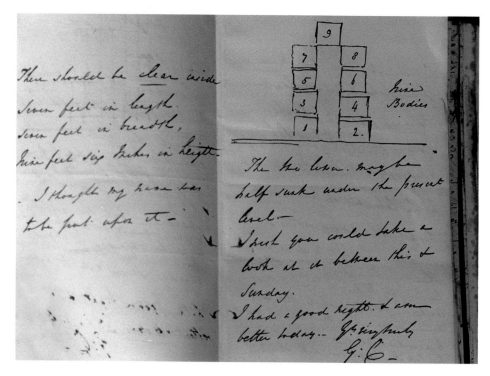

17 – Detail from letter written by George Cockburn to Nicholas Ellis, 20th May 1845, in which he sets out design and measurements for his tomb in Harolds Cross Cemetery (private collection)

George died at home on the morning of Wednesday 18th August 1847. Although not well, the previous Monday he had insisted on going downstairs to attend prayers with all the household, including the servants, to mark the anniversary of the death of his youngest daughter, Mary, the year before. That was the last time he was able to leave his bed. His wife Eliza described his last moments in a letter to her nephew Charles Caldwell:

> The Docr came at nine and on going to him, he could not speak and the pulse was nearly gone – strong wine, brandy and water were given but all was of no avail, the vital spark had fled. You may imagine my horror on going into the room, expecting to find him strengthened by so much sleep, to see him actually expiring. Oh, I shall never forget it'.[95]

He was eighty-three years old, and at the time of his death was fourth general in seniority in the British army. Eliza lived on for another three-and-a-half years, and was interred with him (and probably their daughter Mary, if the building had been completed at the time of her death) in the 'pretty tomb' he had designed in Harold's Cross 'Pere la Chaise' cemetery.

18 – George Cockburn's family tomb in Harolds Cross Cemetery

George Cockburn had lived his life to the full, never regretting his decision to join the army, travelling widely, building up his collection of Classical artefacts, devoting himself to his wife and family and their Shanganagh home, becoming a magistrate for the counties of Dublin and Wicklow, and, on occasion, committing his strongly felt political views to paper.[96] Long before she died, his proud grand-mother had already become aware that he had, indeed, made the 'Good Figure' she had so confidently predicted for him in the days of his turbulent youth.

ACKNOWLEDGEMENTS

My first thanks are due to the owners of the private collections I have been privileged to consult, and to Dr Ray Astbury, without whose generous sharing this article could not have been written. It would also have lacked some crucial information without Rob Goodbody's help. For his photographic work on the Hugh Douglas Hamilton portrait of Lady Cockburn and her two children I'm especially grateful to Michael Gray, independent curator and image consultant, and I'm also indebted to Brendan Dempsey of the Photographic Centre, Trinity College Dublin, for valuable photographic assistance and advice. I thank Andrew Bonar Law for spending time seeking out appropriate map references for me, Philip McEvensoneya for always so promptly responding to my queries, Niall O'Donoghue for his help on Martello towers, and the Knight of Glin for reminding me, every time we met, that I should consider submitting an article for this journal. Finally, as ever, I thank Dr Edward McParland for reading this article, and for his constant support and encouragement.

ENDNOTES

The following abbreviations are used:

CP   Caldwell Papers, private collection, Suffolk

NAM   Cockburn Papers in National Army Museum, London

[1] Edward McParland, *James Gandon* (London, 1985) 38.

[2] Luisa Vertova, 'A late renaissance view of Rome', *Burlington Magazine*, July 1995, 445.

[3] CP. The estate finally passed to the Land Commission in February 1932 when Charles Henry Bulwer, as the landlord, received a net amount of £28,804, payable in 4 % land bonds.

[4] CP.

[5] This portrait, painted by Robert Hunter, and one of George Cockburn senior, used to hang on either side of the drawing-room fireplace in the home of the late Patricia Heyman. (George Cockburn's daughter Eliza married Augustus Heyman in 1822.) Disturbed before they had finished the job, the burglars escaped with George, but had perforce to leave Ann behind.

[6] Walter G. Strickland, *A Dictionary of Irish Artists*, 2 vols (Dublin 1913) I, 536.

[7] Anne Crookshank, 'Robert Hunter', *Irish Arts Review*, 1989-90, 169-185.

[8] Bodleian Library, Oxford, MS Eng. letters c.15, f.109-110, Andrew Caldwell to Edmund Malone, 5th February 1802.

[9] CP, George Cockburn to Mrs Elizabeth Caldwell, 7th June 1763.

[10] The online *Oxford Dictionary of National Biography* (OUP 2004-07) gives George as having been born in 1763, but the family pedigree, compiled by Mr Tuckett, gives 1764 as the year of his birth, and other letters in the Caldwell Papers confirm this date.

[11] British Library, Cockburn Papers, Add 48314.

[12] Irish Architectural Archive, Curran notebook, 14.

[13] CP, Charles Caldwell to Elizabeth Caldwell, 26th August 1769.

[14] The Strand Street congregation subsequently merged with that of Eustace Street Meeting House to form, in 1863, the core congregation of the new Dublin Unitarian Church on St Stephen's Green. The joint archives of Strand Street and Eustace Street meeting houses, which

were held in the Unitarian Church, have recently been entrusted to the care of the Royal Irish Academy, where they will be available for general consultation.

[15] British Library, Cockburn Papers, Add 48315.

[16] NAM, George Cockburn to Andrew Caldwell, 22nd March 1783.

[17] NAM, William Darby to Andrew Caldwell, 3rd April 1776.

[18] CP, Andrew Caldwell to Mrs Elizabeth Caldwell, 26th July 1777.

[19] *ibid.*, 7th August 1777.

[20] *ibid*, 25th August 1777.

[21] *ibid*, 29th August 1777.

[22] CP, Mrs Elizabeth Caldwell to Andrew Caldwell, 31st August 1777.

[23] CP, Fanny Caldwell to Andrew Caldwell, undated.

[24] CP, Andrew Caldwell to Mrs Elizabeth Caldwell, 4th September 1777.

[25] CP, William Cleghorn to Andrew Caldwell, 7th May 1781.

[26] Royal Academy Exhibition, 1781.

[27] CP, George Cockburn to Andrew Caldwell, 7th May 1781.

[28] NAM, George Cockburn to Andrew Caldwell, 20th August 1782.

[29] *ibid.*, 1st November 1782.

[30] *ibid.*

[31] *ibid.*, 1st January 1781.

[32] *ibid.*, 15th February 1783.

[33] John Ingamells, *A Dictionary of British and Irish Travellers in Italy 1701-1800* (New Haven and London, 1997) 222.

[34] NAM, George Cockburn to Andrew Caldwell,15th February 1783.

[35] *ibid.*

[36] *ibid.*, 20th March 1783.

[37] *ibid.*, 22nd March 1783.

[38] *ibid.*, 2nd April 1783.

[39] *ibid.*

[40] *ibid.*, 12th April 1783.

[41] *ibid.*, 23rd April 1783.

[42] *ibid.*, 30th May 1783.

[43] *ibid.*, 9th September 1785.

[44] *ibid.*, 27th September 1785.

[45] *ibid.*

[46] *ibid.*

[47] British Library, Cockburn Papers, Add 48317.

[48] NAM, George Cockburn to Andrew Caldwell, 28th October 1785.

[49] *ibid.*

[50] *ibid.*, 16th November 1785.

[51] CP, Mrs Elizabeth Caldwell to George Cockburn, 26th November 1785.

[52] Was unable to identify this artist.

[53] National Gallery of Ireland, no. 20 in bound volume of catalogues collected by George Meade. *A Dutch Wedding by Ostade*, no. 98 in catalogue for posthumous sale of Caldwell's pictures, framed prints and drawings, held on 1st and 2nd March 1809 at his house, 12 Rutland Square East, by Thomas Jones.

54 CP, Andrew Caldwell to George Cockburn, 9th January 1786.
55 CP, George Cockburn to Andrew Caldwell, 20th August 1788.
56 *ibid.*
57 CP, George Cockburn to Mrs Elizabeth Caldwell, 12th September 1788.
58 CP, Andrew Caldwell to George Cockburn, 18th October 1788.
59 Lawrence Park, *Gilbert Stuart, An illustrated descriptive list of his works*, 4 vols (New York 1926) III, 106.
60 *Oxford Dictionary of National Biography* (Oxford, 2004), Gilbert Charles Stuart (1755-1828).
61 CP.
62 CP, Andrew Caldwell to George Cockburn, 18th October 1788.
63 CP, George Cockburn to Andrew Caldwell, 16th November 1788.
64 *ibid.*
65 *ibid.*
66 *ibid.*
67 *ibid.*, 24th November 1788.
68 NAM, George Cockburn to Andrew Caldwell, 10th December 1788.
69 *ibid.*, 12th February 1789.
70 *ibid.*, 16th March 1789.
71 *ibid.*, 17th June 1789.
72 *ibid.*, 11th August 1794.
73 CP, Andrew Caldwell to Lt Col George Cockburn, 14th August 1794.
74 NAM, George Cockburn to Andrew Caldwell, 23rd September 1794.
75 *ibid.*
76 Registry of Deeds, 528/167/34606; 523/419/346087; 535/576/353035.
77 Registry of Deeds, 199/43/131495.
78 I'm very grateful to Rob Goodbody for giving me the information about Joseph Kathrens' lease of the land, and especially grateful to know that a house was already standing on the land leased by Cockburn.
79 George Taylor and Andrew Skinner, *Maps of the Roads of Ireland* (Dublin (1778), 1783) and unabridged facsimile (Shannon, 1969) 140. My thanks to Rob Goodbody for drawing my attention to this map and Andrew Bonar-Law for emailing the relevant detail to me.
80 CP, Andrew Caldwell to George Cockburn, 17th October 1800.
81 *ibid.*, 28 July 1804.
82 *The Architecture of Richard Morrison and William Vitruvius Morrison* (Irish Architectural Archive, Dublin, 1989) 158-59.
83 James Norris Brewer, *The Beauties of Ireland*, 2 vols (London, 1825-26) I, 273-74.
84 Peter Pearson, 'Shanganagh Castle and the bottle letter', *Irish Architectural and Decorative Studies*, III (Dublin, 2000) 162.
85 CP, C.A. Caldwell to his mother, Mrs Caldwell, 28th August 1806.
86 CP, Peter Walsh to Andrew Caldwell, 26th August 1807. This tower has since been completely eroded by the sea.
87 Ray Astbury, 'Sir George Cockburn an Irish traveller and collector', *Classics Ireland* (1966), 1-17.
88 He was eventually to have a large collection of such artefacts, many of which are now in University College Dublin's Classical Museum.

[89] CP. Notes found among the Caldwell Papers headed 'General Sir George Cockburn, Kt. And GCH', author unknown.

[90] CP, George Cockburn to Charles Andrew Caldwell, 12th November 1820.

[91] *ibid.*, 30th November 1835.

[92] *ibid.*, 28th February 1843.

[93] CP, George Cockburn to Revd George Caldwell, 21st May 1845.

[94] CP, George Cockburn to Nicholas Ellis, 20th May 1845.

[95] CP, Eliza Cockburn to Charles Andrew Caldwell, 20th September 1847.

[96] General George Cockburn, *Six Letters on subjects very important to England* (Edinburgh, Dublin, London, 1831).

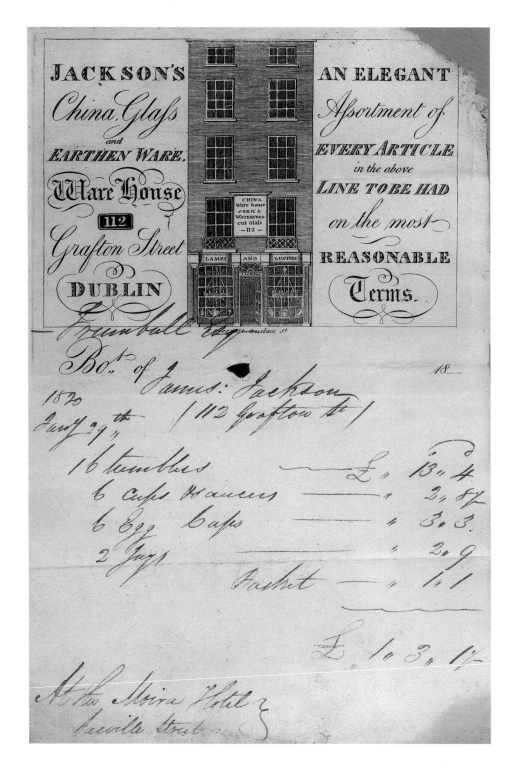

Merchants and material culture in early nineteenth-century Dublin: a consumer case study

ANNA MORAN

O N 29TH JANUARY 1820, NATHANIEL TRUMBULL, A DUBLIN-BASED TOBACCO merchant, purchased a number of objects from the ceramic and glass retailer James Jackson, of 112 Grafton Street, Dublin (Plate 1). His purchases included sixteen tumblers, costing 13s 4d, together with a list of ceramic items, including six cups and saucers, six eggcups and two jugs. As evidence surviving for the consumption of ceramics and glass in late-eighteenth and early nineteenth-century Ireland is sparse, the fact that this bill has survived is fortuitous. Even more exciting, however, is the fact that it is one of a large cache of Trumbull's bills, personal correspondence and business records.[1] Study of this material, combined with newspaper and street directory research, makes it possible to piece together a picture of this man's work and background. The bills for food, ceramics, glass, furniture, clothes and textiles are seen alongside bills for repairs, replacements and redecorations. Letters requesting money, discussing marriage and considering trade survive together with invitations to dinner and letters that once enclosed gifts. These sources allow the material-culture historian to map the acquisitive patterns of Nathaniel and his wife Sarah, establishing a picture of where they shopped and what they purchased, what they gave away, what they sold on, and what they valued enough to have repaired.

Focused on a narrow, but revealing, base of sources, this study cannot convey the Trumbulls' feelings towards their goods or establish broad trends for middle-rank interaction with consumer culture. Instead it provides a valuable case study which points to the existence of a rich material history of early nineteenth-century

1 – Bill for goods bought at Jackson's China, Glass and Earthenware Ware House,
112 Grafton Street, Dublin, January 1820   (courtesy New York Public Library)

Dublin, replacing the very grim picture often presented of exiting peers, a diminishing manufacturing base and a decaying urban fabric. A rare insight is thus provided into the material world of a member of Dublin's burgeoning middle class, a sector of society which provided a crucial market for luxury and semi-luxury goods in the post-Union city.[2]

Historians of material culture have, in various ways, reflected on and sought to contextualise consumers' motives for buying particular goods. The 'trickle down' or emulatory model advocated by Thorstein Veblen in his 1899 publication assumes that beyond material function, the principal role of goods was to communicate status.[3] While forming the bedrock of many historical studies, this model is no longer adopted blindly as the only way to interpret consumption of those of the middle rank. Research published in the fields of sociology, anthropology and design history has contributed greatly to the ways in which material culture of the long eighteenth century is studied. For example, social anthropologists Mary Douglas and Baron Isherwood argue that the primary information goods impart is not status, but character, emphasising the importance of things in the construction of identity.[4] Adopting an approach that allows for innumerable motivations, including those of competition and emulation, they assert that the decisions a consumer makes 'say something about himself, his family, his locality ... the kind of statements he makes are about the kind of universe he is in, affirmatory or defiant, perhaps competitive but not necessarily so.'[5] Therefore, while emulation is certainly one motivation for consumer behaviour, it is naive to attribute all purchasing choices to a desire to 'keep up with the Joneses'. As argued by Amanda Vickery, the acquisition of the same goods by two individuals, or two families, does not necessarily mean that one or other is attempting to copy his or her social superiors, but instead reflects a shared material culture, so often a feature of 'social solidarity and cohesion'.[6] Taking cognisance of such research, and being mindful of the fact that consideration of a consumer's choices will always and inevitably be speculative, an (albeit fragmentary) image of the Trumbulls' material world is presented. Rather than conveying a picture of a family which slavishly aped the lifestyle of the gentry, this valuable collection of bills for a range of necessaries and luxuries provides a rare insight into the material trappings of polite and genteel living amongst the commercial and professional elites of early nineteenth-century Ireland.

Nathaniel Trumbull was one of many middle-rank Dublin residents who, through shrewd investment and successful trading, achieved great financial security. However, Trumbull did not start his business from scratch with nothing. Trumbull's father, also named Nathaniel Trumbull, started out as a silk weaver in Francis Street, later owning part of a silk mercer's shop on Parliament Street between 1766 and 1769.[7] Eager to satisfy gentry demand for the very latest fashion, Trumbull and Mackay imported silks which they promoted in twice-weekly newspaper advertisements between October 1765 and May 1766.[8] However, by 1778 Trumbull is listed as 'Nathaniel Trumbull & Co. Merchants, 149 Abbey Street', having ceased to operate as a silk mercer. Considering the agitation witnessed in the textile industries in the 1770s involving violent riots and anti-importation protests, it is not surprising that a move towards trading tobacco was ventured.[9] By 1792, directories confirm that Nathaniel Trumbull junior had taken over the complete running of the business, Nathaniel senior having stepped down long before to concentrate on his official duties for Dublin Corporation. Being of the Protestant faith, Trumbull senior was able to take up such positions, gaining a more secure foothold in the trading and merchant networks which oversaw Dublin commercial life. In 1765 Trumbull senior was referred to as 'water bailiff', and by 1768 he had been appointed to the Common Council of Dublin Corporation. He continued to move up through the ranks, and by 1778 Trumbull senior had been appointed to the position of sword bearer.[10] The extended and influential network of merchants, officials and guild members with which Trumbull senior would have interacted placed Trumbull junior in a fortunate position.

Nathaniel Trumbull junior was born in 1749.[11] He not only traded in tobacco, but also wine, hops and sugar. His business correspondence shows that over the course of his working life he dealt with a network of 373 retailers around Ireland. He also corresponded with agents and suppliers in America and various parts of the Continent. However, a great proportion of his incoming and outgoing letters were to and from merchants based in Liverpool and London.[12] He spent periods of time in London, evidenced by a series of love letters with Maria Thompson, the daughter of a business associate with whom he stayed while in London. The letters imply that he planned to marry Maria, but it appears this did not come to pass as his wife's name was Sarah.[13] Nathaniel and Sarah Trumbull had a number of children, none of whom followed Nathaniel into the business. Trumbull's personal correspondence indicates that Sarah fell ill around 1817, and was removed to 'Bloomfield', possibly having suffered a breakdown of some description, leaving Trumbull to direct the household and manage the material needs of the home.[14] By that time, Nathaniel had retired to his country residence in Malahide, a short distance north of Dublin, which he had purchased in 1790. In 1814 he had handed over the business to his nephew Nathaniel Anderson, whom he had taken into partnership in 1811.

Trumbull's working life traverses a key period in Irish political and economic history. Important political events such as the granting of legislative independence in 1782, the 1798 rebellion, the Act of Union of 1800, the removal of protective trade tariffs (beginning in 1801, with complete removal in 1816), and the end of the Napoleonic Wars in 1815, punctuated his life, impacting to varying degrees on his work and the city in which he lived. The Act of Union is long thought to have had a deleterious effect on Dublin. It was felt that the exodus of peers returning to London would result in a collapse of the residential property market, the deterioration of the luxury retail market, and the decline of the building industry. Anti-Union lobbyists also showed concern for Dublin's artisan and small manufacturing industries, which had become dependent on the Irish market, assisted up to that point by import tariffs put in place by the Irish parliament. The superb research carried out by David Dickson highlights the fact that while the aristocratic exodus was not completely a myth, the withdrawal was not as sudden as predicted:

Prior to that nemesis, wartime prosperity, shared by rentiers, merchants and rural consumers of Dublin's goods and services, had masked the dislocating effects of the parliamentary exodus. A dozen years of post-Union prosperity stimulated the fresh building on the Gardiner and Fitzwilliam estates and sustained expansion in luxury craft production – silver-plating and musical-instrument manufacture, for example – and in the high-status professions. Indeed, Napoleonic Dublin saw more signs of expansion than contraction, and it seemed to a careful observer like Edward Wakefield a surprisingly lively place, especially in springtime – the new social season – its theatre 'better frequented than the play-houses in London', and respectable society more animated than either London or Paris.[15]

While property prices did drop following 1820, and evidence indicates a general deskilling across many trades in the 1830s, research carried out by Dickson relating to the period pre-1820 clearly points to the growth of the professional, urban and middling sorts.[16] During the last decades of the eighteenth century and the early decades of the nineteenth century, many of the grand town houses lining Dublin's Georgian squares became home to lawyers, physicians and tradesmen. Just as Nathaniel Trumbull was able to buy Beechwood, his country residence in Malahide, in 1790, in the same year the Dublin brewer Mr Farrell was able to entertain the English traveller Charles Topham Bowden at his residence in fashionable Merrion Square.[17] Bowden was also entertained by Farrell's brother-in-law, Mr Byrne, another 'eminent' brewer, and recounted that he 'was never more elegantly entertained in [his] life', both gentlemen being 'held in the highest estimation by all ranks for the most exalted virtues'.[18] Not all contemporary accounts of the new Dublin bourgeoisie were as complimentary. In reference to the smart villas and country houses bought by the middle sort, Lord Colombre in Maria Edgeworth's *The Absentee* declared: 'After the Union these were bought by citizens and tradesmen, who spoiled, by the mixture of their own fancies, what had originally been designed by men of good taste.'[19]

Alongside purchasing his country abode, Trumbull had invested shrewdly in property, owning numerous houses across the city which he rented to tenants at a fixed annual rent.[20] Significant rental income supplemented his mercantile earnings, which were by no means trifling. On 24th July 1809 the *Freeman's Journal* included the following announcement: 'we have to notice an entry on Saturday which will be agreeable intelligence to many persons in this city, 35 Hhds tobacco from New York, by Trumbull & Co'. A list detailing the imports and exports for Dublin on 3rd January 1814 allows us to position this quantity in context.[21] Trumbull & Anderson are listed as having imported fifteen hhds (hogsheads) of tobacco from Liverpool, having to pay an enormous £799 1s 4d in duties.[22] In terms of the amount of duty paid, Trumbull & Anderson were second highest, with Conolly, Maxwell & Co. paying £1660 4s in duties on fifty-four hhds and forty-three tierces of Muscavado sugar. Such quantities highlight the great rise in the amount of sugar imported over the course of the eighteenth century in accordance with the growing practice of putting sugar in tea.[23]

While Trumbull had business contacts in various parts of America, changes within the nature of Irish foreign trade in the early nineteenth century were seen in a decline in Atlantic trade and the increased relative importance of Anglo-Irish mercantile operations.[24] The 1814 flyer produced by Dublin's Custom House records the assortment of ironmongery, piano fortes, Indian floor mats, candles, earthenware, cotton, muslin, flag stones and old drapery that was imported from London, Liverpool and Lancaster. Also recorded is a very short list of cargo coming from outside the United Kingdom, including sugar (from Barbados), port wine (from Oporto) and salt (from St Ures). The very brief list of exports at the very bottom of the page details linen, beef, butter, oats and tongues destined for London, Liverpool and Glasgow, highlighting the prominence of linen within Irish exports, but also the eclipsing of Dublin's Atlantic trade.[25]

Overseeing all aspects of trade was Dublin's Customs House on the far eastern edge of the city, designed by the architect James Gandon and completed in 1791. It replaced the old Custom House (built in 1707) which had been sited been further west along the River Liffey at Essex Bridge, in the heart of the old merchant quarter. This, and other buildings designed by Gandon, were part of an extensive building programme in the eighteenth century which saw Dublin's muddled medieval topography rethought and strategically reordered so that the main symbols of power and wealth were connected by straightened, widened or entirely new streets. This programme of urban redesign was engineered and managed by the Wide Streets Commission, founded by an Act of Parliament in 1757.[26] Architects such as James Gandon, Thomas Sherrard and Henry A. Baker executed designs for the buildings lining these newly constructed streets.[27] Following the Continental fashion, the Commissioners' very enlightened and coherent agenda included the practical combination of shop space on the ground floor with residential space above.[28] This facilitated the construction of not only elegant shopfronts and façades, but also entirely new contexts for fashionable consumption in the form of new shopping streets.[29]

In 1784 a plan was approved to widen and straighten Lower Abbey Street, the street on which Trumbull's office was based, and on which he owned a number of properties. The same plan included a proposal to build a new quay which would link Bachelor's Walk with the new Custom House, creating a new economic hub within that area of the city. The 1790s saw the completion of the Commission-led extension to Sackville Street, also very much in Trumbull's vicinity. The new southern end of the street was designed as a shopping street, and the anticipated diminished appearance of the street provoked controversy within certain circles. In 1786, having studied the proposed designs, one anonymous critic responded to the introduction of shops as 'an absurdity so very gross, that it needs no comment on it; the best, and most spacious Street in Dublin, inhabited, chiefly by the first Nobility in the Kingdom, to be continued, and the Continuation to be occupied by Shopkeepers'.[30] The mixture of upper and middling sorts rubbing shoulders on Dublin's finest street was also alluded to in a description of the street provided by the English visitor, Nathaniel Jefferys:

> The uses to which the houses in this fine street are applied are as various as their external appearance, and afford no small amusement to a lounging spectator, in the different descriptions of the inhabitants, which are to be seen on the brass plate of private houses, and the written inscriptions over the fronts of those devoted to trade for they comprise Peers, Pastry cooks and Perfumers: Bishops, Butchers and Brokers in old furniture, together with hotels of the most superb description, and a tolerable sprinkling of gin and whiskey shops.[31]

Perhaps due to its convenience to their Dublin base and the great variety of shops to choose from, Trumbull and his wife shopped on Lower Sackville Street for a great number of their everyday goods and occasional luxuries. Bills survive from three of Mrs Trumbull's visits to Wedgwood's showroom on Sackville Street.[32] On her visit in February 1809, she bought four queen's-ware tureens, costing 9s 10d (Plate 2). On a subsequent trip in May later that year she purchased four queen's-ware mugs, two blue and white (2s 1d) and two plain (9d), this time choosing objects that were affordable yet still carried the status value of having been bought at Wedgwood's showroom.[33] The shops on Sackville Street were not trade- or product-specific; there was a variety of speciality shops selling everything from fruit to fine silver. Regular trips were made to Hickey's seed and nursery shop at 32 Lower Sackville Street, from which Trumbull bought all manner of seeds for vegetables and foreign fruit to be planted in his nursery and greenhouse at Beechwood. Not far from Hickey's seed shop was Law & Son Goldsmiths, 1 Sackville Street, where Mrs Trumbull brought their table candlesticks, silver breadbasket and plated snuffers to be repaired.[34] Apart from listing the various repairs to be made, the bill for this transaction notes that Law & Son gave her a fruit knife free of charge. Evidently Sarah Trumbull was an

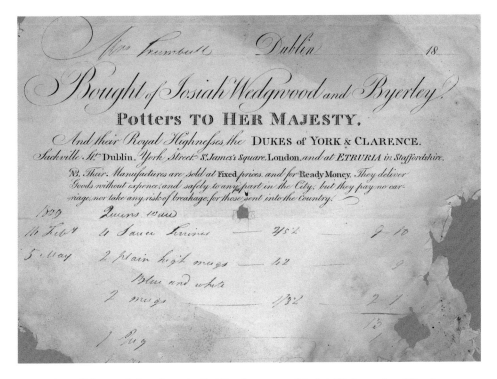

2 – Bill for goods bought at the Dublin showroom of Josiah Wedgwood and Byerley,
Sackville Street, Dublin, February-May 1809 (courtesy New York Public Library)

astute shopper, cognisant of the subtle but crucial social and economic exchanges which occurred in the context of the eighteenth- and early nineteenth-century shop. Perhaps the more impersonal and hurried nature of shopping believed by Helen Berry to characterise early nineteenth-century shopping practices was not yet felt in early nineteenth-century Dublin.[35]

Just across the river on George's Quay was the large high-class china and glass shop run by James Donovan. While nicknamed 'The Emperor of China' due to his reputation for importing ceramics, Donovan was also one of the most prominent glass-sellers in the city. Alongside running his own glasshouse, Donovan ran a workshop where ceramics imported from English manufactories were decorated, and a number of examples survive bearing his name marked on the base.[36] In some instances, Donovan may have imported blue transfer-printed wares, which were already decorated with red and yellow over glaze enamels, to which he then added his name on the base (Plate 3, 4).[37] Over the course of 1812 and 1813, Nathaniel Trumbull bought two tumblers, costing 8d, from Donovan, together with twelve wine glasses, six of which were larger and thus more expensive.[38] While it is likely that the Trumbulls would have had a servant who could be dispatched to acquire

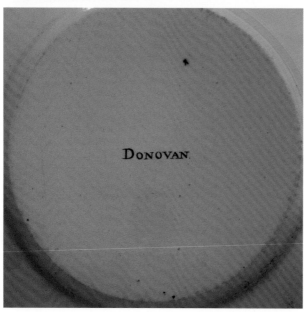

3, 4 – Selection of Minton pearl-ware ceramics decorated in the Water Lilies pattern (Minton pattern no. 333), each piece bearing Donovan's impressed mark on the base, c.1810-20

necessities, it is likely that goods of a luxury or semi-luxury nature were acquired in person.[39]

The scale of Donovan's operation leads one to imagine that it was a fashionable place to shop.[40] This view is supported by a reference to the shop in an autobiographical account written by William Blacker, who, upon moving to Dublin in 1817 to take up his position as vice-treasurer, visited Donovan's shop. In reference to Donovan's concern, Blacker noted that 'in 1817 you were sure of meeting some of elite of the Dublin society or as I should say the society of Dublin there during the day – he got a fair share of my money as did West the silversmith.' Eager to provide adequate quarters for his wife, he moved to Dublin before she did in order to set up home at 8 North Great George's Street, the house of Alderman King. The house, in Blacker's words, 'was in many respects a good one, the rooms large and handsome, but sundry articles of furniture of my own were necessary to complete its plenishing [sic] as we say in the north however I had it so much more reasonable.'[41] Still in reference to Donovan's shop, he recalled how 'a friend of ours, the Honble Mrs Jones, happening to be one day in Donovan's & not minding which way she tumbled headlong down a trap door into the lower regions among the delf & vulgar crockery – old Lord Norbury, on my telling him of it exclaimed "pooh, she meant to be a descendent of In-I-go Jones".'[42]

The route between Trumbull's base in Abbey Street and Dame Street was significantly improved by the construction of Westmoreland Street. The new street of forty-one four-storey houses, each with a shop on the ground floor, linked the Houses of Parliament and Trinity College with Carlisle Bridge, Sackville Street and the Rotunda Assembly Rooms in Rutland Square.[43] In October 1811, Mrs Trumbull, or perhaps a servant running errands for her, brought two hats (one described as 'a white hat', the other 'a feather hat') to James and Robert Wright's Fashionable Hat Warehouse at 33 Westmoreland Street to be cleaned.[44] Two years later a selection of 'china' items were purchased from Samuel Alker's China and Glass Warehouse and Galleries, the shop neighbouring Wright's hat warehouse.[45] The illustration of Alker's shop on the billhead indicates the pride he took in his elegant façade and his awareness of the advertising potential of an impressive billhead (Plate 5). On 1st March 1805, not long after taking ownership of his smart Westmoreland Street shop, Alker had requested permission from the Wide Streets Commissioners to 'introduce balconeys to his Drawing room windows in Westmoreland St'.[46] The minutes of the Commissioners' meetings go on to state that 'Mr Alker wishes to be understood that it is not his intention to lower the window stool, or alter the front in any respect whatsoever.'[47] While not 'altering the front', Alker clearly felt that the addition of a balcony would demonstrably improve the appearance of his façade, distinguishing it from the other buildings in the vicinity. Like the other shops on the street, all being of uniform design, Alker's shopfront was twenty feet in width, fin-

5 – *Bill for goods bought from Samuel Alker's China, Earthen Ware, Glass and Japan Ware premises, 31 Westmoreland Street, 3rd February 1813* (courtesy New York Public Library)

ished in mountain stone, and comprised one window between two doors – one for entering the shop and the other for entering the residence above – each embellished by Ionic pilasters either side.

While matters of economy had thwarted plans to construct a colonnade stretching the length of the street on either side, the grandeur of the shop interiors more than compensated for the flush-fronted façade of the Westmoreland street shops (Plate 6). An article profiling the new street, published in the *Freeman's Journal* on 26th October 1808, described the 'lofty' fourteen-feet-high interiors of the shops, each boasting a mezzanine level comprising a narrow gallery overlooking the shop, from which shop managers could keep check on the 'eccentricities of apprentices and shop-men'.[48]

From the late-seventeenth century, the development of fashionable squares in the eastern half of the city saw Dublin develop in an eastward rather than westward direction, creating fashionable quarters in and around those areas.[49] The evolution of districts or sub-centres of social and economic activity within a city's urban and demographic morphology, each with local loyalties and identities, is typical of cities of the scale of eighteenth-century Dublin.[50] As Sheridan-Quantz points out, certain centres developed due to the retail possibilities available in that area, giving the Parliament Street / Dame Street area, or that found in the College Green / Dame

Street / Castle Street / High Street area, as examples.[51] However, despite the existence of a fashionable shopping area on their doorstep, the Trumbulls did not restrict themselves to one axis of consumption, instead going slightly further afield to patronise as many speciality shops as required or desired, in streets such as Skinner Row, Essex Street or Thomas Street.

It is not known where the ceramics bought from Samuel Alker's shop were manufactured. Alker bought glass on a wholesale basis from the Waterford glasshouse, as did the Jacksons of Grafton Street, but it is very likely that Alker sourced his ceramics in England or on the Continent.[52] While the origin of the ceramics and glass purchased is not noted in the bills, just by the name and identity presented by the retailer it can be ascertained that certain textile items acquired were unequivocally Irish. It is clear from the Trumbull bills that they frequented shops such as the Irish Woollen Warehouse in Castle Street, Robert Fletcher's Irish Tabinet and Silk Warehouse at 2 Essex Bridge, and John Shannon's Irish Silk Mercery & Tabbinet Ware House at 28 Dame Street (Plate 7).

From the late-seventeenth century, the importation of British goods became a politically sensitive subject as prohibitive acts had been introduced preventing the export of Irish goods. During times of political or economic crisis, Irish political

6 – 'Elevation of the West Side of Westmoreland Street extending from the Portico of the House of Lords to Fleet Street as approved by the Commisioners appointed by Act of Parliament for making Wide and Convenient Streets in the City of Dublin, Thomas Sherrard 1800'

(courtesy Dublin City Library and Archive)

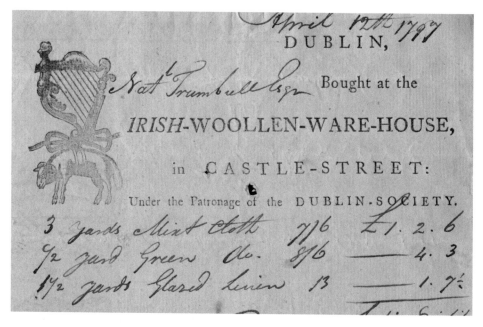

7 – *Bill for goods bought at the Irish Woollen Warehouse, Castle Street, Dublin, 12th April 1797*
(courtesy New York Public Library)

commentators, backed by numerous pamphleteers, rallied against these restrictions, making the sale and consumption of English goods a highly contentious issue.[53] Reaction on the streets was seen in the form of fierce and violent riots and the hanging and burning of effigies wearing foreign (English or French, in particular) cloth. Sarah Foster's research has highlighted the various actions taken by Irish manufacturers, such as the tarring and feathering of merchants and retailers of imported goods and attacks on people thought to be wearing foreign merchandise.[54]

More genteel methods of consumer protest were also seen in the form of 'Buy Irish' campaigns and the conscious donning of Irish cloth at key social occasions. The support of Irish industry was certainly an issue that Trumbull's father was mindful of. Two decades earlier, at the height of the importation protests, Nathaniel Trumbull senior, had entered into resolutions with the board of Aldermen at a quarter assembly 'not to WEAR or IMPORT any goods of the manufacture of England'.[55] Interestingly, however, the lengthy declaration detailing this pledge was printed in the *Freeman's Journal*, the very same newspaper in which Trumbull senior had advertised his extensive stock of imported silks fifteen years earlier.[56]

Foreign goods, particularly those from London or Paris, always held an allure for a great majority of Irish consumers who delighted in the possession of goods that had just arrived from England or France.[57] The vibrant consumer market that had developed over the course of the eighteenth century did not, as anticipated, dissipate as a result of the Union. A growing economy in the first two decades of the nineteenth century was reflected in the development of the legal profession, clearly represented in Dublin by the imposing Four Courts building which opened in 1796.[58] Alongside great numbers of attorneys and barristers, Dublin had a significant concentration of physicians and medical professionals, all contributing to the strong market for consumer goods which kept Dublin retailers in business. However, the various occupations of those comprising the middling sort didn't concern Sir James Brook, a character in Edgeworth's *The Absentee*. In Brook's discussion of post-Union Dublin, they all came under the general heading of 'commerce':

> '[M]ost of the nobility and many of the principal families among the Irish commoners, either hurried in high hopes to London or retired disgusted and in despair to their houses in the country. Immediately, in Dublin, commerce rose into the vacated seats of rank; wealth rose into the place of birth. New faces and new equipages appeared: people, who had never been heard of before, started into notice, pushed themselves forward, not scrupling to elbow their way even at the castle.[59]

The cultural life of Dublin did witness a shift in practices. Maxwell cites the reducing profits at the Rotunda Assembly Rooms as evidence of this.[60] An increased number of gentleman's clubs and smart hotels appeared on the elegant streets of early nineteenth-century Dublin. Trumbull's correspondence confirms that he patronised gentleman's clubs, and numerous bills denote the 'Moira Hotel, Sackville Street' as his Dublin base.[61] While Trumbull was very much a participant in Dublin's changing social scene, the breakfast, lunch and dinner invitations received and sent by Trumbull testify to his position within a network of upper-middling sorts and country gentlemen in the north county Dublin area.[62] In September 1817 Trumbull received a letter from John Hone of Eustace Street, Dublin, thanking him for his kind present, while in December 1820 Trumbull received a present of some game from Arthur Garlen of Longford.[63] Sir Thomas Newcomen of Killester sent a pineapple to Trumbull, but enclosed a letter requesting return of the 'crown'.[64] Richard Brophy wrote to Trumbull in 1817 to express his gratitude for all his kindness, and also to say that he hoped Trumbull's peacock would appear soon.[65]

Letters enclosing gifts were not as common as letters requesting help. In February 1815 Trumbull received a letter regarding the support of 'Mrs Lunt and two of her children', and in November 1816 Trumbull received a letter from 'A Neighbour' thanking him for repairing the hole in a bridge but now 'the bridge was in danger of falling down'.[66] If Trumbull did support the Lunt family, then they were three of a number of his dependents. Apart from financing the schooling of his own children, account ledgers show that he also organised and financed the schooling of two nieces. Alongside paying for Miss Mary Jackson's education, food and clothes for nine years, he also purchased a silver spoon for her to use while at school.[67]

Trumbull's correspondence describes the economic and social networks of exchange, sociable encounters and philanthropic endeavours which delineated the social arenas in which he existed. The world in which Trumbull, or his father, existed was nothing like that described by Richard Twiss, whose account of his tour of Ireland, published in 1776, was the most controversial attack on Irish politeness.[68] The issue of politeness in Irish society was one taken up by many at the turn of the century. *Saunder's Newsletter* printed concerns that the Union would have a deleterious effect on Irish manners: 'with the desolating increase of absentees, our reviving taste for letters, and the incipient study of the arts, must vanish; works of science and ingenuity cannot exist where none remain to encourage them but tradesmen and labourers.'[69] Contrary to this disquiet, the picture created by his papers would seem to indicate that Nathaniel Trumbull's lifestyle was that of a member of polite Dublin society.[70] His great financial capital was matched by social, cultural and religious capital. Like his father before him, his name features in the subscription lists of various publications.[71]

Participation within polite society required the correct accoutrements. A bill from Trumbull's tailor records the making and alteration of various items of clothes for Trumbull, his coachman and his butler. The many maps and surveys commissioned by Trumbull illustrate the size and position of his estate, which comprised close to 150 acres.[72] Alongside a melon yard, pigeon house and a number of stables, Trumbull had a hothouse and an extensive nursery in which grew an amazing selection of foreign fruit and vegetables, which would have been considered highly desir-

Fig. 1 – An undated list of ceramic and glass objects noting either the value or quantities of the items present (Trumbull Papers, NYPL, MS 3039)

Delf		Glass	
Coffee cans	9d	Decanters	7s 4d
Large cups	11s 11d	Tumbler[s]	8s 12d
Small [cups]	9s 4d	Salts	5s 9d
'and one without dish'		Glasses	9s 7d
Large saucer	2s 10d	Cut wine glasses large	22
Small saucers	3d 13d	Small do. [wine glasses]	23
Large plates	6s 6d	Wash hand glasses	18
Small [plates]	9s 9d	Licure glasses	23
Tea pots	3s 3d	Jugs	2
Egg cups	6s 6d		
Cream ewer	1s 1d		
Bowls	2s 3d		

able within the dining rooms of the gentry.[73] However, perhaps unlike many members of the gentry who owned hothouses, the many letters requesting quantities of potatoes indicate that Trumbull ran his as a business.[74]

The extent of his nursery, together with bills for food and drink, provide an insight into the Trumbulls' diet, while his correspondence, as noted above, illustrates his social manoeuvrings. Alongside this, an inventory of silver, and another of ceramics and glass, together with various bills for furniture, gives an indication of the material world in which the Trumbulls lived. Moreover, it provides an insight into the glass items found in an upper-middle-rank Dublin home in the early nineteenth century, and a picture of the constellation of objects of which those glass items were part.

An undated list of ceramics and glass details a list of objects which were primarily for use in the context of eating and drinking (fig. 1).[75] The list does not detail the location of these objects; however, on the basis of other contemporary sources one could speculate that the glass may have been displayed on a sideboard, as suggested by Thomas Cosnett in his *Footman's Directory*.[76] Alternatively, it may have been stored in a larder or displayed in rows on shelves in a dining room cupboard, as described in a work of contemporary fiction by the character Mrs Soorocks, a middle-aged widow.[77] The Trumbulls' collection of wine glasses in small, large, cut and plain varieties ensured that they had appropriate wine glasses for a range of formal and informal occasions. Their possession of liqueur glasses reflects an understanding of the importance of having the correct receptacle for that particular alcoholic drink, and their ownership of wash-hand glasses, generally placed within

Fig. 2 – An undated list of items subdivided into two smaller lists,
one entitled 'Wanted' and the other 'Have' (NYPL, Nathaniel Trumbull Papers, MS 3039)

Wanted	Have
Cut glass decanters	5 Cut decanters
Wine glasses	11 small wine glasses
Ale glasses	1 Ale glass
Common Wine glasses	7 common wine glasses
Kitchen table & chairs	
All kind of saucepans	
4 pairs of servants sheets	
do. Table cloths	
Towels – & dabbers	
Blue and white plates & dishes	
Castle patterns	

reach of each diner from the late eighteenth century, further alludes to their knowledge of fashions in polite dining. Similarly, the range of large and small saucers, ceramic cups, coffee cans, bowls and cream ewer includes the various utensils required for tea- and coffee-drinking in the context of social occasions of varying formality.

A second list of objects, dating to c.1817-24, records in shopping-list fashion the objects he has and the objects he needs (fig. 2). The list indicates that while he has five cut decanters, he would like to acquire some more. Having only one ale glass, he notes that he needs more of those, together with 'wine glasses' and more 'common wine glasses'. In his entry regarding ceramic items, he is specific, describing the plates and dishes desired as firstly 'Blue and white' followed by 'castle patterns'.

The purchase of '8 drawing room chairs', 'a mahogany sofa bordered with bolsters' and a 'spider table' add to the picture of the Trumbulls' objects in use. A bill dated 1795 from the Dublin decorating firm run by Patrick Boylan lists work carried out on two rooms – 'scraping and cleaning of cornice, whitening of ceiling ... wallpapering two rooms' – and in 1807 reference is made to a chimney-piece artist being employed in Beechwood. Three years earlier, in 1804, a substantial amount of money was spent by the Trumbulls on the making and fitting of 'Venetian Ladders' for seven windows: 832 'blades' were made by the King & Dempsey firm of cabinetmakers before being painted in green varnish and hung using ninety-four yards of broad green tape and forty-six pulleys. Apart from the expense of a 'very good house clock' costing £7 19s 3d, further outgoings in the front space areas of hall, drawing room and parlour were focused around repairing particular items already in their possession, suggesting that they may have inherited a collection of furniture. The 1809 bill from Lewis & Anthony Morgan, cabinet-makers of Henry Street, details the repairing and stuffing of a 'parlour chair', 'cleaning, scraping and new painting 6 drawing room chairs', and 'repairing a mahogany card table' (Plates 8, 9).[78] While it is possible that the objects sent to be repaired were treasured either as a result of their age, quality of workmanship or possibly for their sentimental importance as heirlooms, it was quite the norm to have objects repaired, and doesn't necessarily denote value.

Alongside expenditure in the 'front space' areas of the house where objects would be seen, the Trumbull bills testify to extensive expenditure being focused in the bedrooms. In 1804 King & Dempsey billed Trumbull for an 'elegant painted bedstead with elegant painted sweeping cornice' costing £11 7s 6d, not including the cost of making the curtains. By far the most expensive item listed on Morgan's 1809 bill was a 'mahogany bidet with turned legs and a delf pan per agreement' costing £2 10s. Furthermore, a bill for goods and work carried out in October 1811 by the upholders La Crille included a wagon roof bedstead, a four-poster bed and a

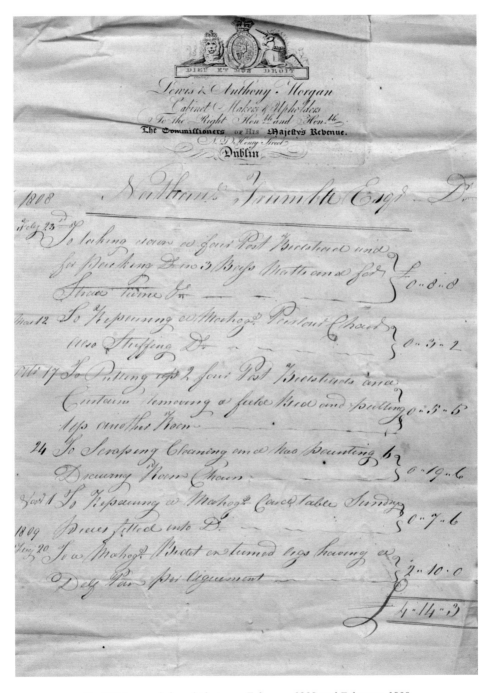

8 – Bill for goods bought between February 1808 and February 1809
from Lewis & Anthony Morgan, Cabinet Makers & Upholders, 21 Henry Street, Dublin
(courtesy New York Public Library)

9 – Two of eight Regency mahogany parlour chairs made by Morgan cabinetmakers, c.1810
The parlour chair which Trumbull wished to have repaired and stuffed was sent to the Morgan firm of cabinetmakers,
as recorded in their 1809 bill. (courtesy Christie's).

mahogany 'fancy child's bedstead' costing £5 2s 4$^{1}/_{2}$ d.[79]

Despite the relative indulgence in bedroom furniture, when the incredibly long list of properties owned by Trumbull is studied, together with the steady income from each house, the Trumbulls' expenditure on luxuries does not seem overly extravagant. The bills evidence caution in outgoings, buying what was needed and desired but focusing expenditure on either renovating or acquiring property. Trumbull was also wary in his banking arrangements, successfully managing to avoid placing money in what would later turn out to be 'bubble banks'. Instead, he kept his money in the Bank of Ireland, having £2,000 in Bank of Ireland stock by 1812. It seems he preferred having money in the bank to having it tied up in silver and plate, as in 1807 he received a quotation of the value of a long list of silver and plate items to be 'sold by Robert Williams'. This detailed and extensive list was compiled by the goldsmith Robert Williams before these items were sold, accruing a total of £511 12s 9d. The list includes a 'Large Gilt Salver' valued at £44 5s 2d, a 'Large Tureen' valued at £ 48 19s 2d, four 'Square cover dishes' valued at £ 72 9s 9d, to all manner of cutlery, asparagus tongs, scallop shells, 'sallad spoons & forks', an epergne, various candlesticks, a bread basket valued at £13 6s 4d and '1 liqure stand & glasses' valued at £13 13s. The list describes a very extensive silver collection, one that would have been assembled by someone who did a lot of entertaining, someone who relied on the power of silver to evoke one's status, taste and wealth. It is likely that at least some of this collection of silver was amassed by Nathaniel Trumbull senior, who may have hosted many dinners throughout his involvement with the upper ranks of Dublin Corporation. For Trumbull junior, however, the monetary value of these items outweighed any sentimental meaning attached to them, and the money accrued may have been spent either in projects such as developing the business or in acquiring more property.

Things, whether bought, not bought, saved, sold or received as gifts, were integral to the communication of Trumbull junior's identity. In his *Inquiry into the Nature and Causes of the Wealth of Nations*, Adam Smith extolled the virtues of merchant expenditure over that of the landowner.[80] He described the way in which 'merchants are commonly ambitious of becoming country gentlemen, and when they do they are generally the best of all improvers. A merchant is accustomed to employ his money chiefly in profitable projects, whereas a mere country gentleman is accustomed to employ it chiefly in expense.'[81] Trumbull hovers between Smith's view of merchants and gentry. His occupation as a tobacco merchant and his tendency to focus his expense around profitable projects positions him as a merchant under Smith's criteria. Yet indications of class, patriotism and confessional identity were communicated through the choices made within his material world. His evident wealth, combined with a country residence and an impressive social network, together with his extensive philanthropic outgoings, places him in a social position which was very close to that of a country gentleman, drawing our attention not only to the highly stratified nature of the middling sorts in early nineteenth-century Ireland, and but also highlighting the difficulties inherent in considering consumers in terms of stereotypes.

———

ACKNOWLEDGEMENTS

I wish to thank the Irish Georgian Society for awarding me the Desmond Guinness Scholarship, which, together with a travel grant from the Thomas Dammann Memorial Trust, financed a trip to New York to view the Trumbull Papers. I am grateful to Peter Francis and Dr Angela Alexander for their help in sourcing illustrations, and to Professor Maxine Berg, Dr Helen Clifford, Sarah Foster, Dr Jennifer Ní Ghrádaigh and Dr Macushla Baudis for their comments on an early draft of the article. Special thanks are also due to Dr Greer Ramsey of the Armagh Museum, Andrew O'Brien of Dublin City Archive, and the staff of the New York Public Library manuscripts department.

ENDNOTES

The following abbreviations are used:

NYPL   New York Public Library, Nathaniel Trumbull Papers

TP, 1983   Trumbull Papers (Galway, 1983) – a catalogue of the Trumbull Papers written and published by Kenny's Bookshop, Galway, prior to the sale of the collection to the New York Public Library.

[1]   The Nathaniel Trumbull Papers are in the collection of the New York Public Library, Manuscripts and Archives Division, MS 3039. I am sincerely grateful to Sarah Foster for alerting me to this collection of papers.

[2]   In falling after Toby Barnard's main period of interest and before the well-trodden Celtic Revival, the material culture of early nineteenth-century Ireland has suffered relative neglect. However, the ongoing research of Angela Alexander on the production and consumption of furniture in early nineteenth-century Ireland and Sarah Foster on the middle-class interior in nineteenth-century Ireland will greatly contribute to our knowledge of middle-rank consumer culture in Ireland.

[3]   Thorstein Veblen, *The Theory of the Leisure Class* (London (1899), 1994).

[4]   Mary Douglas and Baron Isherwood, *The World of Goods: Towards an Anthropology of Consumption* (London (1979), 1996).

[5]   Douglas and Isherwood, *The World of Goods*, 45, cited in Amanda Girling Budd, 'Comfort and Gentility: furnishings by Gillows, Lancaster, 1840-55' in S. McKeller and P. Sparke (eds), *Interior Design and Identity* (Manchester, 2004), 28.

[6]   A. Vickery, *The Gentleman's Daughter Women's Lives in Georgian England* (London and New Haven, 1998) 163.

[7]   Nathaniel Trumble (sic) is listed as a weaver in Francis Street in the *Directory of Dublin for the year 1738*. Surviving Dublin street directories show that Trumbull continued to be listed as a weaver in Francis Street until 1764. Between 1766 and 1769 'Trumbull and Mackay, mercers' of Parliament Street are listed in Dublin street directories. *Wilson's Dublin Directory*, 1761, 1762, 1764, 1766-69.

[8]   The earliest advertisement found featured in the *Freeman's Journal*, 22nd October 1765. The same advertisement was placed twice weekly until 13th May 1766: 'TRUMBULL AND MACKAY Mercers, At the KING'S HEAD in Parliament-street have just imported a great

variety of Gold, Silver and Flowered Silks, brocaded, enamelled and watered Tabbies; Tissues, Damasks, Sattins, Paduasoys, Armazeens, &c. with every other Article in the Mercer's business. NB This being the first Importation made by said Trumbull and Mackay of Gold and Silver Silks, the Nobility and Gentry may depend on their being of the richest kind, and of Fancies entirely new, which they are determined to sell on the lowest Terms.'

[9]   Other families involved in the textile industry, notably the Bewleys, also ventured away following the difficulties witnessed in this area of manufacture. The Bewleys became the most prominent importers of tea, while other families such as the Caffrys went into the brewing business. D. Dickson, 'Death of a Capital? Dublin and the Consequences of Union', *Proceedings of the British Academy*, 107, 2001, 111-31: 129-30.

[10]   Trumbull is listed as 'Sword Bearer' at 2 College Green in *Wilson's Dublin Directory for 1778*. It is likely that Trumbull senior held this position until his death in 1797. The *Calendar of Ancient Records of Dublin*, XV, records that on 6th September 1797, John Minchin was 'praying to be appointed Sword Bearer in the room of Mr Nathaniel Trumbull deceased: whereupon it was ordered that the said John Minchin be and is hereby appointed Sword Bearer to this city, during the city's pleasure, at the yearly salary of £130, to commence this day'.

[11]   TP, 1983, i. The catalogue of the Trumbull Papers, written and published by Kenny's, includes an introduction by Professor John Dillon of Trinity College Dublin. It provides a very useful list of the various letters and account books in the collection. The discovery and sale of the Trumbull Papers are discussed in two newspaper articles: *Irish Times*, 26th November 1983 and *Sunday Independent*, 22nd January 1984.

[12]   There are forty-eight letters from John Orr in Liverpool to Nathaniel Trumbull in Dublin. It is likely that John Orr acted as Trumbull's agent in Liverpool, as in a letter to Martha McTier (1st May 1806) William Drennan makes reference to John Orr 'serving his time' with Nathaniel Trumbull. Jean Agnew and Maria Luddy (eds), *The Drennan McTier Letters 3, 1802-1819* (Dublin, 1999) 475.

[13]   TP, 1983, iii.

[14]   The exact circumstances surrounding Sarah Trumbull's move to Bloomfield are unclear. There are twenty letters from Sarah to Nathaniel between 29th July 1817 and Nathaniel Trumbull's death in 1824. One letter enclosed a lock of hair sent by Sarah to Nathaniel; however, it seems that Nathaniel was advised not to visit her. Eight letters from Joseph Gough, Bloomfield, inform on her 'progress', with one (letter 460) recommending that 'Sarah would not benefit from a visit' from Nathaniel. TP, 1983, 41.

[15]   D. Dickson, 'Death of a Capital?', 111-31: 124-25.

[16]   *ibid.*, 111-31.

[17]   Charles Topham Bowden, *A Tour Through Ireland* (Dublin, 1791) 47.

[18]   *ibid.*, 48.

[19]   Maria Edgeworth, *The Absentee* (London (1812), 1988) 86, cited in M.J. Powell, *The Politics of Consumption in Eighteenth Century Ireland* (Basingstoke, 2005) 230.

[20]   For example, in the years 1803 and 1804 Trumbull purchased 'sundry houses in Abbey Street, [numbers] 147, 148, 151, 155, 156 & 157'. National Library of Ireland, MS 5186, Ledger of Nathaniel Trumbull.

[21]   'Daily List of Goods Imported and Exported into Dublin on 3 January 1814'. This list is illustrated in TP, 1983 (pages bearing illustrations are unpaginated).

[22]   This list is illustrated in TP, 1983 (pages bearing illustrations are unpaginated).

ANNA MORAN

23   Between the 1700s and the 1790s, the national imports of unrefined sugar rose by a factor of eighteen. L. Clarkson, 'Hospitality, housekeeping and high living in Eighteenth century Ireland' in Jacqueline Hill and Colm Lennon (eds), *Luxury and Austerity*, Historical Studies (Irish Conference of Historians), 21 (Dublin, 1999) 84-105: 98.

24   Trumbull's business correspondence gives a good indication of the extent and nature of his trading network. Within the collection there are 1,406 letters from England, eighty-four from Europe (Rotterdam, Oporto, Hamburg and Malaga), eighteen from New York, Virginia and Barbados, and thirty-one from Scotland. NYPL, MS 3039.

25   However, as those involved in the linen trade developed direct contact with British dealers, the importance of Dublin finance became less crucial and Belfast grew into a distinct regional capital, becoming completely autonomous in the latter half of the nineteenth century. D. Dickson, 'The place of Dublin in the Eighteenth-Century Irish economy' in T.M. Devine and David Dickson (eds), *Ireland and Scotland, 1600-1850* (Edinburgh, 1983) 188.

26   E. Mc Parland 'The Wide Streets Commissioners: Their Importance for Dublin Architecture in the Late 18th-Early 19th century', *Quarterly Bulletin of the Irish Georgian Society*, XV, 1, January-March 1972, 1-32: 1.

27   *ibid.*, 1-32.

28   M. Fraser, 'Public Building and Colonial Policy in Dublin 1760-1800', *Architectural History*, 28, 1995, 116.

29   E. Sheridan Quantz, 'The Multi-Centred Metropolis: The Social Topography of Eighteenth-Century Dublin', *Proceedings of the British Academy*, 107, 2001, 280.

30   *Letters to Parliament ... by an Admirer of Necessary Improvements* (Dublin, 1787), cited by M. Craig, *Dublin, 1660-1860* (Dublin, 1969) 247.

31   Nathaniel Jefferys, *An Englishman's descriptive account of Dublin, and the road from Bangor Ferry, to Holyhead* (London, 1810) 86, cited in Sheridan Quantz, 'The Multi-Centred Metropolis, 283.

32   NYPL, MS 3039.

33   Wedgwood's showroom in Sackville Street, Dublin, opened in 1808 and closed in 1812. M. Reynolds, 'Wedgwood in Dublin, 1772-1777', *Irish Arts Review*, I, 2, 1984, 36.

34   NYPL, MS 3039. The total of 5s 5d was 'paid 9 February 1814 per ST'.

35   H. Berry, 'Polite Consumption Shopping in Eighteenth Century England', *Transactions of the Royal Historical Society*, 12, 2002, 375. Berry argues that with the rise of cash-only business at the end of the eighteenth century, there was a shift towards a more hurried and informal form of shopping.

36   M. Reynolds, 'James Donovan 'The Emperor of China'', *Irish Arts Review*, I, 3, 1985, 28.

37   I am grateful to Peter Francis for sourcing these illustrations for me.

38   Trumbull paid 9s 9d for '6 wine glasses', while '6 large do. [wine glasses]' cost 5s 5d. NYPL, MS 3039. The Trumbulls may have been important customers of Donovan's, as in October 1803 Nathaniel Trumbull paid a bill of £37 to James Donovan. However, as Donovan was also a serious property speculator, it is possible that this expense was incurred in some way other than the provision of ceramics or glass.

39   H. Berry, 'Polite Consumption Shopping in Eighteenth Century England', 379.

40   Donovan's shop was certainly extensive. The shop was described as 'having 23 feet frontage onto George's Quay, 22 feet at rear and 95 feet in depth, as well as the land from 25, Poolbeg Street which also had a 22 feet frontage onto that street and stretched 90 feet in depth towards

George's Quay'. Reynolds, 'James Donovan', 28.

[41] Armagh Museum, Blacker Papers, 5-1948, Daybooks of William Blacker, vol. 6, 1817, 98.

[42] *ibid.*

[43] Westmoreland Street was completed by 1805. Christine Casey, *The Buildings of Ireland: Dublin* (Dublin, 2005) 420.

[44] NYPL, MS 3039.

[45] The following items were purchased from Samuel Alker's shop: '1 china bowl, 2s 8d, 1 blue do. [bowl], 10d, 1 jug, 2.6, totalling 6s', NYPL, MS 3039. However, elegant shops such as Alker's were only one source of ceramics and glass. The fact that bills do not exist to evidence transactions between consumers and hawkers, criers and vendors at fairs has led to the underestimation of the prevalence of this mode of acquisition. The collection of drawings known as 'The Cries of Dublin &c Drawn from the Life by Hugh Douglas Hamilton, 1760' illustrates numerous different hawkers who walked Dublin's streets, each specialising in a particular commodity, be it 'old cloaths', 'perukes', 'hard ware' or 'coarse earthen ware'. W. Laffan (ed.), *The Cries of Dublin &c. Drawn from the life by Hugh Douglas Hamilton, 1760* (Tralee, 2003).

[46] Dublin City Library and Archive, Minute books of the Wide Street Commissioners' meetings, 1803-6/Mins/19, p.205.

[47] *ibid.*

[48] The interiors of the Westmoreland Street shops were apparently so bright and 'lofty' that some shopkeepers opted to form 'an apartment out of this extra altitude, to which light is admitted thro' the upper line of panes in the window. But this is not general'. *Freeman's Journal*, 26th October 1808.

[49] Sheridan-Quantz, 'The Multi-Centred Metropolis', 268.

[50] *ibid.*, 265.

[51] *ibid.*, 280.

[52] National Museum of Ireland, 1956.138, Waterford glasshouse account books. For further discussion of glass retailers such as Alker and Jackson, see Anna Moran 'Selling Waterford glass in early nineteenth-century Ireland', *Irish Architectural and Decorative Studies*, VI (Dublin, 2003) 56-90.

[53] For an account of the 'Buy Irish' campaigns of the eighteenth century, see S. Foster '"An honourable station in respect of commerce, as well as constitutional liberty": retailing, consumption and economic nationalism in Dublin, 1720-85' in G. O'Brien and F. O'Kane (eds), *Georgian Dublin* (Dublin, 2008) 30-44.

[54] *ibid.*

[55] *Freeman's Journal*, 29th June 1779.

[56] For example, *Freeman's Journal*, 22nd October 1765.

[57] S. Foster, 'Going Shopping in Georgian Dublin', *Things*, 4, Summer 1996, 33-61.

[58] The legal profession had developed over the course of the eighteenth century. In 1763, seven hundred attorneys and three hundred barristers had Dublin addresses, but by 1800 those figures had increased by fifty percent. D. Dickson 'The Place of Dublin in the Eighteenth Century Irish Economy', 185.

[59] Edgeworth, *The Absentee*, 83 cited in Powell, *The Politics of Consumption in Eighteenth Century Ireland*. See also S. Murphy, 'Maria Edgeworth's representations of Georgian Dublin' in O'Brien and O'Kane (eds) *Georgian Dublin*, 145-55.

[60] 'Between 1795 and 1815 the average profits from the Assembly Rooms at the Rotunda had reduced from £1,450 to less than £300'. C. Maxwell, *Dublin under the Georges 1740-1830* (London, 1936) 136.

[61] On 7th September 1807 Trumbull received an invitation to dinner at the Heathfield Club, TP, 1983, 41. Twelve years earlier, Trumbull received a printed letter from Barthw. Martin, dated 15th December 1795, regarding the establishment of a merchants' club. The letter asked the recipients to signify to any of the gentlemen whose names were at the foot of the letter the desire to become a member, TP, 1983, 118.

[62] Trumbull's correspondents included many noted members of Ireland's upper-middle rank, including among others Arthur Guinness, David and Peter La Touche and Sir Marcus and Richard Somerville. NYPL, MS Col. 3039.

[63] TP, 1983, 36.

[64] *ibid.*, ii.

[65] *ibid.*, 34, Richard Brophy, Richmond Lodge, 1817, to Nathaniel Trumbull. The exchange of gifts, as Margot Finn's research has shown, was important in the 'reinforcement of affective bonds' and the promotion of local sociability. M. Finn, 'Men's things: masculine possession in the consumer revolution', *Social History*, XXV, 2, May 2000, 143.

[66] TP, 1983, 'A Neighbour' to Nathaniel Trumbull, November 1816.

[67] National Library of Ireland, MS 5186, 47, Ledger of Nathaniel Trumbull.

[68] Richard Twiss, in his account of his tour of Ireland, stated that outside of Dublin and its environs, 'nothing is to be expected in making the tour of Ireland, beyond the beauties of nature, a few modern-antiquities, and the ignorance and poverty of the lower class of the inhabitants', *A Tour in Ireland in 1775*, 3rd edn. (Dublin, 1777) 11.

[69] *Saunder's Newsletter*, 2nd January 1799, cited in Powell, *The Politics of Consumption in Eighteenth Century Ireland*, 229.

[70] Further evidence of Nathaniel Trumbull's standing is suggested by the appearance of his name on a panel of individuals from which the jury would be selected for the 'Government versus James Napper Tandy' case, *The King versus Tandy. Proceedings on the trial of James Napper Tandy, Esq. in the Court of King's Bench, before the Right Honourable Lord Chief Justice Clonmell, the Hon. Mr. Justice Boyd, and the Hon. Mr. Justice Hewit, upon an indictment for sending a challenge to John Toler, Esq; His Majesty's Solicitor General* (Dublin, 1792).

[71] For example, Nathaniel Trumbull senior subscribed to W R. Chetwood, *Memoirs of the Life and Writings of Ben Johnson, Esq: poet Laurea* (Dublin, 1756) and Nathaniel Trumbull junior is listed as a subscriber to Jane Elizabeth Moore, *Miscellaneous poems on various subjects* (Dublin, 1796).

[72] NYPL, MS 3039. These include Map 705, survey of the grange, Portmarnock, 'belonging to Nathaniel Trumbull Esq' by Thomas Sherrard, 1789 and copied by John Chesney, 1812. Map 706: a map and survey of the Mill of Portmarnock and the land belonging to it, the property of Nath. Trumbull Esqr. Copied 1815 by David O'Reilly. Map 707: may and survey of the lands of upper Beechwood in the County of Dublin, belonging to Nathl Trumbull Esqr, October 1819 by David O'Reilly, showing 18 different sections, comprising 95 acres, woods, the road, avenue, a melon yard and a number of buildings. Map 708: lower Beechwood in the county of Dublin belonging to Nathl Trumbull Oct 1819 by David O'Reily. 15 fields, and their size totalling 52 acres, a river and bridge are shown as are wooded boundaries.

[73] NYPL, MS 3039. Trumbull's bills for seeds such as those from Charles & Luke O'Toole

Nursery and Seeds-Men of Westmoreland Street, Dublin, list an impressive array of seeds. The bill covering the period between February and August 1814 included many different varieties of cabbage, onions, carrots, lettuce and beans, together with three different varieties of peaches and a further three varieties of nectarines.

[74] TP, 1983, 41. For example, Trumbull received two orders for potatoes from Mrs Norman Luke of Mountjoy Square, dated 17th February 1817 and 3rd August 1818.

[75] This list was written on a scrap of paper and it is likely that it is not an exhaustive list of their ceramic and glass objects.

[76] T. Cosnett, *The Footman's Directory, and butler's remembrancer* (London, 1825) 78.

[77] Stana Nenadic cites Mrs Soorocks' lengthy description of the ceramics and glass displayed in her dining room cupboard. John Galt, *Last of the Lairds*, edited by J.A. Gordon (Edinburgh, 1976) 6, cited in S. Nenadic 'Middle rank consumers and domestic culture in Edinburgh and Glasgow, 1720-1840', *Past and Present*, 145, November 1994, 136.

[78] NYPL, MS 3039. 'Repairing and stuffing the mahogany parlour chair' cost 3s 2s; 'Scraping, Cleaning and new Painting 6 Drawing Room Chairs' 19s 6d; 'Repairing a Mahogany Card table Sundry pieces fitted into do.' 7s 6d. I am grateful to Dr Angela Alexander for sourcing an illustration of a pair of parlour chairs made by the Morgan firm of cabinetmakers.

[79] NYPL, MS 3039.

[80] Adam Smith, *An Inquiry into the Nature and Causes of the Wealth of Nations*, III (London, 1776; reprint 1910) 507-08

[81] *ibid.*, I, 363, cited in Clarkson, 'Hospitality, housekeeping and high living in Eighteenth century Ireland', 84.

———

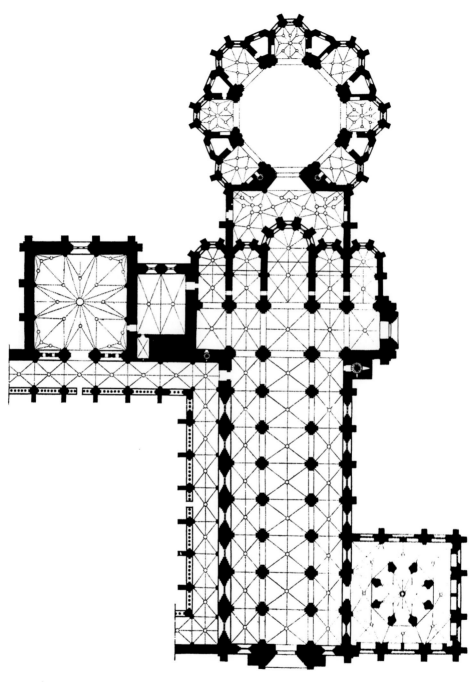

N

Three mausolea and a church:
the drawings of James C. Murphy
for his book on Batalha of 1795

MICHAEL McCARTHY

J AMES CAVANAH MURPHY PUBLISHED TWO BOOKS IN 1795 – *PLANS, ELEVATIONS, Sections and Views of the Church of Batalha* and *Travels in Portugal ... in the years 1789 and 1790*.[1] At the conclusion of the preface to the latter, he wrote:

> As it was principally through the munificence of the Right Honourable William Burton Conyngham that I have been enabled to collect the material of this work, as well as those relating to the description of the Royal Monastery of Batalha, I feel it my indispensable duty most gratefully to acknowledge the many obligations I owe to his constant patronage and friendship.

One of the subscribers to the book on Batalha was the director of the Society of Antiquaries of London, Richard Gough, author of *Sepulchral Monuments of Great Britain*, the second volume of which was published in 1796.[2] In the introduction, Gough repeated his constant encouragement of the recording of the monuments of the Gothic period, and cited Murphy's book as a model, 'done by a single artist, under private patronage, in a most perfect manner, for the monastery of Batalha, which owed its foundation to an intermarriage with a princess of England, and to an English architect' (Plate 1).[3]

Twelve members of the Society of Antiquaries were subscribers to *Batalha*, including its patron and dedicatee, who had been elected fellow in 1790. This is recorded in the sixth volume of John Nichols' *Literary Illustrations of the Eighteenth Century*, where a tribute to William Burton Conyngham from the

1 – Plan of the church and mausolea of Batalha
The chapter house is on the north; the mausoleum of the founder on the south; the unfinished mausoleum on the east. (from Howard Colvin, ARCHITECTURE AND THE AFTERLIFE (Yale UP, 1991) 181)

European Magazine of 1794 precedes an account of the life of James Cavanah Murphy and a transcription of five letters from the architect to his patron written from Portugal in 1789 and 1790. Nichols had copied these from a copybook in the possession of Thomas Crofton Croker. This author, too, was a fellow of the Society of Antiquaries of London, to which he had presented in 1830 'the original drawings of Mr. Murphy's magnificent work on Batalha',[4] which are the subject of this essay. Their presence in the library of the Society has been noted in the literature of the Gothic Revival and in biographical notices of the architect, but they have not previously been examined in detail, nor in the context of the letters of the architect and the antiquarian studies of the patron.[5]

William Burton Conyngham enjoyed a more than modest reputation as a collector of studies of antiquity. The tribute in *European Magazine* reads:

> The collection of drawings relating to Irish churches, abbeys, and castles, in his possession is esteemed the most valuable extant, and there are but few objects of antiquity in Spain and Portugal of which he had not drawings, as he travelled through these countries accompanied by three ingenious artists he employed for that purpose.

This was the immediate context for Murphy's book on Batalha, in the preface to which the artist wrote: 'My first knowledge of this venerable pile, was derived from seeing some sketches of it in the possession of the Right Honourable William Conyngham, taken by himself and two other Gentlemen who travelled with him through Portugal in 1783.'[6] In the first of his letters to his patron, dated simply March 1789, he wrote: 'Your elegant sketches of this fine Building often led me to think on the grandeur of the original, which I think is one of the finest pieces of Gothic architecture in Europe.'[7] Those sketches have not come to light, but they were sufficiently informative to enable Murphy to leave in Dublin a large plan of the church and monastery of Batalha before he had ever seen it (referred to in the same letter). This early study may account in part for the brevity of the period of thirteen weeks it took him to compile the album of drawings now in London, without shirking on details. 'Where any part is executed with uncommon judgment, difficulty or elegance,' he wrote, 'I have drawn it with the minuteness of a Desgodetz.'[8] He also studied a diary kept by his patron on his visit to Batalha, and translated from it *An Account of the modern establishment of the Royal Convent of Batalha*, written in French by one of the friars for William Burton Conyngham.[9] The other literary source he mentions is the account of the buildings given in 1622 by Fr Lewis de Sousa in Portuguese, which Murphy was later to translate for inclusion in his book, 'from forty-five pages of large quarto, which I esteem the more as you charged me to collect as much of the history of this convent as possible'.[10] His one reference to the earlier travel account in English by Richard Twiss is dismissive, justifiably, since Twiss declined an invitation to lodge in the monastery, 'as I saw they had little or nothing to eat, and less to drink'.[11] Murphy seems to be correct in noting the absence of any earlier drawings of Batalha other than those his patron had collected in 1783 and 1784.

There was, however, an earlier written description in manuscript, well known to the fellows of the Society of Antiquaries of London, that made in 1760 by Thomas Pitt, later Lord Camelford, who was also a subscriber to Murphy's book. The original has not come to light, but there is a transcription of it by William Cole, the antiquary from Cambridge, who had travelled in Portugal with Pitt's uncle, Temple West, in 1737 and 1738.[12] Another of Pitt's uncles was the president of the Society of Antiquaries of London, Bishop Charles Lyttelton, a pioneer of the study of the history of Gothic architecture, and recipient of the only letter known to have been written by Thomas Pitt from Portugal, dated 24th March 1760.[13] The Iberian diary of his nephew was passed eagerly among the fellows of the Society, and the copy made by William Cole in 1772 had been given to him by Michael Tyson, who had, in turn, received it from Richard Gough, director of the Society. As we have noted, he too was a subscriber to Murphy's book and was the first to single it out as an exemplar for the study of Gothic monuments.[14] This antiquarian background is the most reasonable explanation for the difference between Murphy's early outline for the book in his letter of March 1789 and the work that was published in twenty-five plates from 1792 to 1795.[15]

The outline had listed nine drawings in all, the first four of which were plans. Of these, only the first, *A General Plan of the Church and Monastery*, was realised in the earliest plate, published on 17th May 1792. The three drawings that followed were elevations of the south, north and west fronts, of which only the north was realised fully in the second plate, published ten days later. These were double-page plates engraved by Samuel Porter, who was responsible also for *West Elevation of the Church*, on a single page, and *The West elevation of the Refectory*, also on a single page. The final two drawings were to have been sections of the entire building from east to west and a separate section of the unfinished mausoleum at large, neither of which was realised.

One senses a shift from enthusiasm for the specifically Portuguese character of decoration at Batalha – the Manueline style of its latest phase, evident in the unfinished mausoleum – to the architecture of the earlier church and monastery, which has more in common with the Gothic architecture of England and France. One-third of the drawings listed in the outline are of the unfinished mausoleum. None was realised. However, three-and-a-half plates of the book are devoted to the mausoleum of King John and his English wife Queen Philippa, not mentioned in that list. The chapter house is ignored also in the outline, though Murphy's admiration of its structural daring cannot be doubted;[16] in the book it receives a separate plate and it shares with the mausoleum of King John the details of the plate *Ornaments, Mottos &c.*

William Burton Conyngham's election to fellowship of the Society of Antiquaries of London in 1790 may well account for this major shift in emphasis. He was, perhaps, in London for his election, and may have been introduced to the Pitt account of travels in Portugal and Spain by Richard Gough or other fellows of the Society, who would have been aware of his very recent publication in the current issue of *Transactions of the Royal Irish Academy* on the theatre at Saguntum in Spain, and inscriptions found there.[17] James Cavanah Murphy was certainly in London at the end of October 1790 at the conclusion of a brief tour that included the study and sketching of Gothic architecture in York, Cambridge and Ely.[18]

Thomas Pitt's first reaction to the sight of Batalha was one of wonder and amazement – 'the most elaborate and exquisite Gothic architecture I ever saw', he wrote. 'It requires the pencil of a painter, rather than the pen of description, to give an idea of it, to one who has not seen it.' He gave a brief but admiring account of the great west front, 'adorned with a multitude of decreasing mouldings, in pointed arches without columns; the mouldings being filled with little images in tabernacle work, which being continued in the moldings of the arch seem suspended in air.' He also emphasised the connection with England:

> the Founder, John I and his wife, Philippa, daughter to our John of Gaunt, Duke of Lancaster, lies in a most lovely Chapel ... the pillars with clustered columns, & ribbing of the vaulting, are the last degree of lightness & elegance, particularly the centre stone, which is the finest open lace-work I ever saw. The Building, for the honour of our Country, was executed by an Englishman, who lies in the nave, with an inscription over him

His account of the unfinished mausoleum makes reference particularly to the 'most curious' architecture of the entrance arch:

> A trefoil of prodigious size with different foliage of the most beautiful kind imaginable. The variety of the work is surprising, as well as the skill in the execution of it being quite hollow. Tho' carved in the same stone, the tabernacles for images carved quite into the middle of the stone, where one would think no tool could reach, without spoiling the rest.[19]

It is unnecessary to labour the point that the plates devoted to the unfinished mausoleum in James Murphy's book, confined to discrete parts such as the entrance, arches, and *Columns, Ornaments and Hieroglyphics*, conform far more closely to the written description of Thomas Pitt than do the plans and section at large of the outline proposed by Murphy in 1789. So too does the amount of attention given to the mausoleum of the founder and its tombs, not mentioned in that outline. The change of emphasis would have special appeal for the director of the Society of Antiquaries, who had authored a first successful volume of *Sepulchral Monuments* and was about to produce its sequel. Murphy's book on Batalha must be seen at least in part as inspired by the agenda of the Society of Antiquaries of London at the end of the eighteenth century, under the direction of Richard Gough.

Another fellow of the Society of Antiquaries who was of first importance to William Burton Conyngham during these years was Francis Grose, author of several books on the antiquities of the British Isles, who had died in Dublin in 1791 when extending his research into the antiquities of Ireland. His work was continued textually by Edward Ledwich, and published in two volumes between 1791 and 1796, using the drawings in the collection of William Burton Conyngham as illustrations.[20] The second volume was dedicated to Conyngham in recognition of his generosity in making the drawings (mostly by Gabriel Berenger) available for engraving by Samuel Hooper in London. It includes one plate, *View of the Lavabo at Mellifont Abbey*, stated to be by James Murphy, who presumably kept a watchful eye on that publication during the process of engraving in London, which coincided with the engraving of his plates for his book on Batalha.

William Burton Conyngham died at the end of May 1796. It is to be hoped he lived long enough to appreciate the dedications to him of these major works which owed so much to his generosity. His energy and persistence in the promotion of the recording and publication of Irish antiquities has long been recognised: 'Through his membership of the antiquities committee of the Dublin Society, his presidency of the Hibernian Antiquities Society, and his founding membership of the Royal Irish Academy he played an important facilitative role in the advancement of antiquarian scholarship,' James Kelly has written. 'He was deserving of the accolade of *superior patriot* bestowed on him by Charles O'Connor.'[21]

While this is true, its emphasis on the Irish dimension of his achievement may well obscure the impetus his patronage gave to the Gothic Revival internationally in providing the Society of Antiquaries of London with an exemplar for monographs on medieval monuments at a time when this body of scholarly literature started to flourish under the direction of Richard Gough. 'It was the first volume illustrative of medieval antiquities comparable in standard to the great volumes on classical antiquities published earlier in the century.'[22] It neglects also the theoretical dimension of James Murphy's book on Batalha, the aspect to which foreign editors were particularly attracted. A translation in German of Murphy's *Introductory Discourse on the Principles of Gothic Architecture*, with twelve plates, appeared in Leipzig in 1813, and his book was already well known to propagandists of the Gothic Revival in that country.[23] The impact of the book upon the practice of architecture of the Gothic Revival, evident particularly in the work of James Wyatt and his nephew and associates, several of whom were subscribers to *Batalha*, is a further dimension of the patronage of James Burton Conyngham that is overlooked in the emphasis on his contribution to Irish antiquity.[24] These will be the subject of a later study.

THE CHAPTER HOUSE

There is no mention in the account by Thomas Pitt in 1760 of the chapter house of the monastery, which had served as repository for the tombs of King Alphonso V, who died in 1481, and his grandson Prince Alfonso, both removed to the west wall of the mausoleum of the founder in 1901. Richard Twiss, however, had described its principal architectural features: 'a cube of twenty-three paces ... The roof of this chapel is vaulted in the shape of a star with eight points, and is without support.' He specifies that the bodies lay 'in two chests'.[25] Three altars for the celebration of masses for the deceased were also in the room, but they were removed at some time before it was dedicated to its present use in 1924 as the repository for the national Tomb of the Unknown Warrior to commemorate the Portuguese dead of the First World War.[26] Neither chest nor altar, this is a slab in the floor, which does not obstruct the view of the marvel of structural engineering that is the vault, with its slender ribbing springing elegantly from the walls to the starred centrepiece without any intervening support. This has attracted legends from the start, which, like the inscriptions on all the tombs, are recorded by Murphy at second-hand from the Portuguese of Fr Lewis de Sousa in his book on Batalha.[27] But it evoked spirited drawings and admiring comments from him, and he wrote the following description in his *Travels in Portugal*:

> In point of construction the Chapter-House might be considered a master-piece of architecture. Its plan forms a square, each side of which measures sixty-four feet, and is covered with a vault of hewn stone. The principal ribs spring from slender shafts, and branch out in different directions as they approach to the centre, where all the radiating nerves, in the form of a star, encircle an ornamented patera.[28]

Six drawings are devoted to the meticulous measuring of the structural and orna-mental features of the chapter house, the inscription of which reads: 'Note the extream arch is about a semi-circle' (Plate 2). The dimension of the arch is 31:6, noted with the height of the small columns and their capitals, 10:6 and 1:4 respec-tively, to give the 'Whole height from floor to crown of center part 43:4'. On the same sheet is a detail of the capital of the small columns, noting a flower over each shaft, and a second detail outlines the tracery of the circular window over the entrance. In the lower-left of the sheet is the admiring comment: 'N.B. The front

2 – Section and details of the chapter house (f.45)
(Unless otherwise stated, all illustrations are by James Cavanah Murphy from the album BATALHA, ORIGINAL DRAWINGS
*in the library of the Society of Antiquaries of London, ref. MS 260. All are pen and wash over pencil on paper, each
36 x 26 cm, except where noted differently. Reproduced by permission of the Society of Antiquaries of London.)*

entrance of this Hall will make a fine drawing. The Door and windows on each side
are admirably contrived and extend the whole length.' This is the preparatory drawing, therefore, of the plate *A Section of the Chapter House at Batalha*, engraved by
Wilson Lowry, though for the plate it is combined with f.49, titled *Principal
Entrance to Chapter room*, an elevation drawing taken from the cloister, the inscriptions of which repeat the sentiments of f.45 (Plate 3).

The most extensive sheet of measured profiles of mouldings rendered with
hatching are devoted to the chapter house (ff. 47, 48), the first of which carries the
note: 'N.B. the columns at the door at E the same height as the columns in Cloyster
and 10in. diameter. The top of the small columns ranged with those at the door.' The
right-hand of the sheet bears the measured profiles of the bases of the small columns
to the windows and the larger columns at the entrance. This folio is shorter than the
normal sheets, 35 x 22 cm as opposed to 36 x 26 cm, and the profiles are repeated at
large and without hatching, but minutely measured, on the following sheet, f.48
(Plate 4).

The chapter house also occasioned the finest sheet of bases and capitals rendered in wash on f.46. The architect-artist was struck by the delicacy and depth of

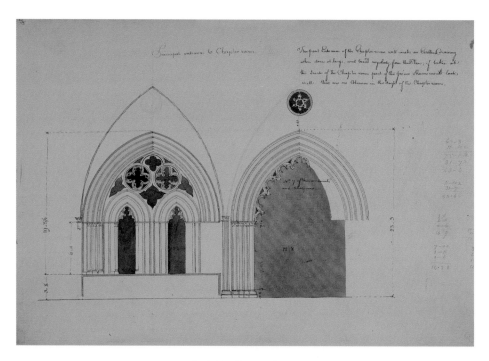

3, 4, 5 – Chapter house
Entrance (f.49), profiles of columns (f.48), and (opposite) details of columns (f.46)

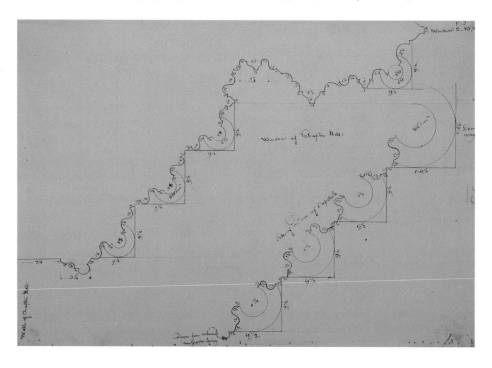

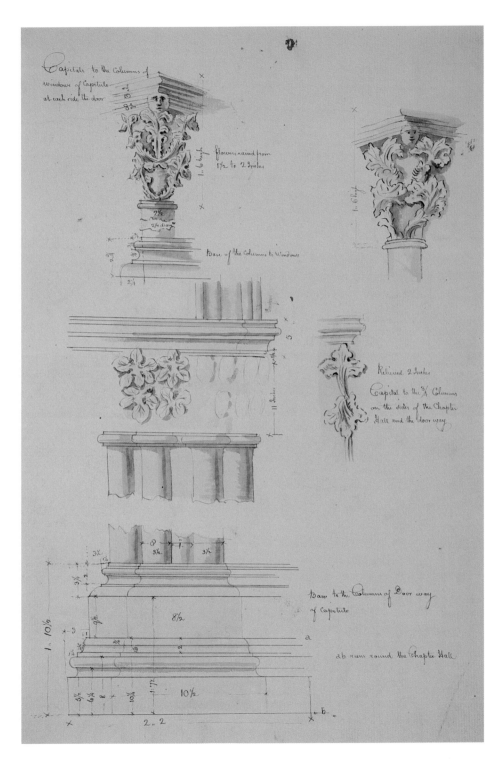

above 6 – *Figure in the south-east corner of the chapter house, said to represent the architect (f.50)*

left 7 – *Sepulchral effigies of King John I and Queen Phillipa (f.23)*

carving of the floral ornament of the capitals, remarking of the capitals of the columns on each side of the entrance: 'Flowers raised from one and a half to two inches', and of the capitals of the three-quarter columns on the sides of the entrance: 'Relieved 2 inches' (Plate 5). A detail from the chapter house is drawn on f.50, labelled: 'Figure in the SE corner of Chapter House placed under one of the ribs of the Groins, supposed to be the architect of the Church'. He is described with a wash-shadow and bistre accents in the drawing, holding a measuring rod with an alert and lively expression. That was unfortunately lost in the engraving found on the plate titled *Ornaments, Mottos &c.*, out of place among the details from the mausoleum of the founder in one sense, but not in the sense that it represents the master builder, probably named Huguet, who designed and supervised the construction and ornament of both memorial spaces (Plate 6).

THE MAUSOLEUM OF KING JOHN I

THE INTERIOR OF THE MAUSOLEUM OF KING JOHN IS REMARKABLE FOR ITS COM-
bination of spatial complexity and geometric simplicity. An octagonal core
of clustered columns rises within a square chamber through two storeys to a
star vault, the ribs of which collect the energies of the upward movement of
columns and arches in an area filled with light from the eight windows of the walls
of the octagon. This is supported by flying buttresses that transfer the weight to the
buttresses of the lower walls, allowing those walls, too, to be pierced by windows
originally filled with stained glass. Beneath the vault of the octagon is placed the
tomb of the founder, King John I, shown recumbent and with his hand in that of his
wife Queen Philippa (f.23), a drawing in ink and wash that differs from the engraving in the book, *Effigies of King John and Queen Philippa*, mainly in the absence of
the canopies over their heads, described as 'a triple canopy of curious workmanship,
in the Gothic manner' (Plate 7).

Surprisingly, there is no further verbal description of the mausoleum of the
founder, though admiring accounts had been written by Thomas Pitt and Richard
Twiss, who had each mentioned the connection with the English queen. Inscriptions
on the tombs are given at length in *Batalha* and repeated in *Travels in Portugal*.[29]
The external elevation from the south is shown in one of the plates, and the similar
west elevation is on the right side of the engraving by Samuel Porter titled *West
Elevation of the Church*, for which f.2 is the preparatory drawing. Both show the
structure completed with an octagonal spire of pierced stonework with ornamented
ribs, though no such spire exists today. Nor did it exist in 1789, because it had been
destroyed in the aftermath of the Lisbon earthquake of 1755. The preparatory drawing for these plates is f.21, exceptional in being a gatefold sheet (45 x 33 cm),
bound into the volume (Plate 8) The non-existent spire is sketched without its perfo-
rations and with only two ribs ornamented. The architect-artist could not resist the
temptation to restore this structure, and he claims to have taken the design 'from an
old painting in one of the windows of the Church'.[30]

No such window exists today, and it is probable that for his reconstruction
Murphy looked to the structure of the Great or Stork Tower adjoining the chapter
house in the royal cloister. This tower also suffered in the calamity of 1755, but had
since been repaired. It is the subject in plan, elevation and section of the plate titled
The Spire of the North end of the Transept. This is based on f.44 for the plans of the
three storeys of the tower and ff. 40 and 41 for the elevations in outline and detail
(Plate 9). Ornamental motifs are described at large in ff. 42 and 43, the last
inscribed 'Ornament running up the angle of the Great Spire taken on the spot',
indicating that his study of the details was made at some danger to life and limb for
the architect. His reconstruction of the upper stage of the founder's mausoleum is

---

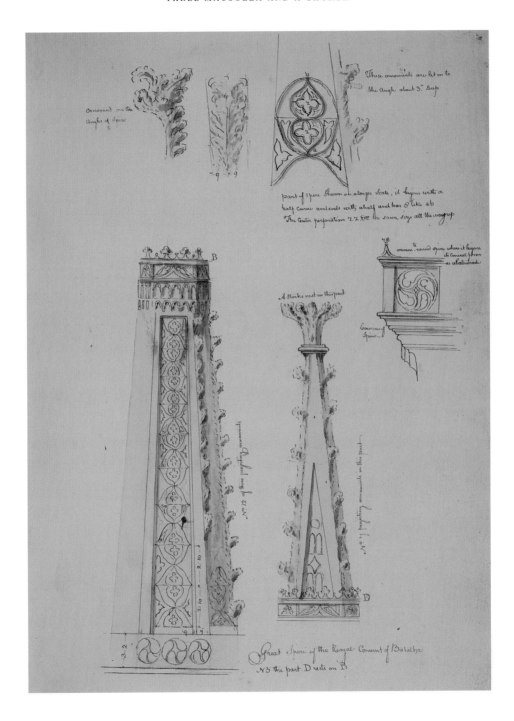

9 – Elevation of the great spire of Batalha with details (f.41)

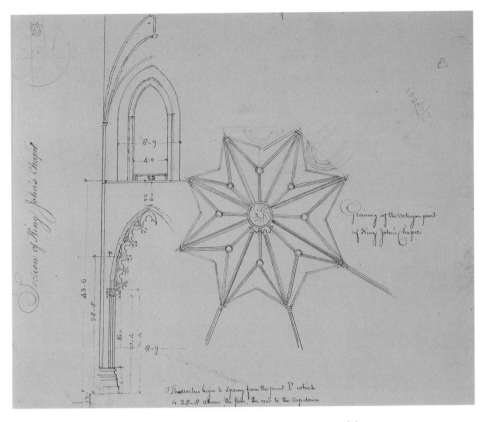

11 – Section of the mausoleum of the founder with groining of the octagon (f.11)

opposite 10 – Proposal for the completion of the unfinished chapels or mausoleum of King Emmanuel
pen, ink and watercolour on paper on board, 472 x 308 cm (British Museum, Prints and Drawings, 16AN216076)

quite convincing, but his use of the same motifs in the later reconstruction of the upper stages of the buttresses of the unfinished mausoleum – seen in the plate *Design for completing the mausoleum of King Emmanuel* – is less happy. The preparatory drawing for this plate is in the collection of the British Museum (Plate 10).[31]

A measured elevation of one bay of the internal core of the mausoleum of the founder is described in an ink drawing titled 'Section of King John's Chapel' on the left of the sheet, f.11, and 'Groining of the Octagon point of King John's Chapel' on the right (Plate 11). It is a beautiful drawing in displaying the admiration the architect-artist clearly felt for the integrity of the architecture and its ornamental features. These are elaborated in coloured wash in f.22, inscribed 'Centre part of King John the First Chapel', followed by dimensions and the remarks: 'The centre part is covered with a cobweb under which is to be seen a shield with a figure on each side. The whole has a beautiful effect, the incisions are very much sunk, which gives it

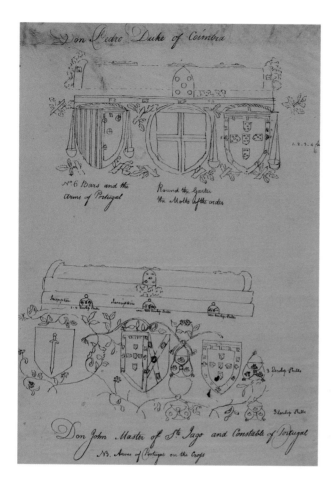

12 – Drawing by J. Taylor Jnr of coats of arms from the mausoleum of the founder (f.24)

great relief.' Below are detailed drawings of three smaller bosses, labelled 'Pateras in the groining of the side ailes of King John's Chapel – the leaves are coloured red, yellow, green &c.' All these are reproduced in the plate *Ornaments, Mottos &c.*, which also shows the helmet, battleaxe and sword on the same sheet, and the variety of floriated capitals of the columns of the mausoleum, shown with measured profiles in ink and wash in f.12 and itemised on page 20.

The plate titled *Section of the Mausoleum of King John I* shows the four tombs installed against the east wall, with the names and coats of arms of their occupants. The preparatory drawing is f.15 in ink and wash, with dimensions, inscribed 'Sketch of the Tombs in K. John's Chapel. Note the four are alike except in the arms cut on the Dado part'. These arms are drawn on light onion paper glued to the sheets of ff. 24 and 25, and the legend of the plate reads on the right 'Etched by the author. Finished by J. Taylor', who is also mentioned on the title page of the book, where he was responsible for the figures (Plate 12).

THE UNFINISHED MAUSOLEUM

'HAD IT BEEN FINISHED, IT WOULD HAVE BEEN THE RICHEST PIECE OF GOTHIC work in Europe', Thomas Pitt had exclaimed on examining the mausoleum of King Emmanuel or *Capellas Imperfectas* at the east end of the church.[32] Richard Twiss had expressed admiration for the carving, but had offered only a summary description – 'a spacious octagon chapel without a roof, as it was left unfinished'.[33]

There are five preparatory drawings in pen and ink for doorways and arches of the unfinished mausoleum on the same light paper glued to ff. 58, 59 (which has subtle touches of wash), 60, 61 and 64. Two further drawings devoted to the unfinished mausoleum are technical in character and delineated in outline – f.63 titled 'Plan of the Second Story', which also contains an outline of an arched doorway and several ornaments, and f.78, 'Groins of the Capellas Imperfectas'. But in ff. 51-55 and f.62, a grey wash is used sensitively to convey depth in larger structural features – in f.55, for instance, 'Elevation of an Arch' (Plate 13) and f.54, 'Column of Capellas Imperfectas externally' (Plate 14), as well as in details such as the architrave and cornice of the arch to the right of the former drawing, with the remark:

> very finely executed in the original. It is undercut 4 or 5 inches and shews quite detached in the middle that makes so great a contrast of light and shade as to shew the smallest part to advantage: in making these ornaments at large they should be drawn very full and the intermediate parts made very black to shew it highly relieved.

Such enthusiastic admiration for the art of the sculptor responsible for the decoration of the cornice is echoed in the crispness of the engraving by James Walker in the lower-left of the plate titled *Columns, Ornaments, and Hieroglyphics in the Mausoleum of King Emmanuel I*. It compensates a little for the draughtsman's rueful comment: 'The frieze was never finished. They must have intended some rich ornament for it.' The crowned letters RM are also on that plate, as are mottoes and ornament from f.62. The delicately ornamented columns above these are from a subtle wash drawing of a half-elevation of the entrance, marked TC in the upper right of f.59, to which f.58 is preparatory and bears the warning: 'Do not depend on this. Look at TC drawing'. Unfortunately the delicacy is lost in the engraving by Wilson Lowry and the otherwise unmentioned assistant (one Clare), *The Entrance of the Mausoleum*, the plate dedicated to the Prince of Brazil, the future King Jaoa VI.

The upper curve of the inside of the entrance arch to the mausoleum is a very graceful composition of intersecting segmental and triangular arcs outlined in ink in ff. 60 and 61. The left half of the arch is drawn in f.52, 'Entrance to the Capellas

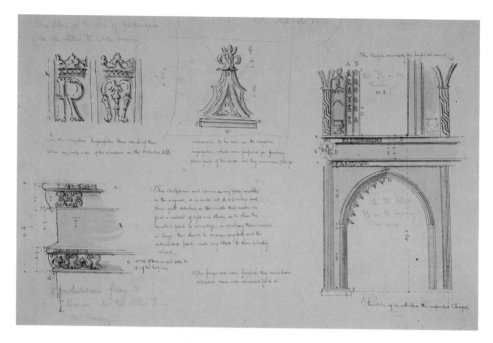

The unfinished mausoleum

13 – Arch, with details of ornament *(f.55)*
opposite 14 – Columns, with details of ornament *(f.54)*
15 – Arch detail in entrance door *(f.52)*

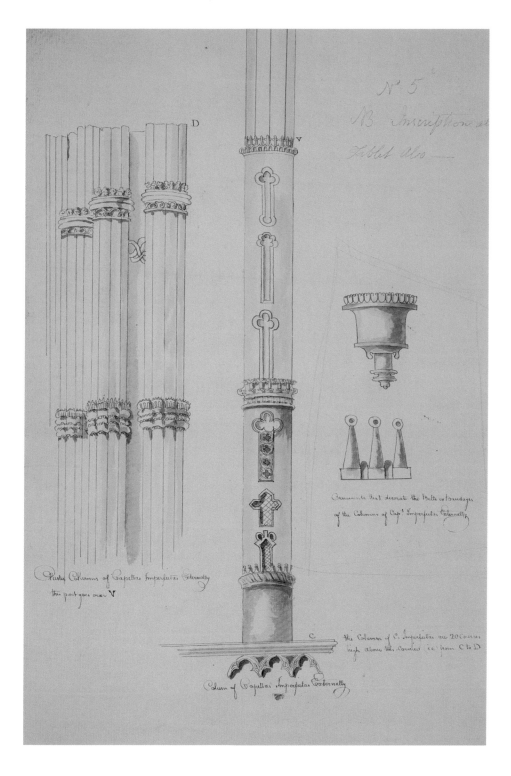

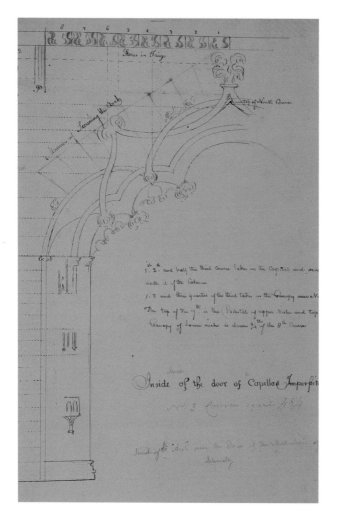

The unfinished mausoleum

16 – Interior of the door (f.53)

opposite 17 – Plan (f.51)

Imperfectas. Inside' (Plate 15). This is one of the most attractive renderings in wash of the energetic movement of the springing of the elaborately decorated composition. The print in the upper part of the plate titled *Arches appertaining to the Mausoleum*, the engraver of which is not named, deadens the design, alas, by inking in the interstices. Fortunately, the same error was not made in the lower part of the plate, a doorway whose purpose puzzled the architect, as is has other commentators, but whose artistry compelled his admiration: 'It would make a fine effect from the body of the Church', he wrote.[34] There are two drawings for this doorway, f.53 for its internal elevation (Plate 16) and f.51 for the exterior, the one fancied to make a grand impression (Plate 18). It is shaded with differing densities of wash in the turn of the arch, and neat hatching gives the meticulous measurements of the profiles of

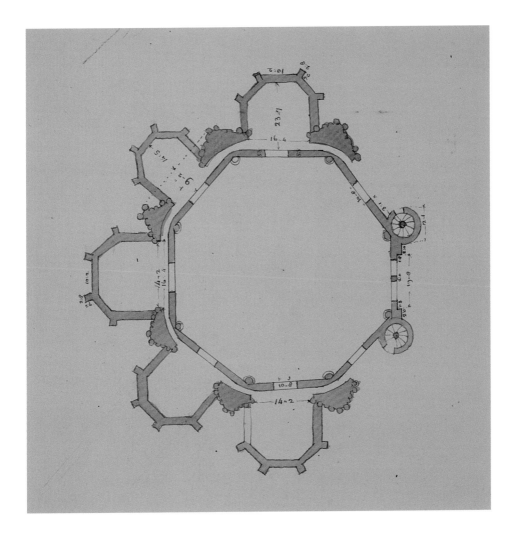

the clustered columns, which are also rendered in outline to the left with their floriated capitals.

The plan of the unfinished mausoleum is in the upper-right of the double
plate, *A General Plan of the Church and Royal Monastery of Batalha*, for which
f.57 is a preparatory drawing in ink and wash, scaled and with measurements (Plate
17). There is also a measured plan in outline of the second story of the mausoleum,
which was not engraved, although originally an engraving was intended. No elevation drawing of the exterior is known, though f.56, which is of the exterior of the
chancel and apse of the church, is misleadingly titled in the hand of the author,
'Capellas Imperfectas' (Plate 19). The elevation of the mausoleum is at the extreme
left of the double plate engraved by Samuel Porter, *The North Elevation of the*

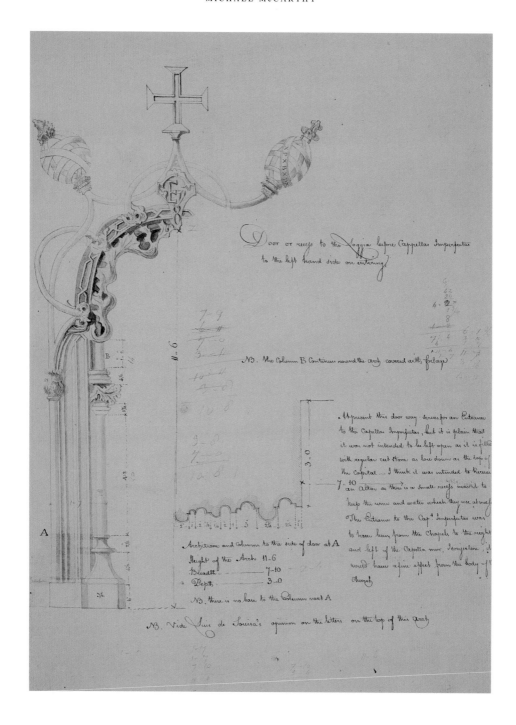

18 – Exterior of the door of the unfinished mausoleum (f.51)

Church of Batalha. The author gives a verbal description in *Travels in Portugal*:

> At the rear of the church is an unfinished Mausoleum of a curious form,
> wherein the architect has exhibited no superficial knowledge of geometry, or
> the principles of sound and elegant design. In point of workmanship, neither
> the pen nor the pencil is adequate to express its real merits; for, though most
> objects, when transferred to the canvas appear to advantage, this, on the con-
> trary, though delineated by the most ingenious artist, upon examination, will
> appear more beautiful than any representation of it. And for these reasons,
> the marble is polished, the sculpture in many parts detached from the centre
> of the block, and so minutely carved, that to preserve all the expressive
> marks and touches of the chisel, it is not possible to condense them into a
> smaller compass: so that, to convey a true idea of the whole, the picture
> would require to be as large as the prototype.[35]

THE CHURCH OF OUR LADY OF VICTORY

THE CHURCH TO WHICH THESE SPLENDID MAUSOLEA ARE APPENDED IS RELATIVELY
unadorned internally, though we and the architect-author are not privileged
to witness its former glories since the destruction wrought to the stained-
glass windows by the earthquake of 1755. Whatever ornaments are employed in it',
wrote Murphy,

> are sparingly, but judiciously disposed; particularly in the inside, which is
> remarkable for a chaste and noble plainness: and the general effect, which is
> grand and sublime, is derived, not from any meretricious embellishments, but
> from the intrinsic merit of the design.[36]
>
> The forms of its mouldings and ornaments are also different from
> those of any other Gothic building that I have seen. The difference chiefly
> consists in their being turned very quick, cut sharp and deep, with some other
> peculiarities which cannot be well explained in writing.

The author-artist is to be congratulated in the circumstances for his renderings of six
capitals and the base of a column in f.36 (Plate 20). They are engraved on the top
line of the plate *Ornaments, Mottos, &c.*, but with inevitable loss of liveliness in the
detail. 'The flowers are so highly relieved', reads one inscription, 'that they appear
detached from the capital.' These capitals reappear in measured profiles in the plate
engraved by Wilson Lowry, *Elevation of one of the Pillars of the Church*, for which
there is no preparatory drawing. Murphy concluded his account of the architecture:

> Throughout the whole are seen a correctness and regularity, evidently the

Church of Our Lady of Victories

19, 20 – East end (f.56) and (opposite) capitals of the columns (f.36) result of a well-conceived design: it is equally evident that this design has been immutably adhered to, and executed in regular progression, without those alterations and interruptions to which such large buildings are commonly subject.

This is a considerable analysis by comparison with that of Thomas Pitt, who asserted that Alcobaca had been the model for Batalha, or Richard Twiss, who wrote, 'a very fine Gothic building, much like King's College in Cambridge'.[37]

Justice is done to the size and consistency of the structure of the church and chancel in the plate *Longitudinal Section* by Samuel Porter, and two plates by Wilson Lowry, *The Elevation of the Chancel* and *Interior View* from the west entrance to the altar. This distance of seventy-four feet and four inches appears more lengthy and lofty because of the relative narrowness of breadth of the nave viewed in perspective through the series of eight columns to the chancel. This consists of five chapels – four of equal breadth, and the centre one, which rises uninterrupted through two storeys to the vaulted roof, slightly broader. That is the only part of the interior to which a drawing, taken from the front of the transept, is devoted, f.37 (Plate 21).

Since the south side of the church was obstructed by the monastery buildings,

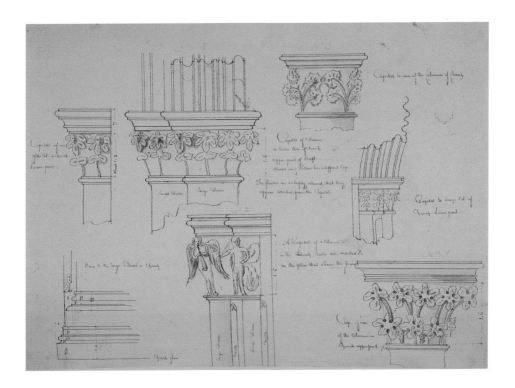

 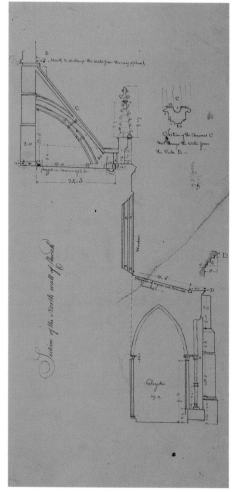

Church of Our Lady of Victories

21, 22 – Interior view of east end (f.37) and section of the north wall (f.28)

opposite 23 – Section of the north wall, with details of ornament (f.33)

the measuring was done on the north side. The lower part of the walls is detailed in f.28, 'Section of the North wall of the Church', which notes the channels for discharge of water from the roof to the ground at the buttress of the cloister. 'This is roofed', Murphy noted, with a 'platform of regular cut stone well cemented', while the level of the springing of the buttress is 'flagged in courses of 18 inches' (Plate 22). The factual recording of materials and dimensions is continued in f.33, 'Section of the North side of the Church showing window, ornaments &c' (Plate 23). Once the physical constituents of the structure had been itemised, the artist-architect was in a

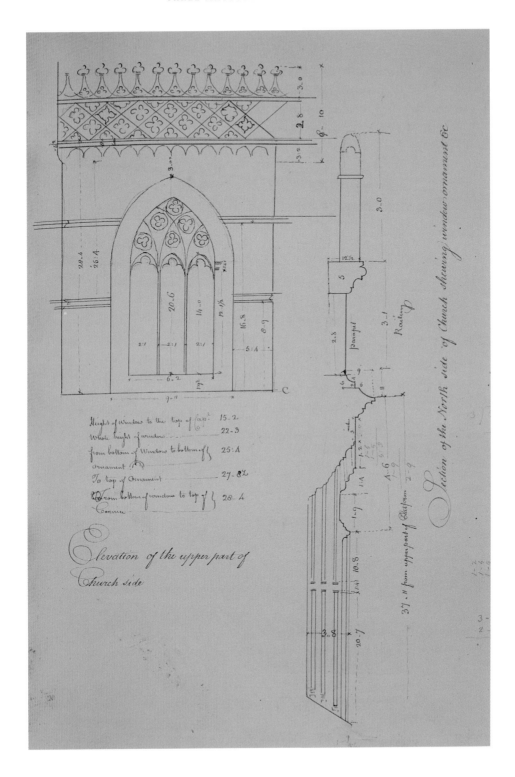

Height of Window to the top of arch 15.2
Whole height of window 22.3
from bottom of Window to bottom of ornament 25.4
To top of Ornament 27.8½
from bottom of window to top of Cornice 28.4

Elevation of the upper part of Church side

Section of the North side of Church shewing window ornament &c

position to reconstitute them in f.27, an ink drawing to the right side of the double plate by Samuel Porter, *North Elevation of the Church of Batalha* (Plate 24).

The comprehensiveness and care of Murphy's survey is particularly apparent in f.29, 'Section of the roof of the Church'. The upper part of the sheet has five sketches of technical details in ink and wash, with dimensions: 'manner of securing the fleur de luce ornament, manner of uniting the stones in the roof of K. John's Chapel, roof of church centre aile: there is a strong cement in the joints', and 'form of ridge stones over the Church' (Plate 25). On the lower part of the sheet are 'Memorandums relating to the Height of Church':

> Height of the column of Church. NB measured only as (triangle)
> From cap of col to top of arch 28 feet
> About 90 feet from the church to the bottom of upper groin
> No. 128 steps from the church floor to the tops of the fleurs de luce ornament on the side of Church upper part. NB each step is $9,^1/_2$in high.
> 66 feet 6in from the floor of Church to the bottom window inside of Church – upper part of slope
> 101 f. 0.in. from the floor of the church to the top of the fleurs de luce ornaments on the side of Church upper part
> 71:8 Height of Col in Church from the base to top of cap
> 91:8 from the Church floor to top of arch of Church
> 121:8 to the part where the Steeple begins in conic form

The mensuration complete, the author-architect was in a position to make the drawing for the engraving by James Walker, *Transverse Section of the Church*, for which the preparatory drawing is with the album but not bound in it, so it has been creased and is torn at the edges. It contains the outline figure of the Vitruvian man standing in the nave of the church. Above the roofs of the aisles are placed the diagrams of f.29 under different designations (Plate 26):

> Longitudinal section of the roof;
> form of the ridge tiles;
> the manner of morticing the pinnacles into the acroterias; Section of the arch buttress at B; D water conduit.

Murphy could justifiably claim to his sponsor and patron William Burton Conyngham: 'I have endeavoured to penetrate into every part of the building, from the foundation to the top.'[38]

A separate plate engraved by Wilson Lowry for the entrance on the south side of the church is titled *Elevation of the Transept Entrance*. The preparatory drawing is a tipped-in sheet (f.38), which has been cropped to 35 x 27 cm. It is marked and measured in ink with inscriptions in pencil, and differs from the engrav-

Church of Our Lady of Victories

24, 25 – Elevation and part-section of the north of the church (f.27) and details of the roof (f.29)

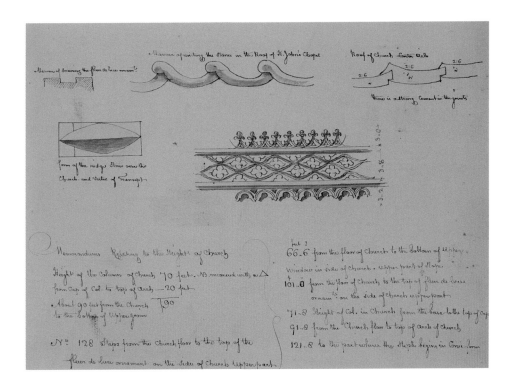

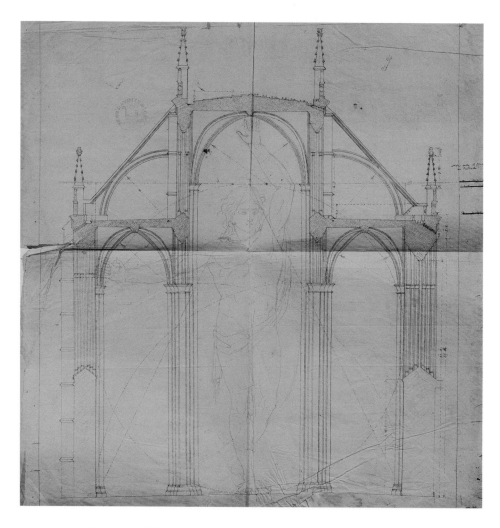

ing principally in simplifying the fenestration above the doorway. This is set within an arched and pinnacled porch of five receding columns. The only sculpture, however, is armorial in character, placed in the triangle above the entrance (Plate 27).

The principal entrance on the west, in contrast, is a veritable gallery of sculpture (Plate 28), described as follows in *Travels in Portugal*:

> In every thing that constitutes the ornamental or the elegant, the principal Entrance certainly stands unrivalled by any other Gothic frontispiece in Europe. The Portal, which is twenty-eight-feet wide by fifty-seven high, is embellished with upwards of one hundred figures in alto relievo, representing Moses and the prophets, saints and angels, apostles, kings, popes, bishops, and martyrs, with their respective insignia. Each figure stands on an ornamental pedestal, beneath a canopy of delicate workmanship; they are separat-

Church of Our Lady of Victories
27 – Elevation of transept entrance (f.38)
opposite 26 – *Section with the Vitruvian man inscribed in the nave* (unnumbered)

ed from each other by an assemblage of mouldings, terminating in pointed arches.

Below the vertex of the inferior arch is a triangular recess, where there is seated on a throne, beneath a triple canopy, a figure with a celestial crown, his left hand resting upon a globe, the other is extended in the act of admonition. This figure represents our Saviour dictating to the four Evangelists who surround him, attended by their respective attributes.[39]

It is surprising that a separate plate is not devoted to the main entrance, which shares a plate, engraved by Samuel Porter, with the west elevation of the mausoleum of King John I (Plate 28). There are seven preparatory drawings, two of which are sheets glued to the page – f.5 of ink drawings of figure statuary and ornament, and f.8, inscribed 'Plan of the side of the West Door of Batalha'. A measured elevation of the upper stage of the entrance front is given with details of moundings and ornaments on f.4, whose title has been corrected from *South Front* to *West Front* (Plate 29).

The window over the great west door is the subject of ornamental details in wash on f.2, an elevation of the entire façade marked off in thirty-eight courses from ground to top for measuring purposes, and of f.6. 'A large window of singular workmanship,' wrote the author, 'it consists of tablets of marble, formed into numeous compartments, whose interstices are filled up with stained glass' . Folio 7 has only a slight sketch of the arch of the door, but it is important in detailing the sculpture of the entrance. Titled 'Memorandums relative to West Door', it reads in part:

> 1st row 8 female saints; 2nd 7 martyrs; 3rd Moses at right David and Kings; 4th 6 Patriarchs; 5th 6 Angels with instruments ... clothed; 6th 5 Angels praying with their hands lifted up ... their bodies are naked.

> On right hand 1st a pipe; 2nd a pipe; 3rd diagram; 4th a Guitar, 5th a fiddle; 6th a cymbal.

> Left hand: 1st a viol with strings; 2nd a Harp; 3rd diagram; 4th a fiddle; 5th Stag; 6th Stag kneeling....

> N.B. All the Kings with David sitting with globes on the right

> Left hand: 1st with a Globe; 2nd with a Globe; 3rd young with a different crown and two books in his left hand; 4th with a large scroll on lap; 5th a scroll in right hand; 6th a scroll unfolded; 7th a scroll and book.

Such precision in itemising the figure sculpture leads one to expect a parallel exactness in draughtsmanship in the visual part of the book *Batalha*, but it is not present

28 – The west door of the church of Our Lady of Victories
(photo the author)

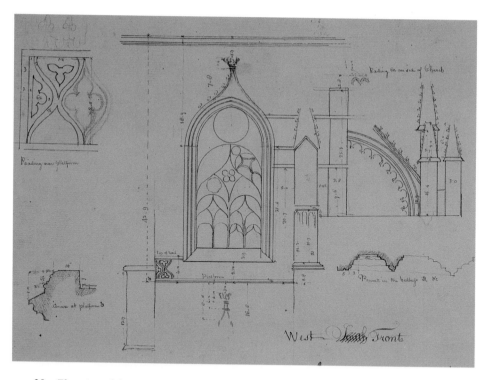

29 – Elevation of the upper stage of the west front of the Church of Our Lady of Victories, with details (f.4)

there nor in *Travels in Portugal*, plate III of which shows the entrance from the north-west, with the wall of the refectory of the monastery abutting the great west entrance. That is the subject of a plate by Samuel Porter, 'The West Elevation of the Refectory', most notable for the gaiety of the railings on top of the wall, contrasting with the sobriety of the walls and buttresses. This feature is shown in the lower right of the plate 'Rails, Cornices and Arched Modillions'. That plate receives no mention in the text, but the window openings are offered as an example of Greek architecture in no. 23 of figure 1 and cited on page 6 of the introductory discourse. Precision of detail was clearly of great importance to the architect-author, but he entrusted the figures of the title page of the book on Batalha to J. Taylor Jnr., so we may presume that figure-drawing was not one of the talents to which he laid claim.

———

ACKNOWLEDGEMENTS

Particular thanks are due to the Society of Antiquaries of London for permission to quote the text and reproduce the drawings of MS 260. The librarian, Bernard Nurse, was most helpful in discussion of the work, and Adrian James arranged for the photography, which was financed by the Irish Georgian Society and executed by Roy Fox. Oliver Grogan kindly provided me with a translation of the catalogue by Paolo Pereira, *James Murphy e o mosteiro da Batalha* (Instituto Portugues do patrimonio cultural, 1989), and Jonathan Carroll provided access to his MA dissertation of 1997 for UCD, 'James Cavanah Murphy: description of the palace of the Alhambra and related literature'.

ENDNOTES

The following abbreviations are used:

Batalha   James C. Murphy, *Plans, Elevations, Sections and Views of the Church of Batalha* (1795)

Travels   James C. Murphy, *Travels in Portugal ... in the years 1789 and 1790* (1795)

[1]   For the bibliographic details of these books and their editions and translations, see Paul W. Nash et al (compilers), *Catalogue of the British Architectural Library Early Imprints Collection, Volume 3: M-R* (Bowker-Saur, 1999), 1198-202. I owe thanks to David Griffin, director of the Irish Architectural Archive, for this and other references in connection with this study, and for use of the Archive's copy of *Batalha*. Murphy was also the author of *A General View of the state of Portugal* (London, 1798), and *The Arabian Antiquities of Spain* (London, 1815-16).

[2]   For Gough and the importance of his *Sepulchral Monuments*, see Rosemary Sweet, *Antiquaries: the discovery of the past in Eighteenth-Century Britain* (London, 2004) 273-76.

[3]   John Nichols, *Literary Illustrations of the Eighteenth Century*, VI (London,1815-1817) 294.

[4]   This album of drawings is no. 260 of Pamela Willetts, *Catalogue of the Manuscripts in the Society of Antiquaries of London* (London, 2002).

[5]   It was introduced to the literature in Megan Aldrich, 'William Beckford's Abbey at Fonthill: from the Picturesque to the Sublime', 117-35, of Derek E. Ostergard (ed.), *William Beckford, 1760-1844: an Eye for the Magnificent* (Yale UP, 2001). I am grateful to Megan Aldrich for an introduction to the drawings and for advice in the course of this study. For biographical notice of Murphy, see *The Dictionary of National Biography* (*DNB*), XXIV, 1236.

[6]   James Murphy, preface to *Batalha*. The gentlemen are named in a footnote as Colonel Tarrant and Captain Broughton. The only Portuguese artist mentioned by him is in a passage on page 10 of *Travels*: 'Signor Glama was one of the artists employed by the Right Honourable William Burton Conyngham, when on his travels through Portugal, in making drawings and sketches of antiquities &c., which may be seen among this gentleman's valuable collection of papers relating to Portugal.' Atanasi Raczynski, *Dictionnaire historique-artistique du Portugal* (Paris, 1847) 112, names him as Jean Armand Clarma Strebel or Strabile, a German who came to Lisbon in the train of Queen Marianne of Austria. He lived in Oporto and was hghly regarded.

[7]   The letter was partly quoted in the earliest extended biography of the architect and author Count Plunkett, *The Irish Builder and Architect*, 15th May 1909, 295-97. For the complete text

of the letters of Murphy, see Nichols, *Literary Illustrations of the Eighteenth Century*, VI, 435-42. The most recent account of the architect-author is Michael McCarthy, 'Unpublished Drawings by James Cavanah Murphy', *Irish Arts Review*, Summer 2002, 114-17.

[8] Antoine Desgodetz (1653-1728), author of *Les edifices antiques de Rome*, which was famed for the accuracy of its measurements. See Eileen Harris, *British Architectural Books and Writers, 1556-1785* (Cambridge, 1990) 180-82. Murphy's publisher, Taylor, was preparing an English translation of Desgodetz in 1795.

[9] *Batalha*, 58.

[10] Murphy gives an account of Fr Lewis de Sousa in *Travels*, 231-35.

[11] Richard Twiss, *Travels through Portugal and Spain, in 1772 and 1773*, 2 vols (Dublin, 1775) I, 45-47.

[12] British Museum, Add. MSS 5845, 111-46, published in part by the author in 'Art Education and the Grand Tour' in M. Barasch and L.F. Sandler (eds), *Art the Ape of Nature: essays in honor of H.W. Janson* (New York, 1981) 477-94. For the circulation of the manuscript and further drawings from it, see Michael McCarthy, *The Origins of the Gothic Revival* (Yale UP, 1987) 16-19. See also John Frew and Carey Wallace, 'Thomas Pitt, Portugal, and the gothic cult of Batalha', *Burlington Magazine*, 128, 1986, 582-84. A connection between the manuscript of Thomas Pitt on Portugal and the book of James C Murphy is suggested in the final paragraph of the review of *Murphy's Travels*, published in the *Gentleman's Magazine*, XLV, October 1795, 848-55.

[13] For Charles Lyttelton, see Sweet, *Antiquaries*, 249-55. The letter is British Museum, Stowe MSS 754, ff.48-49.

[14] For the importance of Richard Gough, see John Frew, 'An aspect of the early Gothic Revival: the transformation of medievalist research, 1770-1780', *Journal of the Warburg and Courtauld Institutes*, XLIII, 1980, 174-85.

[15] For the printing history of *Batalha*, see Nash, note 1 above. The text of Murphy's letter of March 1789 is given in full in Nichols, *Literary Illustrations of the Eighteenth Century*, VI, 435. What I have called the early outline is the following passage:

> What follow are finished nearly on the same scale with the large plan I made for you in Dublin.
> A general Plan of the Church and Monastery
> Plan of the second story
> Plan of the Second story of Capellas Imperfectas
> Plan of the roof of the Church
> Elevation of the roof of the Church
> Elevation of the South front
> Elevation of the North front
> Elevation of the West front including the Refectory, Kitchen & being the extent of the ancient building
> A general Section from East to West, though Church, Chapel and Caps. Imperfs. Section of the Caps Imperfs.
> I have some views of the building yet to complete before I go to Alcobaca.

[16] He has inscribed f.45: 'NB the front entrance of this Hall will make a fine drawing. The door and the windows on each side are admirably contrived.'

[17] For Conyngham, see now James Kelly's entry in *DNB*.

[18] There is a diary in the Royal Institute of British Architects with drawings of his journey from 8th October 1790 to 25th October 1790, which ends with an ink sketch of a cornice in the house of Sir Joseph Banks, one of the subscribers to *Batalha*. See entry by Jill Lever in *Catalogue of the Drawings of the RIBA, L-N* (London, 1973) 98.

[19] All quotations in the preceding paragraph are from the transcript published by Frew and Wallace, 'Thomas Pitt, Portugal, and the gothic cult of Batalha'.

[20] For Grose and his relations with William Burton Conyngham, see Peter Harbison, *Our Treasure of Antiquities* (Bray, 2002) 215-17.

[21] *DNB*, s.v.

[22] Frew, 'An aspect of the early Gothic Revival'.

[23] Paul Breman (ed.), *The Gothic of Gothick*, Weinreb Catalogue 14 (London, 1966) items 168, 169.

[24] Megan Aldrich, *Gothic Revival* (London, 1994) ch. 3.

[25] Twiss, *Travels through Portugal and Spain*, I, 45-47.

[26] For the history of the church and monastery of Batalha, I have relied on Sergio Guimaraes de Andrade, *Santa Maria da Vitoria, Batalha, Artes Graficas* (Lisboa-Mafra, 1992). See now also José Custodas Vieira de Silva and Padre Rodel, *The Monastery of Batalha* (London, 2007)

[27] For the most recent version of the legend see the current guidebook *Batalha*, 24-25:

> It was necessary to recall Alonso Domingues, who swore to complete the Chapter House. Now completely blind, the aging master builder gave instructions on construct-ing the new vault until the day arrived to remove the lead supports. These were duly taken away and Domingues, convinced that the vault would hold, sat beneath it. He stayed there for three days and three nights. This was the work of his life; either the vault was perfect, or it would kill him. And the vault never fell.

[28] *Travels*, 36.

[29] *ibid.*, 50-68.

[30] Quoted from the letter-press of the plate 'The South elevation of the Mausoleum of King John I'. The same source is given in the preface to *Batalha*, where the date of the earthquake is mis-takenly given as 1745. This is corrected in *Travels*, 33, where, however, the account of the damage is not as extensive as that given in the preface.

[31] *DNB*, XXIV, 1236.

[32] Frew and Wallace, 'Thomas Pitt, Portugal, and the gothic cult of Batalha', 585.

[33] Twiss, *Travels through Portugal and Spain*, I, 45-47.

[34] 'I think it was intended to receive an altar as there is a small recess near it used to receive the wine and water which they use at mass', Murphy wrote on the drawing (Plate 18). See De Andrade, *Santa Maria da Vitoria, Batalha*, 83-85, for the best description of the doorway, which is attributed to Mateus Fernandes and is considered the acme of Manueline architecture.

[35] *Travels*, 37.

[36] *ibid.*, 33-34.

[37] Twiss, *Travels through Portugal and Spain*, I, 45.

[38] Quoted from the first letter of James Murphy to his patron. Nichols, *Literary Illustrations of the Eighteenth Century*, VI, 435.

[39] *Travels*, 35.

Irish civic planting
c.1740-c.1890

PATRICK BOWE

THE EXPANSION OF URBAN AREAS IN IRELAND DURING THE EIGHTEENTH AND nineteenth centuries led to a need for the provision of open areas for the citizens' recreation. The people of many Irish towns had free access to the parks of adjoining demesnes. For example, the townspeople of Ballinasloe, county Galway, had free access to Lord Clancarty's adjoining Garbally Park; the people of Bryansford, county Down, were free to walk in the grounds of Tollymore Park, the seat of the Earl of Roden; the inhabitants of Tuam were afforded a 'pleasant promenade' in the gardens of the Archbishop's Palace.[1] On the other hand, the private bowling green of Kilkenny Castle was open only to those who could pay. William Chetwood wrote in 1748 that the castle was then uninhabited: 'but the Bowling Green is now common for any gentleman that pays for his pleasure. It is generally the rendezvous of both sexes for an evening's Walk ... I have seen the beaumonde here make a very handsome figure.'[2]

Notwithstanding these facilities, civic or public tree-planting was undertaken in Ireland with increasing seriousness from the middle of the eighteenth century. It became an integral part of the urban planning of Dublin and of other Irish cities. It was also a component of many smaller towns and villages. In many places, as in Dublin, the planting was initiated and maintained by the civic authorities. In others, as in the case of the Mall in Armagh, the tree-planting was paid for by voluntary subscription from the community. In yet others, as in the case of the Mardyke Walk in Cork, a single philanthropist was responsible for funding the planting.

The new tree-planting shaded not only streets, but also a variety of other urban areas, such as the malls, walks and greens where the citizens were accustomed to walking for recreation. In some cities and towns, rides and drives were available, since exercise and fresh air were also taken on horseback and by carriage.

1 – The Mardyke Walk, Cork (courtesy National Library of Ireland)

These were also often planted with trees. Trees were also planted to give shade to urban bowling greens, around health spas and in 'pleasure gardens' – those gardens designed for public entertainment that were characteristic of urban social life during the eighteenth century. (The latter are included in this article because though they were fashionable, they were not exclusive in the way that the later Dublin squares such as Merrion Square and Fitzwilliam Square were exclusive to the residents of the respective squares.)[3] Pleasure gardens were public in the sense they were open to all who could pay the relatively small charge, and so were used by a socially mixed company. For example, Thomas Campbell wrote of the crowds in the plea-sure gardens of the Rotunda in Dublin in 1778:

> On these nights the rotunda and gardens are prodigiously crowded and the price of admission being only sixpence, everybody goes. It would perhaps benefit the charity if the price were doubled, for though it might exclude many, it would, I think, bring more money. On the other hand, it must be con-fessed that the motley appearance gives an air of freedom, for the best com-pany attends as well as those to whom another sixpence might be an object.[4]

The tree of choice for the planting of public urban spaces was the lime or linden tree. It was known to be tolerant of the smoke of large cities and towns. For exam-ple, Thomas Fairchild, author of a book called *The City Gardener* (1722), wrote of the planting of the lime tree in the London squares of his time: '...all the squares in London which are already made, are proof the Lime-tree will bear the London Smoke'.[5] The elm tree was also commonly used for urban planting. Its relatively narrow, upright form, like that of the lime, was especially adaptable to confined urban areas. The use of ash, sycamore and chestnut is only occasionally recorded. As regards the layout of tree-planting, trees in confined urban areas were usually planted in orderly rows and spaced along the rows at regular intervals.

Some planted areas were laid out with gravelled walks for exercise. The gravel or sand used in Ireland had a variety of origins. Particularly prized was that from Rathfriland, county Down. Walter Harris described it in 1744: 'the sand dug out of the quarries is of singular use in garden-walks, being of binding quality always dry and clean and of a fine bright colour.'[6] However, the dark colour of the gravel used in many Irish walks was the subject of visitor comment. An English vis-itor, Anne Plumptre, wrote in 1817: 'The gravel of the country is ... of a dark hue unpleasant to the eye, and at the first glance scarcely better than cinder ashes; yet it is fine, besides it binds well, is firm and pleasant to the foot.'[7]

———

THE MALL

MALLS WERE PROMENADES, USUALLY TREE-LINED, THAT WERE LAID OUT IN urban areas to encourage citizens to take exercise by walking. They were also prominent places of social intercourse and display. In the eighteenth century, malls featured in Dublin, Cork and Waterford, as well as other smaller cities and towns. The layout and planting varied. In Cork, for example, trees were planted on one side of the mall only. In Dublin, they were planted on both sides. In Waterford, the mall featured a double row of elm trees on both sides.[8]

Dublin's mall was short-lived. It was laid out on Sackville Street (now O'Connell Street) in the 1740s by Luke Gardiner. Having obtained ownership of one side of the street, Gardiner demolished the houses and widened the street to approximately 150 feet. He then rebuilt, laying out a mall, forty-eight feet wide, down the centre of the newly widened street. First known as Gardiner's Mall, it was enclosed within a low wall and was ornamented with a statue of General Blakeney by the sculptor Van Nost.[9] At the north end was a fountain.[10] However, in 1786, William Wilson reported with approval the mall's subsequent removal: 'Within these few years past, Sackville Street has received very considerable improvements particularly by removing the Mall at its centre, and by opening the entire into one noble street of one hundred and twenty feet wide.'[11]

Cork's mall was a place of fashionable resort in spite of its poor paving and the disagreeable smell emanating from the adjoining canal at low tide.[12] Charles Smith observed in 1750:

> The public walks of this city, in comparison of the number of inhabitants, are few and not very commodious: that most frequented is called the Mall which has little to recommend it except its being planted with trees ... this mall is ill paved yet on public days, it is well filled with the beau monde of the city and, during the assizes, with considerable numbers from the county.[13]

Thomas Campbell described the fashionable crowd in 1778, and remarked with approval on the filling up of the sometimes evil-smelling canal:

> After [Sunday] service, they generally betake themselves to a public walk called The Mall which is no more than a very ill-paved quay on one of their canals, with a row of trees on one side and houses on the other. It is a pleasure to see, however, how they are filling up this canal.[14]

In spite of its shortcomings, Samuel Derrick, writing in 1786, extolled the virtues of the company, especially the ladies, frequenting the place: 'it is paved worse than the streets of London, yet I have seen it filled with very genteel company, and a greater number of pretty women than I have ever seen together in any other town.'[15]

2 – The Mall, Castlebar, county Mayo, in the 1890s
The age of the trees suggest the mall was planted in the eighteenth century. Note the trees on the right,
recently planted to eventually replace the ancient trees. (courtesy National Library of Ireland)

Waterford's mall, on the other hand, earned the unreserved approval of a visitor such as Charles Smith who wrote in 1746:

The Mall is a beautiful walk, about 200 hundred yards long and proportionately broad, situated on the East end of the city. The draining and levelling of the ground, which was formerly a marsh, was done at very considerable expense; it is planted with rows of Elms and the sides of the walk are fenced

with a stone wall. Near the centre facing this beautiful walk stands the Bishop's palace, which not only adds a considerable beauty to the Mall, but also reciprocally receives the same from it. Here the ladies and gentlemen assemble on fine evenings where they have the opportunity of each other's conversation. Nothing can be more agreeable than to see this shady walk crowded with the fair sex of the city, taking the air, enjoying the charms of a pleasant evening, and improving their health; nor need I inform the reader that this city has been long since peculiarly celebrated for the beauties of its female inhabitants.[16]

3 – The Mall, Birr, county Offaly,
in the 1890s

Trees, probably planted in the early nineteenth century,
flank one side of the mall only,
as they did in other malls such as that in Cork city.
(courtesy National Library of Ireland)

4 – The Mall, Bunclody, county Wexford,
in the 1890s

Lime trees flank the narrow, stepped canal constructed
in the mid-nineteenth century.
(courtesy Irish Architectural Archive)

The smaller city of Armagh did not obtain its mall until 1797. Then, a group of local subscribers funded the development of an eight-acre common in the middle of the city:

> A very fine mall or terrace has been lately enclosed with a dwarf wall, dyke and iron gates within which is a neat gravel walk, encompassing a lawn ... This work was completed by subscription which will be returned, as the rent produced from the lawn in some years will repay both principal and interest...[17]

Towns, like Loughrea, county Galway,[18] Castlebar, county Mayo,[19] and Kinsale, county Cork,[20] enjoyed malls on a smaller scale (Plate 2). The mall in Birr, county Offaly, was the scene of musical entertainment:[21] 'The principal public walk is the shaded terrace on Oxmantown Mall. In this place, which is occasionally enlivened on Sunday evenings by the attendance of a military band, the gentry of the town usually seek their afternoon recreation' (Plate 3).[22] The malls of two smaller towns, Westport, county Mayo, and Bunclody (formerly Newtown-barry), county Wexford, boasted formal canals running down the centre (Plate 4). James Fraser reported of the mall at Westport in 1844: '...through the middle of this street [Main Street] flows a clear transparent stream of water banked in on both sides by quays on which are planted rows of trees,

5 – The Mall, Westport, county Mayo, in the 1890s
The river, canalised in the late eighteenth century, was flanked on both sides by trees.
(courtesy National Library of Ireland)

bearing a close resemblance to a street in a Dutch town...'[23] (Plate 5).

The malls in some towns were associated with the town's assembly rooms, so they became the location of the town's indoor as well as outdoor entertainments. Such was the case in Waterford city and in Youghal[24] and Cobh (Cove), both in county Cork. John Barrow reported in 1836: 'At Cove, they have a small parade which overlooks the harbour, and appears well adapted as a lounging place, at one

end of which is an assembly-room, where the club [yacht club] hold their meetings, their dinners and balls.'[25] A small village like Summerhill in county Meath also boasted a mall:

> The village of Summerhill is composed of one street, about 900 feet long, and 200 feet wide, and in this area, a green mall in the form of a parallelogram has been formed, enclosed on each side by a row of full grown lime trees. It is highly ornamental and exceedingly healthful for the inhabitants and their children.[26]

THE STREET

SOME CITY STREETS THAT WERE NOT formally designated as malls or walks were also planted with rows of trees. The most common street tree in Dublin was the London plane, the hardy hybrid between the Oriental plane and the Occidental plane. Lime and elm trees, with their vertical proportions, were also favoured for civic planting. For example, lime trees were chosen to ornament the streets of Castlecomer[27] and Inistioge,[28] county Kilkenny, and Maynooth, county Kildare (Plate 6). Elms were planted along the wide principal streets of Stradbally, county Laois.[29] Other trees were used less frequently. Sycamore was used at Headfort Place in Kells, county Meath,[30] and rows of ash lined a cross street at Castlemartyr, county Cork.[31]

Avenues of trees were also used to mark the approach to some towns. An avenue of lime trees was planted along the Kenmare Road as it approached Killarney, county Kerry.[32] An avenue of elms marked approaches to towns such as Maynooth, county

6 – *Main Street, Maynooth, county Kildare, in the 1890s*
Young trees on clear trunks planted along the edge of the wide, flanking pavements.

7 – *Castleblayney, county Monaghan, in the 1890s*
The main street 'borrows' the view of the trees in the avenue leading to Blayney Castle. Note the clipped street trees on the left.

(photos courtesy National Library of Ireland)

Kildare,[33] and Castlemartyr[34] and Doneraile,[35] county Cork, and the ash was selected for avenues approaching the town of Templemore, county Tipperary,[36] and the village of Gracehill, county Antrim.[37] The latter avenue of ash trees met to form a graceful archway over the road. In a town like Castleblayney, county Monaghan, the main street 'borrowed' the view of the avenue of trees leading to Blayney Castle (Plate 7).

Some towns were ornamented with more informal planting schemes. For example, walnuts that had been planted in and around Lambeg, county Down, gave the village a distinctive arboreal character.[38] Of the town of Hillsborough, county Down, Arthur Young observed in 1775: 'Lord Hillsborough has marked the approach to his town by many small plantations on the tops of the hills through which the road leads.'[39] Of Doneraile, county Cork, William Wilson reported in 1786: 'It is a very agreeable place being surrounded by fine, stately groves of fir which, flourishing at all seasons of the year, render the town extremely pleasant.'[40]

8 – The Mardyke Walk, Cork

A view by Sir John Carr published in 1806, when the
elm trees were about eighty years old.
Note the walk raised over the surrounding meadows
and the views back towards the city.

THE WALK

W HEREAS A MALL AND A STREET WERE SPACES THAT WERE DISTINCTLY URBAN in character, a 'walk', on the other hand, was usually on the edge of or outside a town. Typically, they stretched along the banks of a river or a canal, and were usually drained, levelled, gravelled and planted with trees. Cork city boasted two public walks known respectively as Friars Walk and the Mardyke. Friars Walk was a little out of the city, and though shaded by trees and enjoying a good view, it was relatively little used. The Mardyke was the more important of the two (Plates 1, 8, 9).[41] Charles Smith wrote:

> [The] Mardyke is a pleasant walk, being a bank walled on both sides and filled up, extending westwards from the city near an English mile and washed, on either hand, by a channel of the river. This bank is carried through a marshy island and was done at the private expense of Mr Edward Webber

9 – The Mardyke Walk, Cork
The trees in the 1890s were approximately 170 years old.
(courtesy National Library of Ireland)

anno 1719 who also built a house at the West end where are good gardens planted with fruit for the accommodation and entertainment of those who frequent the walk.[42]

From the shade of the Mardyke's tall elms, it was possible to enjoy extensive and varied views of the city and countryside. However, by the time John Barrow reported in 1836, the Mardyke, like many walks in other cities, had fallen into disuse as the fashionable promenade of the notables of the city.[43]

Dubliners enjoyed two waterside walks. One was around the City Bason (*sic*) and the other was along the banks of the Grand Canal. The City Bason – the reservoir of the city's water supply – was located in a walled enclosure on the western edge of the city. It was about a half-a-mile in circumference. Of its recreational use, Walter Harris observed in 1766:

> This is the pleasantest, most elegant and sequestered place of relaxation the citizens can boast of; the reservoir being mounded and terraced all round and planted with quickset hedges, limes and elms having beautiful walks between; in a situation that commands a most satisfactory prospect of fine country to the south, bounded by a view of that enchanting chain of hills, called the Dublin mountains ... The entrance is elegant by a lofty iron gate.[44]

10 – The Harcourt Lock, Grand Canal, Dublin.
This early nineteenth-century print shows the elm trees that were planted for some miles on both sides of the canal.
(courtesy Irish Architectural Archive)

opposite – 12 – The Grand Canal, Dublin, in the 1950s
The elm trees on the canal banks were then almost 150 years old. (courtesy National Library of Ireland)

11 – Lithograph by John Irwine Whitty of Baggot Street Bridge, Grand Canal, Dublin (1851)
'A delightful place of exercise for the citizens'. The elm trees were then about fifty years old.

The trees were formally planted in rows. The walks between the rows were of grass, not of gravel, as was more usual in public walks.[45] At one end of the basin was a Chinese-style bridge and palisades, over which there was a fine view of the Grand Canal.[46] However, in 1837, Samuel Lewis noted it as a place of declining fashion. He described it as 'formerly a favourite promenade'.[47]

The Dublin reach of the Grand Canal – the canal that traversed the south side of the city – was completed in 1796 (Plate 10). Its banks were planted with elm trees, and a gravel walk was laid out between the trees and the water. William Wilson reported their recreational use: '...the sides of the canal for some miles into the country are planted with elm-trees which render its banks in fair weather a delightful place of exercise for the citizens.'[48] The canal banks continued to be a much-used place of recreation throughout the nineteenth century (Plate 11). The trees reached splendid maturity during the last century (Plate 12).

Kilkenny city enjoyed two walks, one along a canalised section of the river and another by the castle walls. The latter extended for about a mile (Plate 13).[49] A. Atkinson, reporting in 1815, admired the shimmering dresses of the promenading Kilkenny ladies:

> ...the banks of the river are richly planted with lime trees, which gives the approach to the latter [Kilkenny] a rich and picturesque appearance, and in the summer season, constitutes this walk, to the citizens and their families, a cool retreat from the noise and bustle of the town, and an elegant promenade in the hours of relaxation from business. The reflection of so many light dresses, together with the crystal waters of the Nore, through the foliage on the banks of the river, was rather an entertaining prospect to the traveller in his progress.[50]

The town of Cavan also enjoyed a promenade. Samuel Lewis reported in 1837: 'A large garden handsomely laid out in walks and planted was left by the will of the late Lady Farnham ... as a promenade for the inhabitants.'[51] By contrast, the promenade of the city of Londonderry was along the city's walls. Samuel Lewis noted: 'the walls were eighteen hundred yards in circuit, twenty four feet high, and of sufficient thickness to form an agreeable promenade on top.'[52] The walls of the town of Clonmel, county Tipperary, likewise, served as a walk for the townspeople until they were taken down in the early nineteenth century.[53]

13 – The Avenue, Kilkenny, in the 1890s
Kilkenny boasted two walks shaded with lime trees, one along the riverbank and the other, shown in this illustration, by the castle walls. (courtesy National Library of Ireland)

THE RIDE

RIDING WAS REGARDED AS AN EXERCISE AS BENEFICIAL AS WALKING. RICHARD Lewis wrote of the banks of the Grand Canal in 1786: 'It is adorned with trees on either side for several miles, and having fine gravel walks, is a most agreeable place either for riding or walking.' [54] A prime location for recreational riding and carriage driving was the Circular Road around Dublin. It formed a circuit of nine miles, and was greatly enjoyed by visitors to the city as well as the residents. Richard Lewis wrote in 1786:

This road nearly surrounds the city and is carried on in as circular form as the situations would admit. It begins on one side of the river and terminates on the opposite shore. It forms a very pleasant and agreeable ride, and adds much to the entertainment and recreation of the citizens of Dublin.[55]

Carr added his praises in 1806:

I rented a jingle, and took an airing on the circular road which surrounds the city, and has been made on the site of an old Danish wall, formerly erected for the protection of the capital. The view almost everywhere on this superb road is delightful.[56]

Anne Plumptre remembered 'evenings spent pleasantly in drives ... around the Circular Road'.[57] Its shortcoming, according to Bowden in 1790, was the lack of trees. He observed: 'if both sides of the road were planted with trees at equal distances, as I observed on the Grand Canal, I do not believe there would be so fine an environ in Europe.'[58] By 1837, parts of the road were already flanked by new buildings associated with the expanding city.[59] Less rural in atmosphere, it ceased to be attractive as a ride or drive for visitors and citizens alike.

THE GREEN

14 – *Engraving by James Malton of St Stephen's Green, Dublin (1796)*
The walk on the near side, known as Beaux Walk, was the most fashionable in Dublin. The trees were lime trees.

MANY TOWNS AND VILLAGES had what were known as greens. Richard Pococke noted in 1752 that the town of Donegal was 'built almost all around a sort of triangular Green'.[60] The greens were usually derived from ancient 'commons'. These had been areas of rough, unimproved open space, or green, to which there was common access. On an everyday basis, a commons was used for a variety of activities such as the pasturing of sheep or cattle or the drying of clothes. Some commons were level and were suitable for use for large gatherings, like that situated in the village of Brideswell, county Roscommon, where a huge annual patronal festival was held.[61] Some towns, like Carrick-on-Suir, county Tipperary, had a commons that was called a fair green, on which horses, cattle, sheep and pig fairs were held at regular intervals.

A civic authority or a local community sometimes adopted a commons legally for the purpose of improving it and laying it out for more formal recreation. This was the case in Dublin where the marshy and insalubrious common that was known as St Stephen's Green was first enclosed in 1664. It was subsequently drained, levelled and surrounded with formal public walks. It was, in its day, the most substantial green in Ireland and among the largest in Europe (Plate 14).[62] Each side measured nearly a quarter-of-a-mile in length. Walter Harris wrote of its subsequent development in 1766: 'This spring the lime trees were planted on each side of the walks around St Stephen's Green.'[63] In another part of his book, he described the layout of the green at that time:

> It is enclosed by a low wall, with entrances from every side by gates and turnstiles at proper distances. The outer walks are gravelled and planted with trees on each side; the interior walks (seldom used) are enclosed by thorn hedges on each side and divided from the others by a fosse, which serves for a drain to carry off the water from the walks and the green. The inside is a spacious lawn at the centre of which is a curious equestrian brass statue of his late Majesty George II by Van Nost. In the walks may be seen, in fine weather, a resort of as much beauty and gaiety as the Ranelagh Gardens [London], St. James' Park etc.[64]

The walks on each side of St Stephen's Green came to have their own names. The north side (the most fashionable side) was called Beaux Walk; the east side, Monks Walk; the west side, French Walk; and the south side, Leeson Walk.[65] Thomas Campbell wrote in 1778 that the most popular times for ' genteel company' to walk in the green was during the evenings and 'on Sundays after two o'clock'.[66] However, within a short span of thirty years, the green was no longer fashionable as a place to walk. Charles T. Bowden reported in 1790: 'Stephen's Green is a fine extensive square, once the most fashionable place of resort but now I understand much in decline.'[67] In 1806 Sir John Carr wrote of a decline in the green's maintenance: '...it is a fine meadow, walled and planted with a double row of trees but is disfigured by a dirty ditch on every side, the receptacle of dead cats and dogs.'[68]

In 1817 Anne Plumptre reported that the neglected green was being taken in hand again and that it was in the process of being transformed into a more conventional public park. The low wall with which it had been previously surrounded was being replaced by an iron railing. The interior, which had previously been in the form of a meadow as the walks had been confined to the green's perimeter, was being laid out in walks and shrubberies. Although the old thorn hedges had been removed and the unpleasant ditch filled in, she saw, to her regret, that not one of the old trees had been left standing in the process of these improvements. (This new layout was to be itself transformed in 1880.).[69]

Formally laid-out greens featured also in smaller cities and towns. Samuel Lewis described the green (better known as Eyre Square) of Galway city in 1837 as 'protected by a handsome iron railing, and ... tastefully laid out in walks, and decorated with planting'.[70] He also noted the green at Castlebar, county Mayo, as 'a pleasant promenade'.[71] Clonakilty, county Cork, had also been improved by the formation of a spacious green, 'the centre of which was planted and laid out in walks so as to form an agreeable promenade'.[72] On a smaller scale, villages with greens included Harold's Cross and Sandymount, now absorbed into the city of Dublin.[73] At Gracehill, county Armagh, the Moravian village was laid out in 1758 around three sides of a green, 'the interior of which was surrounded by a paling and a double row of trees, and which contained a gravel walk, a fishpond and a shrubbery in the centre'.[74]

THE BOWLING GREEN

BOWLING WAS A POPULAR SPORT DURING THE SEVENTEENTH AND EIGHTEENTH centuries. It required the creation and maintenance of a level lawn of fine grass if the bowl or ball that was used in the game were to run true. Already in the seventeenth century there were private bowling greens in the gardens of great magnates, such as that previously referred to at Kilkenny Castle. Public bowling greens in cities such as Dublin, Cork and Waterford were recorded in the eighteenth century.

Rocque's 1760 map of Dublin locates three bowling greens in the city.[75] The grandest and most impressive of the three appears to have been the Marlborough Bowling Green. It was located on Marlborough Street, was surrounded by formal plantations of trees and adjoined the garden of the impressive Tyrone House. A second bowling green indicated on the map lay behind the Mayoralty House (now called the Mansion House) on Dawson Street, and a third – more informal in layout – is shown at Oxmantown Green adjoining a barracks (now called Collins Barracks). This green was also used as an archery green.[76]

Trees were also planted around Cork's bowling green. Charles Smith, noted in 1750 that they were regularly trimmed:

> On Hammonds marsh is a large pleasant bowling green, planted, on its margin, with trees kept regularly cut whose shade makes it an agreeable walk: it is also washed by a branch of the Lee; and, on it, a band of music has been supported by subscription for the entertainment of the ladies and gentlemen who frequent it. Adjacent to it is the assembly house...[77]

Chetwood had reported in 1748 that the shady walks around the bowling green were considered pleasant for walking in the mornings before the bowling enthusiasts came to play on the green in the afternoon.[78]

Trees were also planted around the bowling green in Waterford city. Charles

Smith reported in 1746:

> Near the Mall is a pleasant Bowling-green for the diversion of the citizens
> which is a most innocent and healthful exercise when, in summer time after
> the business of the day is ended, they sometimes recreate themselves. This
> Bowling-green is situated on the east end of the kay [*sic*], a little beyond the
> Ring-tower, from where to the Mall, trees are planted, as also on the sides of
> the Bowling-green, which makes this part of the town (affording the prospect
> of the river and shipping) very agreeable.[79]

15 – Engraving by James Malton of the Rotunda Gardens, Dublin (1793)

On the left of the picture is one of the Doric pavilions and the new iron railing with lamps, erected c.1785.

Smaller towns like Kinsale, county Cork, also supported a bowling green.[80]

THE PLEASURE GARDEN

D UBLIN, LIKE LONDON, PARIS and other European cities in the eighteenth century, had its pleasure gardens. These were gardens laid out in the cities as places of outdoor entertainment during the summer season. Shady promenades, alcoves for taking tea, areas for dancing and for concerts, both vocal and instrumental, as well as special lighting effects in the evening, ensured that pleasure gardens were fashionable places of assembly. On occasion there were special events such as concerts by military bands, fireworks displays and acrobatic performances.[81] The Rotunda Gardens were Dublin's principal pleasure gardens (Plate 15). They were laid out in 1738 and continued to be fashionable a century later. The entrance charge in 1778 was sixpence. On certain evenings of the year, upwards of fifteen hundred people were recorded in attendance.[82]

The gardens were originally designed by a professional landscape gardener, Robert Stevenson, who 'was engaged for over two years to lay out the gardens at a fee of £10 a month. In the last three months of 1738, over 600 elms were planted and in the following year the gardens opened to the public.'[83] John Bushe described the gardens in 1764:

a large square piece of ground enclosed, and three sides of the four prettily laid out in walks and plantations of groves, shrubs, trees etc., on the fourth stands the hospital. In the middle, nearly of this garden, is a spacious and beautiful bowling green. On the side of the green, opposite the hospital, the ground being much higher, is formed into a high hanging bank of nearly 30 feet slope, on the top of which is laid out a grand terrace walk, commanding a fine view of the hospital: on the upper side of this terrace, and nearly encompassed with groves and shrubberies, is built a very pretty orchestra.[84]

In 1786 elegant iron railings, set on a low stonewall, were erected around the garden to replace the original high wall. Lighting globes were erected along the railings to give a truly magnificent effect at night,[85] and pavilions, with columns in the Doric order, were erected in the north-east and north-west angles.[86] In the same year, Richard Lewis wrote:

The Rotunda and Gardens are open three evenings a week, during the summer season, when there are excellent concerts of vocal and instrumental music. At such times, and on Sunday evenings, when they are much resorted to, there is a numerous and brilliant assembly of the first people in Dublin.[87]

A second pleasure gardens for Dublin was opened in 1768. An entrepreneur purchased the house and grounds of Willbrook, Ranelagh, to create what became known as the Ranelagh Gardens. This was a commercial venture, unlike the Rotunda Gardens, the proceeds from which went to defray the expenses of the adjoining hospital. F. Elrington Ball described the Ranelagh Gardens as 'gardens of entertainment, with a theatre and gardens laid out with alcoves and bowers for tea drinkers. A fine band was constantly in attendance, the favourite vocalists of the day appeared in the theatre and some of the earliest astronauts made their ascents from the gardens.'[88] Ball is referring to the balloon ascents that took place from the gardens, the best known of which was that of Mr Crosbie in 1785. Unfortunately, the popularity of the Ranelagh Gardens, unlike that of the Rotunda Gardens, was short-lived.

THE SPA

'TAKING THE WATERS' WAS A COMMON WAY OF CURING AILMENTS DURING THE eighteenth century. It consisted of bathing in or drinking medicinal spring waters once or twice a day, usually in the morning, and, then, in the evening during the summer months. A variety of entertainments were devised to keep the visitors occupied during the long hours that separated the twice-daily partaking. Tree-lined promenades, gardens and parterres were laid out. Assembly rooms, breakfast rooms, marble fountains and other ornamental structures were erected.

The most prominent spa in the south of Ireland was at Mallow, county Cork. Arthur Young observed in 1775 that the spring was in the shade of some noble poplars.[89] Richard Twiss wrote in the same year of the spring, and the setting that had been created for it: the 'waters, which burst out of the bottom of a great limestone rock, are at the end of a straight, well planted walk and canal of about a furlong and a half in length'.[90] Visitors were entertained by a walk in the meadows of the town. William Chetwood reported in 1748: 'The meadows where the company walk are very pleasant. Here is a very beautiful shell house and grotto built by subscription of which, they say, a worthy Doctor of Divinity was the contriver.'[91] Visitors to the Mallow spa also enjoyed riding or driving in a carriage along an informal circular drive around the town, which was shaded for the most part by lofty trees.[92]

The most prominent spa in the north of Ireland was at Ballynahinch, county Down. Samuel Lewis recorded the arrangements in 1837:

> In a picturesque and fertile valley south of the town is a powerful chalybeate spring; there are two wells, one for drinking, one for bathing. The grounds adjoining are tastefully laid out in walks, parterres etc. An assembly room and a newsroom have been erected.[93]

Sir Charles Coote described the arrangements made for visitors to the spa at Swanlinbar, county Cavan. It was set in an ornamental garden with neat plantations:

> The celebrated spa is in an ornamental enclosure, which is very handsomely improved with pleasant walks and neat plantations. The breakfast room is contiguous to the well, and here the company generally partake of this sociable meal, and ride or walk till dinner, when an excellent ordinary is provided.[94]

Pleasant walks for the entertainment of visitors were also laid out around the spa in the grounds of Lucan House, near Dublin. Richard Lewis described them in 1786: 'Lucan boasts a celebrated spa .. the well is sheltered in a deep niche neatly executed in hewn stone. There is a rural thatched seat for those who drink the waters, and space allowed for their walking about.'[95]

There was a multiplicity of smaller, lesser-known spas throughout the country. They were usually surrounded by planting. For example, birch trees shaded the mineral spring at Clonbella, near Birr, county Offaly.[96] A small resort with residential accommodation was developed in the grounds of Tollymore Park, county Down. It was unusual in that it was not developed for drinking mineral water but for drinking medicinal goats' whey 'in May and June, when the milk on account of the flow-ers on which the goats feed is in greatest perfection'.[97]

CHURCHYARDS, CEMETERIES AND SHRINES

THE TREE-PLANTING OF RELIGIOUS SITES CONTRIBUTED DECISIVELY TO MANY urban environments. The tree-lined approach to the church in Virginia, coun-ty Cavan, made a major impact on the aspect of the town. The central avenue to the church and the adjoining avenues were in the form of a crow's foot or *patte d'oie* design, the three avenues radiating from a central point (Plate 16). Charles Smith wrote in 1746 of an area by the church in the town of Dungarvan, county Waterford, that was 'handsomely laid out into gravel walks and planted with trees, from whence may be seen a prospect of the harbour and the ruins of an oppo-site abbey and church which makes the place a pleasant walk'.[98] Richard Lewis wrote 1786: 'Near Howth-house stands the family chapel, a small but neat modern

16 – The Square, Virginia, county Cavan, in the 1890s
The avenue to the church in the centre and the flanking avenues form a crow's-foot or patte d'oie
radiating from a central point. (courtesy National Library of Ireland)

structure encompassed with a grove of ash trees.'[99] The church at Castlemartyr, county Cork, dating from the eighteenth century, was located in a spacious plot of ground surrounded by lofty elms.

Trees were also planted to augment the picturesque quality of ancient abbeys and churches. For example, St Mary's Church in Callan, county Kilkenny, was set in 'a small lawn environed by gravel walks and bounded by the King's river. This stream is crossed by a neat wooden bridge leading onto the abbey field in which are situated the venerable ruins of an ancient friary.'[100] An avenue of ash and sycamore formed the approach to the ruins of the Franciscan abbey at Desertmore, county Cork.[101] Horse chestnut, lime and sycamore trees surrounded the ruins of an old church at the Grange, Baldoyle, county Dublin.[102]

The tradition of planting trees around holy wells, the waters of which were believed to affect cures, is also well attested. For example, William Chetwood noted of St Bartholomew's Well, Cork, in 1746: 'The Well is enclosed with green trees, close to the side of the road and even the sight of it looks refreshing.'[103] William Wilson in 1786 noted that the holy well in St Lazerian, Old Leighlin, county Carlow, was 'shaded by many great ash trees'.[104] The grounds around Mullins Wells near Ballinahinch, county Galway, were tastefully laid out, according to Samuel Lewis.(105)

CONCLUSION

THE IRISH TRADITION OF CIVIC PLANTING PRODUCED SOME REMARKABLE URBAN landscapes. The waterside landscapes of the Grand Canal, Dublin, and the malls in Westport, county Mayo, and Bunclody, county Wexford, are just some that survive to enhance their urban environments today. However, many civic planting schemes, such as those at the Rotunda Gardens and the City Bason (*sic*) in Dublin, which were notable in the, have been swept away. Some civic planting schemes such as that in Eyre Square, Galway, have been modernised to such an extent that their traditional virtues are no longer evident. In other instances, such as in Merrion Square, Dublin, and The Square in Clonakilty, county Cork, the traditional planting has been abandoned. This is a situation that contrasts with the strict conservation of the buildings around them, yet such squares were conceived as an aesthetic unity of buildings and planting. The fact that traditional civic-planting schemes are as important a part of our physical heritage as the buildings that surround them needs affirmation.

———

ENDNOTES

The following abbreviations are used:

Lewis, *Topographical Dictionary*   Samuel Lewis, *A Topographical Dictionary of Ireland*,
                                     2 vols (London, 1837)
Lewis, *Dublin Guide*   Richard Lewis, *The Dublin Guide* (Dublin 1786)

[1]   Lewis, *Topographical Dictionary*, II, 600.
[2]   William R. Chetwood, *A Tour through Ireland* (1748) 85.
[3]   Dublin City Council, *The Georgian Squares of Dublin* (Dublin, 2006)
[4]   Thomas Campbell, *A Philosophical Survey of the South of Ireland* (London, 1778) 27.
[5]   Todd Longstaffe-Gowan, *The London Town Garden* (New Haven and London, 2001) 189.
[6]   Walter Harris, *The Ancient and Present State of the County of Down* (Dublin, 1744) 12.
[7]   Anne Plumptre, *Narrative of a Residence in Ireland* (London, 1817) 22.
[8]   Richard Pococke, *Pococke's Tour in Ireland in 1752*, edited by G.T. Stokes (Dublin and London, 1891) 133.
[9]   Richard Twiss, *A Tour in Ireland in 1775* (London, 1776) 30.
[10] Lewis, *Dublin Guide*, 45. General Blakeney was a hero of the Seven Years War with France. The fountain, one of a number erected in Dublin's streets at the time, remained in position until 1807 when it was removed because the wind blew its water onto the road. The water froze in bad weather making the road around the fountain hazardous.
[11] William Wilson, *The Post Chaise Companion ... through Ireland* (Dublin, 1786) xii.
[12] Chetwood, *A Tour through Ireland*, 56.
[13] Charles Smith, *The ancient and present State of the City and County of Cork* (Dublin, 1750) 349.
[14] Thomas Campbell, *A Philosophical Survey*, 182.
[15] Samuel Derrick, *Letters from Leverpole, Chester, Corke etc.* (London, 1767) 44.
[16] Charles Smith, *The antient and present State of the County of Waterford* (Dublin, 1746) 193.
[17] Sir Charles Coote, *Statistical Survey of the Co. of Armagh* (Dublin, 1804) 322. The rent derived from the mall presumably was the financial return from selling the hay from the lawn. The common was used as a horse racecourse from 1731 to 1773.
[18] Lewis, *Topographical Dictionary*, II, 279.
[19] *ibid.*, I, 178.
[20] Smith, *City and County of Cork*, 226.
[21] Thomas Cook, *Pictures of Parsonstown* (Dublin, 1826) 244.
[22] *ibid.*, 230.
[23] James Fraser, *A Handbook for Travellers in Ireland* (London, 1844), 473.
[24] Lewis, *Topographical Dictionary*, II, 679.
[25] John Barrow, *Tour round Ireland* (London, 1836) 332.
[26] A. Atkinson, *The Irish Tourist* (Dublin, 1815) 358. James Fraser, in *A Handbook for Travellers in Ireland* (1859) 558, notes that the village of Summerhill (and presumably the mall) had already fallen into decay.
[27] Atkinson, *The Irish Tourist*, 460.
[28] Lewis, *Topographical Dictionary*, I, 680.
[29] Sir Charles Coote, *General View of the Queen's County* (Dublin, 1801) 169.

30 Atkinson, *The Irish Tourist*, 275.
31 Lewis, *Topographical Dictionary*, I, 293.
32 *ibid.*, II, 93.
33 *ibid.*, II, 187.
34 *ibid.*, I, 293.
35 *ibid.*, I, 462.
36 *ibid.*, II, 564.
37 Plumptre, *Narrative of a Residence in Ireland*, 160.
38 John Dubourdieu, *Statistical Survey of the county of Down* (Dublin, 1802) 161.
39 Arthur Young, *A Tour in Ireland...* (London, 1775) 133.
40 Wilson, *The Post Chaise Companion*, 341.
41 Campbell, *A Philosophical Survey*, 103. He refers to 'another public walk, west of the city, called the Redhouse Walk, cut through very low grounds, for a mile in length, planted on each side, where the lower sort walk'.
42 Smith, *City and County of Cork*, 349.
43 Barrow, *Tour round Ireland*, 323. Although the Mardyke had by then fallen into disuse as a fashionable promenade, it remains to this day an important recreational facility for the city.
44 Walter Harris, *The History and Antiquities of the City of Dublin* (Dublin, 1776), 482.
45 Wilson, *The Post Chaise Companion*, xxvii.
46 Lewis, *Dublin Guide*, 33.
47 Lewis, *Topographical Dictionary*, I, 515.
48 Wilson, *The Post Chaise Companion*, xxvii.
49 Twiss, *A Tour in Ireland in 1775*, 159.
50 Atkinson, *The Irish Tourist*, 422.
51 Lewis, *Topographical Dictionary*, I, 307.
52 *ibid.*, II, 263.
53 John Loveday, *Diary of a Tour through Ireland* (1790) 36.
54 Lewis, *Dublin Guide*, 78. Of course, the extensive Phoenix Park was also used for riding. The staff of Dublin Castle used the garden of the castle occasionally for riding: 'There is a very large garden adjoining the lower castle yard, but which having neither beauty or elegance, is only occasionally made use of as a place for riding or walking by His Excellency and his servants.' See *Dublin Guide*, 86.
55 *ibid.*, 104.
56 Sir John Carr, *The Stranger in Ireland* (London, 1806), 127.
57 Plumptre, *Narrative of a Residence in Ireland*, 81.
58 Charles T. Bowden, *A Tour through Ireland in 1790* (Dublin, 1791) 10.
59 Lewis, *Topographical Dictionary*, II, 515.
60 Richard Pococke, *Pococke's Tour in Ireland in 1752*, edited by G.T. Stokes, 69. Some Irish towns are characterised by a central square or green that is triangular or diamond-shaped. Triangular squares occur, for example, in Donegal town, Castleblayney, county Monaghan, and Clones, county Cavan. Some town squares are called 'The Diamond', usually indicating a square of an irregular trapezoidal shape, as in Monaghan town, and Coleraine and Kilrea, both in county Derry.
61 Lewis, *Topographical Dictionary*, I, 215,
62 Twiss, *A Tour in Ireland in 1775*, 13.

[63] Harris, *The History and Antiquities of the City of Dublin*, 343.

[64] *ibid.*, 481. Harris also comments on the extraordinary number of snipe that wintered on the green, enjoying its marshy character.

[65] John Bushe, *Hibernia Curiosa* (London, 1764) frontispiece: map of Dublin.

[66] Campbell, *A Philosophical Survey*, 6.

[67] Bowden, *A Tour through Ireland in 1790*.

[68] Sir John Carr, *The Stranger in Ireland*, 130.

[69] Plumptre, *Narrative of a Residence in Ireland*, 51. This layout can be examined in the engraved bird's-eye view of the city of Dublin presented as a supplement to the readers of the *Illustrated London News* in 1865. In 1880 Sir Benjamin Lee Guinness Bt. (later Lord Ardilaun) sponsored the redesign of the square by William Brodrick Thomas and William Sheppard. The redesign included artificial rockwork by Pulham & Sons, and buildings by James Franklin Fuller.

[70] Lewis, *Topographical Dictionary*, I, 633.

[71] *ibid.*, 335.

[72] *ibid.*, 278.

[73] *ibid.*, 664. Harold's Cross Green was laid out as a public park in 1898 to the design of William Sheppard.

[74] *ibid.*, 134.

[75] John Rocque, *Map of the City of Dublin, 1760*.

[76] Cook, *Pictures of Parsonstown*, 241.

[77] Smith, *City and County of Cork*, 349.

[78] Chetwood, *A Tour through Ireland*, 89.

[79] Smith, *County of Waterford*, 193.

[80] Smith, *City and County of Cork*, 226.

[81] Lewis, *Topographical Dictionary*, I, 526.

[82] Samuel Carter Hall and Anna Maria Hall, *Ireland: its scenery, character, etc.* (London, 1841-43) 47.

[83] Edward McParland, *Public Building in Ireland* (New Haven and London, 2001) 13 and 84. McParland also reported that Stevenson was gardener to the Earl of Meath in 1734. Stevenson may have been responsible for the extension of the formal garden of the Earl of Meath at Killruddery, county Wicklow, that took place in the early eighteenth century. A plan for a formal garden by Stevenson found at Headfort House, county Meath, survives. See Edward Malins and the Knight of Glin, *Lost Demesnes* (London, 1976) 92.

[84] Bushe, *Hibernia Curiosa*, 13.

[85] The lighting globes are shown on a drawing of Frederick Trench's *Proposed elevation to Cavendish Street, 1784, for the new rooms of entertainment* (Rotunda Hospital, Dublin, 1784).

[86] See James Malton, *Perspective and Descriptive View of the City of Dublin, 'Charlemont House, Dublin', c.1793*.

[87] Lewis, *Dublin Guide*, 176.

[88] F. Elrington Ball, *A History of the County of Dublin*, 6 vols (Dublin, 1802-20) II,109.

[89] Young, *A Tour in Ireland...*, 309.

[90] Twiss, *A Tour in Ireland in 1775*, 153

[91] Chetwood, *A Tour through Ireland*, 122.

[92] Lewis, *Topographical Dictionary*, II, 301. In 1828 a new Spa House in the Early English style

was built. It and the canal survive.

[93] *ibid.*, I, 104.

[94] Sir Charles Coote, *Statistical Survey of the county of Cavan* (Dublin, 1801) 136.

[95] Lewis, *Dublin Guide*, 173.

[96] Cook, *Pictures of Parsonstown*, 232

[97] Pococke, *Pococke's Tour in Ireland in 1752*, 9.

[98] Smith, *County of Waterford*, 88.

[99] Lewis, *Dublin Guide*, 153.

[100] Lewis, *Topographical Dictionary*, I, 236.

[101] *ibid.*, 442.

[102] *ibid.*, 97.

[103] Chetwood, *A Tour through Ireland*, 85.

[104] Wilson, *The Post Chaise Companion*, 319.

[105] Lewis, *Topographical Dictionary*, I, 147.

———

Charles Lanyon at Glenarm

ANNE CASEMENT

S IR CHARLES LANYON (1813-1889) HAS BEEN CALLED THE 'FATHER OF ULSTER architecture',[1] and is arguably the province's best-known and most successful architect. This is primarily due to his association with such landmark Belfast buildings as the Queen's University, the Palm House in the Botanic Gardens, and the Customs House, together with several fine country houses, particularly the home of the linen magnate Andrew Mulholland at Ballywalter Park, county Down.

Charles Lanyon was born in Eastbourne, Sussex, in 1813,[2] but enjoyed a long and distinguished career in Ireland following his appointment as county surveyor for Antrim when merely twenty-three years old.[3] In the early years of his twenty-five-year tenure of the Antrim surveyorship, he established a significant reputation in a variety of fields. His flair for architecture was amply demonstrated by his first country house commission in Ulster – Drenagh House, county Derry, completed around 1836 for Marcus Connolly McCausland. This chaste, carefully wrought design, with its fine central hall, was his earliest essay in the Italianate style he was later to make incomparably his own.[4]

Lanyon had been trained primarily as a civil engineer, having been articled to Jacob Owen (1778-1870) during his time as clerk of works to the Royal Engineers Department in Portsmouth, and subsequently principal engineer and architect to the Board of Works in Dublin. This training enabled him to deal with other, less conventional challenges, such as those associated with the construction of the new Antrim Coast Road. Here his expertise was to be severely tested by the notoriously unstable geology and challenging topography of the coastal strip, and he was to win lasting local fame as the architect of 'The Big Bridge', the triple-arched, eighty-foot-high viaduct which sweeps the Coast Road majestically across the Glendun river (Plates 1, 2). Not surprisingly, Lanyon was proud of this bridge – a handsome and noble structure – completed in 1839.[5] By 1839/40, the construction of the road was in its final stages, and Lanyon was busy with other work, most notably the

1 – *Glendun and the viaduct* (courtesy Ulster Folk and Transport Museum; photo W.A. Green, WAG 1249)

2 – Glendun viaduct
(courtesy Ulster Folk and Transport Museum; photo W.A. Green, WAG 2965)

Palm House in the Belfast Botanic Gardens, one of the earliest examples of a curvilinear glass and cast-iron structure. There was also a series of commissions in counties Down and Antrim for the Church Accommodation Society, where he employed a simple, almost impoverished Gothic style.[6] He was, as it turns out, also engaged on a project for Edmund McDonnell (né Phelps, 1779/80-1852), the occupier of Glenarm Castle, which lay directly beside the route of the Antrim Coast Road.

McDonnell was the second husband of Anne Catherine, Countess of Antrim in her own right, who had died in 1834. They had no children, and under the terms of his wife's will, Edmund retained a life interest in the bulk of her land in county Antrim, and a right of residence at Glenarm Castle. A few years after their marriage in 1817, William Vitruvius Morrison (1794-1838) produced several plans, elevations and sketches for work to the castle,[7] which involved the remodelling of a much earlier house with an already complicated history. The original Jacobean double-pile house had been refashioned in Palladian mode around 1756 by Christopher Myers (1717-1789), who had added a pediment to the entrance front and transformed the original horizontal Tudor windows into Venetian ones, thus giving a vertical emphasis. Curved sweeps linked the main block to adjacent pavilions. It has been suggested that the insertion of a short section of crenellation on the north front, flanked by a pair of mini-bartizans, may also have occurred at this time.[8] This Gothic element was strengthened in the early 1800s by the removal of the pavilions and curved sweeps, and the insertion of pointed arched windows on the ground and first floors and an arched entranceway on the south front, flanked by pointed sidelights. A small extension was also added to the east in the Regency style.

This was the situation inherited by Morrison, who was renowned for his mastery of the Tudor Gothic, a style which his contemporaries credited him with introducing into Ireland,[9] and which might be expected to have had a particular appeal to a family whose lands were secured to them by Queen Elizabeth. At Glenarm, he drew on his earlier work, most notably at Miltown House, county Kerry, and proposed to throw an Elizabethan cloak over the existing building.[10] Three schemes are known to have been suggested by Morrison, all including the addition of four corner towers, a porch on the south front, and a multiplicity of gables around the perimeter of the roof. Myers's pediment on the south front was to be removed, changes made to the existing fenestration, and the south-east wing remodelled and substantially extended. The evidence for a scheme involving the enlargement of the main block is provided by a lively perspective view, in pen and ink, which shows the entrance façade with the outer bays extended to create a U-shaped front, and a large porch filling the centre at ground level. Corner bartizans flank the central section, and high gables link the main block to the corner towers (Plate 3). The entrance front of this scheme is similar to Morrison's unexecuted design for the front of Miltown House (Plate 4), though at Glenarm the Tudor-arched doorway has been replaced by a more Palladian porch. One of the remaining schemes is illustrated by a single perspective view (Plate 5), whilst a number of finished design drawings exist for the other (Plate 6). Both these schemes show the house encased in a new Elizabethan or Jacobean skin, with Flemish gables and an elaborate porch projecting in the centre. The perspective view shows a Palladian-style porch, similar to that envisaged in the enlarged scheme, whilst the porch depicted in the set of design drawings offers clear evidence of Morrison's knowledge of the forms of sixteenth- and early seventeenth-century English Classicism.[11]

A sketch of the south and west fronts, executed by Anne Catherine's brother-in-law, Lord Mark Kerr (1776-1840), in 1828 (Plate 7),[12] shows that the alterations were carried out in more than one stage, and that the proposal to enlarge the house was abandoned, presumably on the grounds of cost. By this time, only the addition of the four Morrisonian corner towers and the south-east wing had been undertaken,[13] creating a visually disconcerting, but presumably perfectly serviceable hybrid house.[14] Curiously, when the work was finally completed, the designs adopted for the porch, the windows on the ground and first floors, and the chimneys differed from Morrison's proposals for Glenarm.

3 – William Morrison
Untitled sketch of
Glenarm Castle
n.d., pen and ink drawing
(courtesy Viscount Dunluce)

4 – William Morrison
Front elevation of Miltown
House, c.1818 (unexecuted)
(courtesy Irish Architectural
Archive)

FRONT ELEVATION FOR GLENARM CASTLE.

5 – William Morrison
A FIRST DESIGN FOR
IMPROVEMENT & RESTORATION
OF GLENARM CASTLE
n.d., wash drawing
(courtesy PRONI)

6 – Richard and William
Morrison, FRONT ELEVATION
FOR GLENARM CASTLE
c.1821-22 (courtesy PRONI)

7 – Lord Mark Kerr, GLENARM CASTLE S&W FRONTS
1828, wash drawing, 11.5 x 18 cm (courtesy Hector McDonnell)

A variety of factors, such as the availability of funds,[15] and the reorganisation of the estate following Anne Catherine's death in 1834,[16] probably contributed to the postponement of the project. Such factors, together with evidence gleaned from contemporary written accounts and drawings, have led to the suggestion that the remodelling might not have been completed until the 1840s,[17] substantially later than was previously thought.[18]

Following further investigation of the Antrim Papers, it is now possible to date the commission for the completion of the work to 1840, and to identify the architect involved not as either William or Sir Richard Morrison, but Charles Lanyon.[19] An agreement, dated 27th February, between Edmund McDonnell and three Belfast builders, John Robinson,[20] Thomas Kelly and John Brown, sets out clearly the terms and conditions of the contract agreed between these parties. This relates to the expenditure by 1st July 1840 of £1,020 on a scheme of works for the castle in the Gothic style, all the stone to be sourced from the Pollockshaws quarry in Scotland.[21] Detailed specifications are provided for the stonework cladding of the south front and the mullioned windows on its ground floor, together with the porch facing this front, including the perforated balustrade over the arches, the several pinnacles or turrets on the point of the gables, and external and internal detailing. Reference is also made to the finishing of the several gables built on the north and west fronts, and the Gothic windows on their ground floors – to be of cut stone; and to the chimney shafts on each elevation – to be of stone perforated with a circular hole thirteen inches in diameter. The details specified concur with those shown on William Lawrence's late-nineteenth-century photograph of the south and west fronts (Plate 8), and that still exist today.[22] The appearance of the porch on an 1844 water-colour of the house has been taken to indicate that originally it was open.[23] No glaz-ing contract survives which would settle this point.

Lanyon's role in relation to the proposed work at Glenarm Castle is apparent in the wording of the 1840 agreement which states that 'the said Edmund McDonnell hath appointed Charles Lanyon Esquire to be the Architect to superin-tend the said Works, during the pleasure of said Edmund McDonnell'. Despite the absence of any correspondence between Lanyon and McDonnell, or signed draw-ings by Lanyon for Glenarm Castle, the architect's specific connection with the works set out in the 1840 agreement strongly suggests that he was also responsible for their design and for providing 'such full size drawings as may be furnished', as described in this agreement – for instance, for the mouldings on the south front. At this time, Lanyon is unlikely to have had architectural assistants capable of under-taking such work, as was later the case.

There is also a second, subsidiary contract between Edmund McDonnell and James Cameron for the expenditure of £217 17s 6d by 1st July 1840 on a carefully detailed scheme of improvements to the roof, involving re-slating with Bangor blue slates and work to the gutters and flashings. Again the architect in charge is Charles Lanyon.[24]

By 1840, almost twenty years had elapsed since William Morrison drew up proposals for the castle. The emergence of firm evidence that his scheme was not completed within his lifetime poses the question as to whether procrastination on the part of the family was partly due to their dissatisfaction with some of his propos-als, perhaps especially for the porch. With Morrison out of the picture, Edmund McDonnell was completely at liberty to select another architect. He may have been drawn to Lanyon not only because he could not fail to be aware of the talent and capabilities of this aspiring young county surveyor,[25] but also because they almost certainly shared an affinity for Italian architecture.[26] Lanyon has been credited with work to the court house in Glenarm, carried out in 1838 under the auspices of the Antrim Grand Jury, and is said to have carried out several private commissions for Jury members in the 1840s.[27] Edmund McDonnell had served as foreman of the aforesaid Jury, and it is interesting to contemplate whether he and Lanyon conspired together to grace the Glenarm court house with an Italianate campanile.[28]

The design of Glenarm Castle, as completed under Lanyon's supervision in the 1840s, was clearly influenced by some of Morrison's unexecuted proposals for Glenarm, especially for the porch and stepped gables. The porch reflects elements of two of Morrison's schemes, most notably in the incorporation of Tuscan-style pillars with partly fluted shafts. Lanyon would have been constrained by the need to integrate any new work with the existing Morrison features. That he succeeded in his task may be judged from the fact that no commentator appears to have suggested that the porch, for instance, might be a substantially later addition by an architect other than the Morrisons. Yet stylistic evidence to support such a contention is not hard to find. For instance, the string courses at the bases of the corner towers do not align with those at the bases of the slender corner shafts of the porch, and the string courses at the bases of the towers supporting the corner turrets do not align with the string courses at the bases of the finials crowning the corner shafts of the porch. Though Charles Lanyon was never a committed student of medieval architecture, his early Gothic churches are said to display some real knowledge of historical detail.[29] Certainly, at Glenarm, the design of the Gothic tracery which was inserted into the ground floor windows – a mullioned shaft surmounted by a cusped quatrefoil – is convincingly neo-medieval.

To conclude, there is now strong evidence to suggest that the final appearance of Glenarm Castle in the

GLENARM CASTLE. Co. ANTRIM. 2.

8 – Glenarm Castle
late nineteenth-century (courtesy National Library of Ireland)

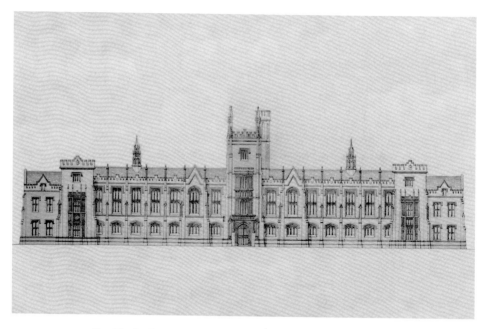

9 – Charles Lanyon, front elevation of Queen's College, Belfast
(courtesy Northern Ireland Environment Agency)

1840s was due as much to the intervention of Charles Lanyon as to William Vitruvius Morrison. In such a case, Glenarm has a claim to be considered Lanyon's earliest essay in a Tudor revival style. It is this style that he would later elaborate and refine in a variety of commissions, ranging from schools at Whitehouse and Craigs, almshouses at Carrickfergus, the courthouse at Ballymena (all in county Antrim), and the Institute for the Deaf and Dumb and Blind in Belfast. This manner reaches its apogee in the Queen's College (later the Queen's University of Belfast) (Plate 9), which must be considered as the high point of early Victorian architectural achievement in Belfast.[30]

ACKNOWLEDGEMENTS

I wish to thank Professor Alistair Rowan for his assistance in the preparation of this article, Viscount Dunluce for showing me the Morrison sketch in his possession, and Philip Smith of the Northern Ireland Environment Agency for discussing the implications of the Ordnance Survey valuations with me. Also Frederick O'Dwyer for information relating to the building history of Glenarm Castle, and Ann Martha Rowan and the staff of the Irish Architectural Archive for being their wonderfully helpful selves. My thanks are also due to Viscount Dunluce, Hector McDonnell, Deputy Keeper of the Records at PRONI, National Library of Ireland, Ulster Folk and Transport Museum, Irish Architectural Archive and Northern Ireland Environment Agency for permission to reproduce photographs and drawings in their possession.

ENDNOTES

The following abbreviation is used:
PRONI   Public Record Office Northern Ireland, Belfast

[1]   Paul Larmour, 'The father of Ulster architecture', *Perspective*, May-June 1994, 53-54.

[2]   Paul Larmour, 'Sir Charles Lanyon', *Irish Arts Review Yearbook, 1989-90*, 200-06. This account has been used throughout this article as the authoritative source of material pertaining to Lanyon's life and career.

[3]   Prior to this he briefly held the county surveyorship of Kildare, but only one possible commission dates from this time.

[4]   Alistair Rowan, 'Ballywalter Park, Co. Down – I and II', *Country Life*, CXLI, 2 and 9 March 1967, 456-60, 516-20; 'Palazzo Mulholland' in Peter Rankin (ed.), *Ballywalter Park* (Belfast, 1985) 13-21; and *North West Ulster: The counties of Londonderry, Donegal, Fermanagh, and Tyrone* (Harmondsworth, 1979) 249-50.

[5]   C.E.B. Brett, *Buildings of County Antrim* (Belfast, 1996) 276.

[6]   Larmour, 'Sir Charles Lanyon', 202, notes that so long as Lanyon carried out his county duties efficiently, there could be no objection to him undertaking private commissions.

[7]   PRONI, D/3560/3/1-7, c.1825; D/3560/1, 1811-50, album entitled 'Glenarm Castle and its Vicinity' and endorsed 'Lady Louisa Kerr, 1835' and 'Lady Letitia MacGregor, 1870': D/3560/1/38. Terence Reeves-Smyth, 'Jewel of the Glen', *Irish Arts Review*, 23, no. 3, Winter 2006, 126-31: 130 notes that final drawings were prepared in 1821-22 and exhibited at the Royal Academy in 1823.

[8]   For more details, see Frederick O'Dwyer, 'In search of Christopher Myers: pioneer of the Gothic revival in Ireland' in Michael McCarthy and Karina O'Neill (eds), *Studies in the Gothic Revival* (Dublin, 2008) 51-111: 66-69.

[9]   John Morrison, 'Life of the Late William Vitruvius Morrison, of Dublin, Architect' in John Weale (ed.), *Quarterly Papers on Architecture*, I, part 1, paper 3 (1844) 1-8: 4.

[10] Terence Reeves-Smyth, 'An Elizabethan Revival House in Ireland. Edward Blore and the Building of Crom, Co Fermanagh', in Terence Reeves-Smyth and Richard Oram (eds), *Avenues to the Past: essays presented to Sir Charles Brett on his 75th year* (Belfast, 2003) 321-52: 327, notes that by the 1820s the term Elizabethan embraced 'Tudor Gothic', 'Elizabethan' and 'Jacobean' revivals, all of which often tended to merge into one another.

[11] PRONI, D/3560/3/1, *c.*1825, Front elevation for Glenarm Castle by Richard and William Morrison; PRONI, D/3560/1, 1811-50, album entitled 'Glenarm Castle and its Vicinity' and endorsed 'Lady Louisa Kerr, 1835' and 'Lady Letitia MacGregor, 1870': D/3560/1/38, sepia watercolour 'A first design for Improvement & Restoration of Glenarm Castle, by William Morrison, Esq. Archt.' The sketch showing the enlarged scheme is in the private collection of Viscount Dunluce. Although its authorship is unclear, it can be attributed to W.V. Morrison on stylistic grounds.

[12] M.R. Kerr, 'Scratches from Nature', 3 vols, unpublished MSS, II, Oct 1828.

[13] The design of the towers is similar in all three Morrison schemes, and reflects the design of the towers as built, but the design of the south-east wing is different in each scheme, and the design as built accords with none of Morrison's proposals.

[14] For a fuller discussion of the building history of the castle, see Anne Casement, 'The Irish world of Lord Mark Kerr...', *Irish Architectural and Decorative Studies*, IX (Dublin, 2006) 40-85, 56-65; Reeves-Smyth, 'Jewel of the Glen'.

[15] Which might have been expected to improve following the opening up of trade and communication resulting from the construction of the new coast road, which was completed in 1842.

[16] She was succeeded by her sister Charlotte, who died the following year, resulting in further disruption.

[17] The first known depiction of the castle with the present porch and without the Myers pediment is dated 1844 (see note 23), and no accounts written prior to this date have been found which specifically mention either the porch or the gables on the main block of the castle. For further details, see Casement, 'The Irish world of Lord Mark Kerr...', 40-85: 62-63.

[18] Reeves-Smyth, 'Jewel of the Glen, 130, gives the date of execution as 1831-32. O'Dwyer, 'In search of Christopher Myers', 69, acknowledges the possibility that the work may have been completed substantially later than previously thought, with the caveat that, if this were the case, operations would have been supervised by William Morrison's father, Sir Richard Morrison, William having died in 1838.

[19] PRONI, Earl of Antrim Estate Papers, D/2977, D/2977/43, Glenarm Castle, 1840-1931: D/2977/43/1, Edmund McDonnell and John Robinson, et al, 1840.

[20] Probably the John Robinson who, according to the Irish Architectural Archive, *Dictionary of Irish Architects* (ww.dia.ie), appears to have remodelled Rockhill House, county Donegal for John Vandeleur Stewart in 1853, though Rowan, 'Palazzo Mulholland', 20, attributes this work to Charles Lanyon.

[21] The agreement specifies the Pollockshams quarry in Scotland, but this is almost certainly a misspelling of Pollockshaws. Residents of Pollockshaws worked the fine sandstone in the Giffnock quarries, which was extensively used for building work in nearby Glasgow. Trade also took place with Belfast. The tender price excluded the cost of transporting the stone from Scotland, which was to be borne by McDonnell. The choice of Pollockshaws may have been influenced by the need to blend the new stonework with that of the existing corner towers.

[22] PRONI, Lawrence Photographs, T/1248: T/2418/2/323, late nineteenth-century photograph of Glenarm Castle, Co Antrim, 2321 W.L.

[23] PRONI, D/3560/1 1811-50, album entitled 'Glenarm Castle and its Vicinity' and endorsed 'Lady Louisa Kerr, 1835' and Lady Letitia MacGregor, 1870': D/3560/1/39, sepia watercolour of Glenarm Castle by Lady Louisa Tighe, 1844; Reeves-Smyth, 'Jewel of the Glen', 128. If the porch had been open, and thus not a habitable room, it might explain why it was not itemised

in the 1859 valuation, despite the fact that the valuation sheet includes a sketch plan of the ground floor of the castle, where the porch is specifically identified. A porch of this size would customarily have been valued separately. The failure to do so might support the idea that it was unglazed if it were not for the fact that the corner towers were valued separately, and they were filled with rubble and thus also uninhabitable. No later nineteenth-century valuations exist to act as a comparison for a period when the porch is known to have been glazed.

24   PRONI, Earl of Antrim Estate Papers, D/2977, D/2977/43, Glenarm Castle, 1840-1931: D/2977/43/2, articles of agreement between Edmund McDonnell and James Cameron..., 1840.

25   The line of the new coast road immediately east of Glenarm traversed a former deer park belonging to the McDonnell family, and construction involved blasting back the chalk head-land to create a platform wide enough to accommodate the road, and high enough to prevent it being washed away.

26   Edmund McDonnell left Glenarm for Italy in 1850, and died and was buried in Rome in 1852.

27   Larmour, 'Sir Charles Lanyon', 202.

28   This campanile resembles that added by the 9th Earl of Antrim in 1852 to the former market house in the centre of Ballymoney, county Antrim, which W.D. Girvan in *Historic Buildings, Groups of Buildings, Areas of Architectural Importance in North Antrim* (Belfast, 1971-72) 38, likens to the clock tower in the stable yard at nearby Dundarave, also by Lanyon.

29   Larmour, 'Sir Charles Lanyon', 203.

30   *ibid.*, 203-04.

———

Gallwey's castle June 23. 1877

'Gallwey's Castle, Carrick': Edward Cheney's drawings of Ormond Castle in the early nineteenth-century

JANE FENLON

'MUCH OF THIS FINE OLD BUILDING HAS BEEN TAKEN DOWN; THE HABITABLE part and two square towers alone remain...'[1] This quotation from William Shaw Mason's statistical account written in 1816 describes the appearance of Ormond Castle, Carrick on Suir, county Tipperary, during the early decades of the nineteenth century. An album of drawings with several views showing this notable Irish building around that time has recently come to light.[2] These previously unpublished drawings have been attributed to the English artist Edward Cheney (1803-1884), and a watercolour of the same building by his brother Robert Henry Cheney (1801-1866) was also included in the sale.

Ormond Castle is famous mainly for its interiors,where elaborate decorative plasterwork survives from the sixteenth century when Thomas Butler, 10th Earl of Ormond, added new buildings around 1565 to two towers and other earlier structures on the site (Plate 2). The Cheney drawings are important because they are comprehensive and they show views of the buildings that comprise Ormond Castle from all four points of the compass. The views of the west elevation are unique in that no other drawings of that elevation with such detailed architectural features have been found. Dating from the month of June 1837, the drawings make an interesting comparison with earlier views of the castle by Purcell of 1782 and Thomas Sautelle Roberts (1760-1826) of 1796 (Plates 3, 4), and later drawings from 1855 by George du Noyer (1817-69) (Plates 8-11).

---

1 – Edward Cheney, EAST ELEVATION OF ORMOND CASTLE
(all Cheney drawings courtesy Office of Public Works; photos Con Brogan)

2 – Principal elevation of Ormond Castle, Carrick on Suir
(courtesy Dept of the Environment, Heritage and Local Government; photo Con Brogan)

Edward Cheney and his brother Robert Henry (generally known as Henry) were members of a well-known English military family from Badger Hall in Shropshire. Following the death of their father, General Robert Cheney, in 1820, Henry and his mother went to live in Italy, where they settled in the Palazzo Sciara in Rome around about 1825. Edward followed later. The brothers moved in artistic circles, while their mother and sister also painted. Peter de Wint (1784-1849), who was the most successful watercolour teacher of his time, is known to have influenced Henry's work, although Edward's watercolours are thought to have been painted in the manner of Antonio Senapé (1788-1859).[3]

Henry travelled back and forth to England looking after the maintenance of Badger Hall, and while there he also painted the houses and parks of his friends. On the evidence of albums of dated drawings, they are both known to have toured Ireland, and the drawings of Ormond Castle were executed over four days, from 23rd to 26th June 1837. The Cheney brothers also travelled extensively in Europe, drawing and painting scenes in Rome, Venice, France and Austria among other places.

Ormond (Carrick) Castle

3 – Thomas Sautell Roberts, 1796 aquatint, engraved by J.W. Edy (courtesy National Library of Ireland)

4 – Purcell, 1782 engraving (detail) (courtesy National Library of Ireland)

THE DRAWINGS

FOR THE ARTIST, THE APPEAL OF ORMOND CASTLE, APART FROM ITS AGE, PROBA-
bly lay in its ruinous appearance with tall towers and ivy-clad walls. Much of
the external render had fallen off, ivy clung to some of the walls and there
were overgrown gardens with unkempt shrubbery, all elements for creating a picturesque riverside scene, popular subject matter at that period.

At the time of the Cheney drawings, the castle appeared semi-derelict. Early
structures in the lower courtyard and between the towers had been taken down.
According to Shaw Mason, this had happened shortly before 1816, the date of his
publication, *A Statistical Account or Parochial Survey of Ireland*. All of the drawings in question are inscribed 'Gallwey's Castle, Carrick' and dated to various days
in June 1837. The inscriptions refer to John Galwey's occupancy of the building.
Galwey, who acted as the Ormond agent in Carrick on Suir, had lived there for at
least six years (1774-80). He has also been described as a Waterford wine merchant
and as 'a very rich Roman Catholic merchant'.[4] Mr Wogan, a solicitor, who was
appointed seneschal for the Marquess of Ormonde at his Manor Court, succeeded
Galwey as tenant of the castle. It was during Wogan's tenancy that the old buildings
were taken down.

The drawings are uneven in the quality of detail they provide, with those of
the east and west elevations being the most accurate architecturally. In these depictions, the window details and other features, including the decorative render, are
faithfully reproduced. A more generalised approach is taken in the depiction of the
north and south elevations, where the buildings are shown as more ruinous, possibly
to create a more 'romantic' image.

THE WEST ELEVATION (Plate 5)
all drawings 1837, pen and ink and brown wash, 16 x 27 cm
inscribed 'Gallwey's Castle. Carrick. June 22, 1837'

This is the only known drawing from this viewpoint that shows clear architectural
detail. It is also the earliest of the four drawings, and is a carefully finished work.
On the exterior of the buildings, the render on the walls may be clearly seen, as well
as decorative quoins to the corners of the north range and the tall west tower.
Render has also been used to add emphasis to the angles on the staircase tower.[5] It is
difficult to say whether this is part of the original sixteenth-century decoration,
although it is known that the buildings were rendered at that time. Ormond Castle
was described by the Gaelic poet Flann McCraith, writing about 1590, as 'this
snow-white mansion and ... handsome, rustic-planned, white-washed'.[6] In this draw-

Gallwey's Castle. Carrick June 22.

5 – Edward Cheney, WEST ELEVATION OF ORMOND CASTLE

ing, the west tower is shown fairly intact, rising through an impressive five storeys; its eastern wall collapsed in the early twentieth century. A section of the roof of the tower is also shown in place. Adjacent to it is another tall staircase tower, and beyond, the conical base of the missing oriel window that probably lit the dais end of the demolished Great Hall. Ruined ivy-covered walls extend down to the river. Horizontal string courses and similar window styles link the tower and north range. These would have been inserted in order to unify the disparate structures during the sixteenth century building programme. The garden area shown in this view was previously the site of the earl's privy garden that was approached through a doorway at the foot of the angular staircase tower. What appears as a low wall to the right of the drawing may be part of a sixteenth-century garden building.[7]

THE VIEW FROM THE SOUTH-WEST (Plate 6)
inscribed 'Gallwey's Castle. Carrick. June 28, 1837'

This drawing inscribed serves only as an addendum to the view above because it is

Gallweys Castle - June 25. 1837

Gallweys Castle Carrick. June 24. 1837

neither as detailed nor as well finished.[8] Details such as windows have been fudged; also the condition of the staircase tower is concealed behind shrubbery, and the west tower is shown in a more ruinous condition. Overall, its main value is to depict the proximity of the river at that time, while also showing the ruined walls and buildings of the lower courtyard from a different viewpoint.

THE EAST ELEVATION (Plate 1)
inscribed 'Gallwey's Castle. Carrick June 23, 1837'

Like the west elevation, here the render is carefully delineated, and it can be seen that a panelled effect has been created in this medium above the multi-light oriel window.[9] The windows on the ground floor of the main building in this view appear to be single-light, and do not have hood mouldings above them, which, it has been suggested, was the original form of all of the windows at that level.[10] Once again the decorative quoins on the corners of the tall tower are delineated. Old arrow loops from earlier days are visible also, and the windows on the upper storeys are mainly of a pattern that served to unify the disparate buildings.

THE NORTH ELEVATION (Plate 7)
inscribed ' Gallwey's Castle. June 24, 1837'

This is similar in treatment to the view from the south-west in that it is composed without much detail as a picturesque image. Here the tall towers, depicted in a semi-ruinous state, dominate the lower north range, while trees and overgrown shrubs mask other details Once again the panelled effect in the render is visible above the oriel window of the principal entrance.

COMPARISONS

WHEN COMPARISON IS MADE BETWEEN THE CHENEY DRAWINGS AND TWO depictions dating from the late eighteenth-century by Sautelle Roberts and Purcell respectively, the main difference may be seen in the view of the lower court, which is shown to be packed with buildings (Plates 2, 3). Some of these buildings were similar in type to the north range, indicating a sixteenth-centu-

---

6 – Edward Cheney, A VIEW OF ORMOND CASTLE FROM THE SOUTH-WEST

7 – Edward Cheney, NORTH ELEVATION OF ORMOND CASTLE

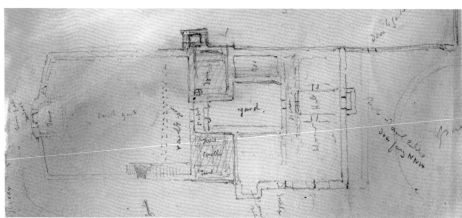

8 – George du Noyer
ORMOND CASTLE *FROM THE EAST*
1855, watercolour, inscribed 'Thomas Butler Earl of Ormond's castle of Carrick on Suir erected a.d. 1565'

9 – George du Noyer
ORMOND CASTLE, *THE ORIEL WITH MASON'S MARK*
1855, pencil, inscribed 'Part of oriel windows oak room the castle of Carrick on Suir'

opposite

10 – George du Noyer
ORMOND CASTLE, *GROUND PLAN*
1855, pencil, inscribed 'Plan of the castle of Carrick on Suir built a.d.1565 by Thomas Butler Earl of Ormond'

(Plates 8-11 courtesy Royal Society of Antiquaries of

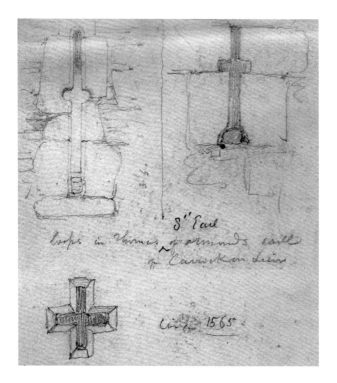

11 – George du Noyer
ORMOND CASTLE, THE LOOPS
1855, pencil, inscribed 'loops in
Thomas 8 Earl of Ormond's castle
of Carrick on Suir, Oct 1850'

ry build, while others, such as the Great Hall, would have been from an earlier phase of building. The architectural details depicted by Cheney are more accurately drawn in the views from east and west than those in the engravings, where the orientation of some of the buildings in the lower court cannot be easily determined.

Another interesting comparison may be made with a collection of drawings executed during 1855 by George du Noyer (Plate 8). Du Noyer's drawings reveal a more antiquarian interest in the buildings, and he must have examined the structures closely to have discovered the mason's mark on a stone mullion in the earl's chamber (Plate 9), and also when he drew the ground plan to a minute scale (Plate 10). While du Noyer's views of the buildings are accurate enough, his more detailed drawings focus on features such as the 'loops' in the walls (Plate 11) and the eighteenth-century painted portraits in the entrance hall.

Overall, the Cheney images, particularly those of the west and east elevations, which are clear and concise architecturally, emphasise the building's antiquity while adding to our store of information about this evocative structure. They also confirm that decorative render was used on the exteriors so that when it was newly applied they would have appeared as gleaming white rather than the pervasive grey stone now accepted as a feature of early buildings in the Irish countryside.[11]

ACKNOWLEDGEMENTS

I would like to thank Michael Ramsden, David Hayes, Tony Roche of the photographic service at the Department of the Environment, Heritage and Local Government, Aighleann O'Shaughnessy, staff at the Royal Society of Antiquaries of Ireland, and Honora Faul and staff of the prints and drawings department at the National Library of Ireland for their assistance with the images used in this text.

ENDNOTES

1. W. Shaw Mason, *A Statistical Account or Parochial Survey of Ireland* (Dublin, 1816).
2. Christie's, South Kensington, sale, 12th October 2005, lot 116, Edward Cheney, an album of 167 works.
3. Introduction to catalogue of sale, Christie's, South Kensington, sale, 12th October 2005, and *New Oxford Dictionary of National Biography*.
4. W. Nolan, 'Patterns of living in Tipperary, 1750-1850' in William Nolan (ed.), *Tipperary History and Society* (Dublin, 1985) 296.
5. It is probable that the decorative render dates from the original sixteenth-century scheme, and some later eighteenth-century plastering has been applied over it. Remnants of sixteenth-century decorative render may still be seen to the side of the gateway in the inner court.
6. Flann McCraith, stanzas from 'Panegyric to the Earl of Ormond', *Journal of the Butler Society*, I-VI, 473.
7. For more information on this garden building, see J. Fenlon, *Ormond Castle* (Dublin, 1996; revised 2008) 56.
8. There is another, slightly later drawing of the same view by Cheney that is inscribed and dated 'Carrick July 13. 37'. Initially it appears to be a sharp and detailed image. However, the artist has omitted the west tower staircase altogether, while the proportions of the west side of the north range are too broad.
9. There are similar plasterwork panels on the interior of the oriel in the Long Gallery.
10. See reference to the windows of Myrtle Grove, county Cork, Tadhg O'Keefe, 'Plantation-era great houses in Munster' in Thomas Herron and Michael Potterton (eds), *Ireland in the Renaissance c.1540-1660* (Dublin, 2007) 280, and in conversation with Maurice Craig.
11. Among other notable buildings in Ireland that have whitish render with decorative elements either in the quoins or incised details are Portuma Castle, Roscommon Castle and Burntcourt, county Tipperary.

———

IRISH ARCHITECTURAL AND DECORATIVE STUDIES

––––––––

This is a volume-by-volume listing of contents for volumes I-X of IRISH ARCHITECTURAL & DECORATIVE STUDIES. For a comprehensive, cumulative index – and an authors' index – to these volumes, see IA&DS — INDEX I-X (Irish Georgian Society, 2008).

— I —

ISBN 978 0946846 160 (ISBN-10: 0946846 162)   (IGS, 1998)   ed. Seán O'Reilly
224 pages   24 x 17 cm   128 illus   €20 pb

— II —

ISBN 978 0946846 320 (ISBN-10: 0946846 324) (IGS, 1999) ed. Seán O'Reilly

208 pages   24 x 17 cm   110 illus   €20 pb

— III —

ISBN 978 0946846 481 (ISBN-10: 0946846 480) (IGS, 2000) ed. Seán O'Reilly

192 pages   24 x 17 cm   143 illus   €20 pb

— IV —

ISBN 978 0946846 726 (ISBN-10: 0946846 723)   (IGS, 2001)   ed. Seán O'Reilly
224 pages   24 x 17 cm   109 illus   €20 pb

— V —

ISBN 978 0946846 962 (ISBN-10: 0946846 960)   (IGS, 2002)   ed. Nicola Figgis
208 pages   24 x 17 cm   136 illus   €20 pb

— VIII —

ISBN 978 0948037 214 (ISBN-10: 0948037 210)   (IGS, 2005)   ed. William Laffan
272 pages   24 x 17 cm   138 illus (incl. 98 col)   €20 pb

— IX —

ISBN 978 0948037 368 (ISBN-10: 0948037 369) (IGS, 2006) ed. William Laffan
288 pages   24 x 17 cm   203 illus (incl. 122 col)   €20 pb

— X —

ISBN 978 0948037 566 (IGS, 2007) ed. William Laffan
272 pages   24 x 17 cm   203 illus (incl. 122 col)   €20 pb

—— INDEX ——

ISBN 978 0948037 368   (IGS, 2008)   ed. William Laffan   64 pages   24 x 17 cm   €10 pb

————

X

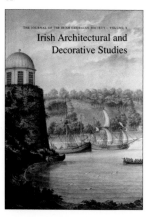

INDEX

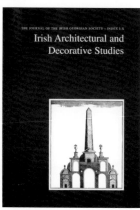

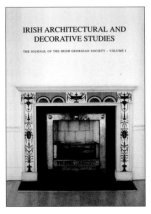

I

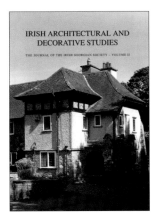

II

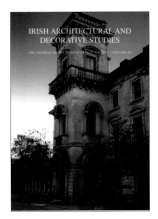

III

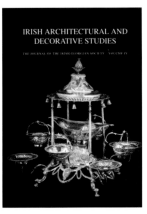

IV

V

VI

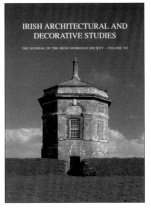

VII

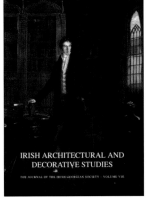

VIII

IX

IRISH ARCHITECTURAL AND DECORATIVE STUDIES

IRISH ARCHITECTURAL AND DECORATIVE STUDIES is the annual journal of the Irish Georgian Society. It is the much-enhanced and dramatically expanded successor to the *Bulletin*, which was published from 1958 to 1997. The journal reflects the Irish Georgian Society's present wider remit, which is no longer concerned solely with Georgian architecture, but acknowledges the importance of the entire spectrum of Ireland's post-medieval architecture and its special need for protection, interpretation, understanding and appreciation. The content of each volume of the journal is wide and varied, testimony to the diversity and scholarship of the series.

■ ORDER FORM – These books can be ordered from any good bookshop, the Irish Georgian Society or Gandon.

_____ Volume I	(1998), 224pp, 11 essays, 128 illus	ISBN 978 0946846 160 (ISBN-10: 0946846 162)	€20 pb
_____ Volume II	(1999), 208pp, 8 essays, 110 illus	978 0946846 320 (0946846 324)	€20 pb
_____ Volume III	(2000), 192pp, 6 essays, 143 illus	978 0946846 481 (0946846 480)	€20 pb
_____ Volume IV	(2001), 224pp, 7 essays, 109 illus	978 0946846 726 (0946846 723)	€20 pb
_____ Volume V	(2002), 208pp, 5 essays, 136 illus	978 0946846 962 (0946846 960)	€20 pb
_____ Volume VI	(2003), 240pp, 11 essays, 120 illus	978 0946846 979 (0946846 979)	€20 pb
_____ Volume VII	(2004), 272pp, 10 essays, 159 illus	978 0946846 511 (0946846 510)	€20 pb
_____ Volume VIII	(2005), 272pp, 10 essays, 131 illus	978 0948037 214 (0948037 210)	€20 pb
_____ Volume IX	(2006), 288pp, 9 essays, 203 illus	978 0948037 368 (0948037 369)	€20 pb
_____ Volume X	(2007), 272pp, 10 essays, 148 illus	*clothbound edition* 978 0948037 290	€39 hb
_____		*paperback* 978 0948037 566	€20 pb
_____ Index – Cumulative Index to Volumes I-X (2008), 64pp		978 0948037 641	€10 pb
_____ Volume XI	(2008), 272pp, 9 essays, colour illus	978 0948037 702	€20 pb

❏ payment enclosed by € euro / stg £ / US $ cheque for _____ (post free in Ireland, elsewhere at cost)

❏ charge to Laser / Mastercard / Visa __ __ __ __ __ __ __ __ __ __ __ __ __ __ __ __

expiry date __ __ / __ __ , security code (last 3 digits on signature panel) __ __ __   MasterCard VISA

name _____ date _____ PRINT NAME & ADDRESS

address _____

■ IRISH GEORGIAN SOCIETY   74 Merrion Square, Dublin 2 – T 01-6767053 / F 01-6620290 / E info@igs.ie
■ GANDON DISTRIBUTION   Oysterhaven, Kinsale, Co Cork – T +353 (0)21-4770830 / F 021-4770755
E gandon@eircom.net / W www.gandon-editions.com   (trade orders to Gandon)